KINETOSCOPE

CELESTE YOST

Copyright 2018 Celeste Yost. All rights reserved.
No part of this book may be reproduced, stored in a retrieval system, or transmitted by any means without the written permission of the author. Printed in the United States of America.
Because of the dynamic nature of the Internet, any web addresses or links contained in this book may have changed since publication and may no longer be valid. The views expressed in this work are solely those of the author and do not necessarily reflect the views of the publisher, and the publisher hereby disclaims any responsibility for them.

ISBN-9781729257081

IN LOVING MEMORY OF
WILLY & PAULINE

"It is in the middle that human choices are made; the beginning and the end remain with God.

The decrees of God are birth and death, and in between those limits man makes his own distress or joy."

"A man's heart deviseth his way;
But the LORD directeth his steps."
Proverbs 16:9

Celeste Yost

ACKNOWLEDGMENTS

My love and thanks to Artie and Shirley Lippert, Gretchen and Neal Vickers, Trudy and Frank Jacob, and Girard and Bonnie Lippert I miss the late night phone conversations with both my brothers, as they regaled me with funny memories of their lives.

Thank you to all my family members and friends on two continents who provided timely photographs and background information for this book. They showed me a new perspective about my family, their struggles and their triumphs. I'm especially grateful for my daughters, April Martyn and Betsy Barron for the joy of being their mother. How wonderful to watch them develop into beautiful, intelligent, talented women and mothers. They also gave us beautiful grandchildren.

Special thanks to my dear friends, Ruthie Davis and Cyd and Norman Josephy for proofreading and editing. Also special thanks to Mike Ellis for proofreading and editing the manuscript and formatting the cover. Their special insights were helpful and appreciated.

Most of all, I am so very blessed for my husband and best friend, Ralph, who leads us always in a Godly manner. He is my "Mr. Wonderful", the love of my life, and my cheerleader. I tell him his "balloon never lands" and he laughs. He's always supportive and encourages me to "continue to march" no matter what my endeavor. He's the same with April, Betsy and the grandchildren. I can't imagine how any of us could ever do without him.

PHOTO CREDITS
Betsy Barron Fine Art Photography for Author's Photo

Celeste Yost

KINETOSCOPE .ki·net·o·scope   [NOUN; kə-ne-tə-skōp]
The Kinetoscope is an early motion picture exhibition device invented by Thomas Edison. Though not a movie projector, it was designed for films to be viewed individually through the window of a cabinet housing its components.

- The Kinetoscope introduced the basic approach that would become the standard for all cinematic projection before the advent of video. It creates the illusion of movement by conveying a strip of perforated film bearing sequential images over a light source with a high speed shutter.
- Dropping a nickel in a machine allowed a viewer to see a short motion picture, devoid of plot.
- Our minds, like kinetoscopes, capture and retain sequential images and feelings we experience throughout our lives that silently, over time, reveal to us who we really are.

Celeste Yost

CHAPTER ONE

Sarajevo, Bosnia 1914

On June 28, 1914 heir to the Austrian-Hungarian throne, Archduke Franz Ferdinand of Austria and his wife, Duchess Sophie of Hohenberg, were assassinated. Nineteen-year-old Yugoslav nationalist, Gavrilo Princip, and his five Serbian accomplices, all members of the Black Hand of Belgrade, attempted to fire upon the royal couple in their touring car as they traveled from the train station through the City of Sarajevo, Bosnia.

The six conspirators lined the route but lost their nerve initially, perhaps due to heavy police presence and crowds eager to glimpse the royal couple. Only one of the six was able to lob a hand grenade at the Archduke's car. The driver saw the grenade and sped up, and the bomb consequently exploded under the wheel of the fourth car, seriously injuring two of the occupants and additionally injuring spectators with bomb shrapnel.

The driver of the touring car realized he had taken a wrong turn and began to reverse the car, causing the engine to stall and the gears to lock. Princip, standing in front of a café on that street, stepped forward, drew his pistol, and at a distance of about five feet, fired twice into the car, killing both the Archduke and Duchess. Then putting the gun to his own head, he attempted suicide, but the pistol was wrested from his hand before he had a chance to fire another shot.

The assassinations were the beginning of The Great War, which came to be known as World War I. The Great War began July 28, 1914 and pitted the Central Powers of Germany, Austria-Hungary, Bulgaria, and the Ottoman Empire against the Allied Forces of Great Britain, France,

Russia, Italy, Japan, and ultimately, the United States in 1917. The Great War would end November 11, 1918 nearly four-and-a-half long years later, when Germany signed an Armistice with the Allies.

Germany's declaration of war in 1914 brought huge numbers of volunteers of all ages who came forward and were accepted for service in the German Army. In 1915 that number was significantly less than the previous year, as the number of volunteers decreased. By 1917 only about five percent of eligible males volunteered. After medical exams, new enlistees ages 17-20 deemed fit for service were incorporated with reservists joining the class for active duty. Recruits were sorted into four categories: "fit for duty" (sent to depot field units for outfitting and training); "fit for garrison duty in Germany or on lines of communications in the field" (sent to a Landsturm formation); "fit for labor" (also Landsturm); or "unfit". The "unfit" pool represented only a small percentage of recruits who were often reexamined and put into some sort of depot job.

After the class of 1914 was absorbed, the Landsturm 2nd Ban. successively called up the class of 1915 in April, May and June of 1915 after only four months' training. Those soldiers were sent to the front to fill the losses of the 1914 winter campaigns. The 1916 class was called up in August and November of 1915 and after only four to five months of training, was also sent to the front. Even this huge influx of men could not offset the losses of 1915. The pattern continued. The 1917 class was called up in January and May of 1916, eighteen months early, but was used up quickly due mainly to the Verdun and Somme battles. Again, these soldiers received only three months' training. The 1918 class was called up in September 1916 and January 1917, with the remainder completely used by July 1917 due to heavy losses at the front. A small portion of the 1919 class was called up in January and February 1917. The remainder were called up in May and June 1917, two-and-a-half years before their due date. After only three months of training, they were deployed.

The Post-War Years began with the Treaty of Versailles on June 28, 1919 under the terms of which Germany admitted responsibility for starting the war. The determination of the Inter-Allied Reparations Commission obliged Germany to pay war reparations to the various Allies, particularly, France. The reparation amount of 226 billion gold marks, as determined by the Commission, put Germany in a tenuous position. The country had endured great loss of life and incurred severe damage to its infrastructure. German factories were unable to function, causing the decline of the economy which further hampered the country's ability to pay.

In 1921 the Commission reduced the amount of reparations to 132 billion gold marks, but even with the reduction, the debt was too much and the country was in default of promised timber and coal deliveries. Inflation was exacerbated when workers in the Ruhr Valley in Western Germany went on a general strike, and the German government printed more money in order to continue paying them for "passively resisting."

In January 1923 French and Belgian troops occupied the Ruhr coalfields in order to enforce German payment of the reparations. The Germans, unable to resist militarily, responded with acts of civil disobedience, strikes and riots. And, in turn, these actions were met with measures of repression by the occupying forces. By November 1923, the American *dollar* was worth 4,210,500,000,000 German marks

THE ALLIED POWERS
Great Britain
France
Russian
Italy [1]
Japan
United States [2]

THE CENTRAL POWERS
Austro-Hungarian Empire
Ottoman Empire
German Empire
Kingdom of Bulgaria

WORLD WAR I TIMELINE

- June 28, 1914 World War I begins with the Assassination of the Archduke and Duchess of the Austro-Hungarian Empire, known also as Austria-Hungary.
- July 5, 1914 Austria-Hungary received assurances of support from Germany for a war against Serbia, in case of Russian militarism.
- July 23, 1914 Austria-Hungary sent an ultimatum to Serbia to which the Serbian response was unsatisfactory.
- July 28, 1914 Austria-Hungary declared war on Serbia, and Russia mobilized.
- July 31, 1914 Germany warned Russia to cease mobilizing and Russia claimed their mobilization was only against Austria-Hungary.
- August 1, 1914 Germany declared war on Russia.
- June 28, 1919 World War I ends with the signing of the Treaty of Versailles.
- November 11, 1919 Armistice signed, soldiers mustered out and sent home.

---

[1] Italy initially had a treaty with Germany, but recanted and secretly joined the Allied Powers.

[2] The United States joined the Allied Powers in 1917 after the country could no longer stay neutral. Ultimately the Allies comprised 25 nations.

CHAPTER TWO

Dresden, September 1917

Arthur looked at the familiar script on the envelope in his post box. He stood on the porch and opened it slowly. Inside was a picture postcard of a young man in full Army dress, complete with a Mauser rifle and oversized boots.

He read the greeting on the back: "Freiburg 11.9.17 Dear Brother Arthur! I surprise you today with my picture, a remembrance for you of your brother Willy. Auf Wiedersehn!"

Arthur was taken aback that this postcard was mailed to him. Willy had always been closer to Georg. Of seven children, Olga was the eldest, followed by Alma, then Arthur, Georg, Flora, Frieda and lastly, Willy.

Arthur loved Willy more than life itself, and there was never a doubt Willy was the heart of their mother. The elder sons, Arthur and Georg, felt compelled to keep careful watch over him for her sake. It was no easy task. The boy was capricious and their parents, at advanced ages, were no longer able to effectively guide him. Arthur frowned and shook his head. This was Willy's way of entrusting Arthur to share the photograph with their mother, which would be difficult, at best.

Arthur and Georg were both officers in the German military. Both were well-versed in military procedures and each had each spoken with Willy about his military obligation. In compliance with the law, on January 1, 1916, the year of his seventeenth birthday, Willy registered for military service. Registrants would become part of the class of the year of their twentieth birthday. Upon registration Willy was assigned to the class of 1919, the year he would turn twenty, also the year he was expected to be called up, should the war last that long.

Their mother, Auguste Amalie (nee Weissflog) Lippert was quite upset when Willy registered. She insisted an inquiry be made with regard to excusing him from service due to a personal hardship -- her own. Weren't two sons in the military enough? Their father, Ernst Hugo, would have no part of an inquiry and their parents quarreled bitterly over the matter. The younger sisters agreed with their mother, but Arthur and Georg supported their father, knowing full well that Willy was anxious to serve, thus dividing the family on the issue.

His mother's anxiety began on January 1, 1917 when Willy found his name, along with other boys his age, posted on the roster scheduled for muster in May – two years earlier than expected. This was due to the heavy casualties sustained by the Germans as the Great War raged on. When Willy realized he would be part of the first group trained at the new pilot instructional facility in Freiburg, south of Frankfurt, he was overjoyed. His mother was inconsolable. She had only a few months to get used to the idea, but it was not enough time.

In early May 1917 Willy and forty-one others boarded the westbound train for Freiburg. They joked and discussed "military life" as they traveled, but when they reached the training camp, the joking ended. It was time to be serious. Willy passed the medical examination and was deemed fit for duty. He received his uniforms and firearms and multiple training manuals and regulation books for the training that would last three to four months. Upon completion of training, an official postcard photograph for mailing home was taken of each recruit in full military dress.

Arthur tucked the postcard into his pocket and walked two blocks to his childhood home, 30 Langestrasse. He gave their special whistle while opening the back door. He didn't think his mother heard him, for she never whistled in reply, nor did she even look up.

She was engrossed in making Knoedels for tonight's soup. She pressed a bit of plum into each one, then gently rolled them in farina.

Arthur deeply inhaled the rich aroma of roasted meat and fresh bread then kissed his mother on the forehead.

She smiled and when the last Knoedel was stuffed and rolled, she washed her hands and poured two cups of chamomile tea, adding just a touch of honey to her son's.

As they sat together sipping their tea, she gave him what had recently become a familiar look, the one that said she thought it was time for dashing Arthur to marry and settle down.

"Don't say it, Mutti, I am going to marry Hedie, but not just yet . . . when the war ends." He placed the postcard in her hand.

Willy Lippert September 11, 1917 Freiberg, Germany

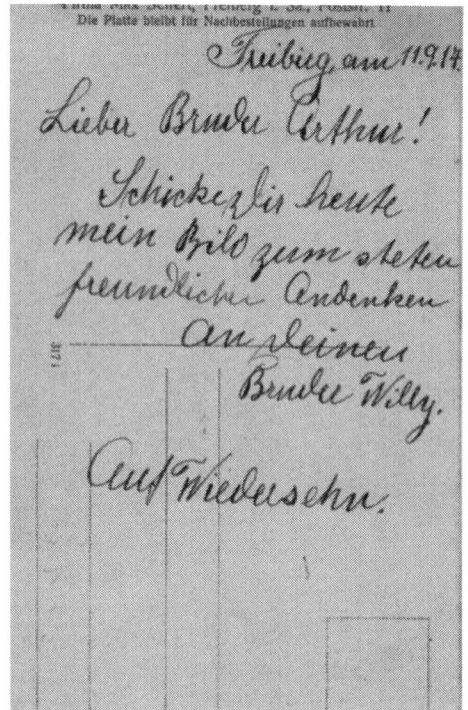

Willy's message to his brother Arthur

Georg, Willy and Arthur

KINETOSCOPE

Alma, Olga, Flora, Frieda

Standing L-R: Arthur,
Flora, Georg, Alma, Olga's husband
Seated L-R: Frieda, Willy, Mother, Father, Olga's son, Olga

Celeste Yost

30 Langestrasse, Dresden, Germany

CHAPTER THREE

Germany-France-America 1917-1923

Willy began his training with twelve hundred other recruits. His new daily life began before dawn with muster in the field, followed by breakfast and continual classes all morning. Afternoons were spent in hands-on training in close combat weapons, defensive fighting, trench warfare, and survival. In addition, all recruits were required to receive instruction in tethered observation balloons and Zeppelins.

The recruits rotated in and out of the various classes. Before lights-out, evenings were for studying the numerous training manuals. As the casualties continued to rise, hundreds of recruits were practically pushed through early completion of training to be immediately dispatched into various branches of combat. They were then replaced by another group of new recruits who also received limited training and were dispatched out before they were ready.

Aerial photography had emerged into an indispensable tool to guide artillery attacks and assess damage afterward, but the most important mission was that of support for the ground forces. Willy's Commander spoke with him and another pilot privately about reconnaissance training for the *Luftstreitkrafte*, the Imperial German Army Air Corps. Willy was elated and very interested, as was his friend. They were to be transferred to a reconnaissance unit near the border with France. They would be flying the radio-equipped, unarmed, two-passenger fixed-wing Rumpler C.VII or *Rumpler-Bildflugzeug* (photography-aircraft) which had distinguished itself for long-range and high-altitude, reaching 21,000 feet. Specialized German Gorz and ICA cameras were mounted on the side of the aircraft for accurately photographing the designated subjects through the large box-type cameras. The Germans also used a standard 70 cm focal length and 13×18 cm plates. Germany alone reportedly generated 4,000 images a day in 1918.

Over the course of the war, the role of the military aviator progressed from one of mere observation to a deadly offensive role. Early on, pilots would fly off armed only with pistols or sometimes completely unarmed. Older technologies, like tethered balloons and kites were still used on the front lines to gain an upper-hand. As aircraft became more of a threat, anti-aircraft weapons and tactics were developed, and pilots had to devise new ways to avoid being shot down from land artillery and from the sky. The pilots of these new aircraft took tremendous risks. They were most vulnerable to enemy fire, at the mercy of the weather, and flying new, often experimental aircraft. Crashes were frequent, and many paid with their lives.

Problems included the shortage of trained and experienced photo-interpreters and lack of timely distribution of interpreted prints to the specific Commanders needing them. There was deficiency in overall coordination and centralized interpretation of common air photographs. Field Commanders demanded risky and repeated flights for objectives, only to learn the photos became lost in files somewhere in the process.

By spring 1918, the British successfully blockaded seaports from the Somme River to the English Channel. The blockade cut off the supply routes to the German Army. Fuel, equipment, repair parts, medical needs, and rations were in short supply. The Battle of Lys, also known as the Spring Offensive, part of the 1918 German offensive in Flanders, was originally planned by German General Erich Ludendorff. The objective was to capture Ypres, forcing the British back to the Channel ports and out of the war, thus opening the supply route for the German troops.

To curtail fuel usage, the German army switched to the smaller one-man recon planes for surveillance. These planes were unable to fly at high altitudes, nor were they equipped with machine guns. Thus, pilots were required to carry their own weapons, fly the airplane, and take the necessary recon photographs. Willy and his fellow co-pilot were transferred to different locations and never saw each other again.

Although apprehensive about piloting his plane alone and taking the recon photographs, Willy felt privileged to serve his country in this special unit of the air corps. Throughout the Spring Offensive, the weather was miserably cold and damp and the continual intense fog greatly hampered a pilot's visibility for taking accurate photographs. He was a perfectionist and sometimes missed his targeted landmark and would have to repeat the assignment. The continual barrage of machine gun fire unnerved him. The lack of visibility, except for when the sky lit up with artillery fire, kept him on edge. The scarcity of fuel was of major concern; he feared running out and being forced to make an unplanned landing in the foggy darkness. Even more so, he feared being shot down or captured by the enemy.

Willy never saw the aircraft approaching through the fog, but he heard the barrage of rapid gunfire and felt the intense jolt and updraft of his plane when it was struck. The cockpit filled with smoke and the plane teetered precariously off balance by the partially torn off left wing where his camera was mounted. In the distance he heard rapid machinegun fire. He forced himself to focus on keeping his disabled plane under control to avoid being shot at again. Cold damp air rushed into the cockpit from breaches in the plane's undercarriage. The plane careened crazily downward. Icy wind and damp fog enveloped him. The wing banged against the fuselage, and strong fumes from fuel leakage made him nauseous. He feared the plane would catch fire.

His mind went blank, immediately forgetting his emergency training. No amount of training prepared him for what was to come. The horrific high-pitched whining of the engine as the plane lost altitude made his heart pound. He could barely discern the open field rising quickly toward the belly of his aircraft as it pitched from side-to-side. He clung desperately to the stick attempting to control the descent but he was now scraping treetops causing pieces of the plane to give way as it continued to break apart. Wind and rain rushed into the cockpit from the damaged floor boards. He felt like an acrobat as his plane now bounced off low scrub. A loose strap caught his neck and he choked on his own vomit.

Willy didn't know how long he had been unconscious when he was awakened by the cold rain and intense pain all over. His torso was tangled in the safety apparatus and even the slightest movement caused severe chest pain. He could feel the warm wetness of his own blood in the left calf which he knew had been shot. He was trembling and scared. He peered through the gaping hole where a remnant of the wing that was torn off hung. His camera was gone. He panicked over its loss and the realization that all his recon photos were gone, too. Could he be court-martialed for losing military equipment and valuable information that enemy combatants could use against his beloved country?

The plane rested awkwardly in a field and he was relieved to be alive. The fuel fumes were pervasive, but the plane had not burned. He untangled himself; then leaned over the side of the aircraft and retched. On his first attempt to get out of the plane, his left leg was utterly useless and the pain so intense he blacked out again.

When he revived, his pant leg above the boot top was drenched in blood which had seeped into his boot. His rucksack was still jammed under the seat. Relieved it was not missing, he pulled it out and found bandage strips which he managed to tie around his throbbing leg hoping to staunch the bleeding. He dropped the rucksack to the ground and hefted himself backward over the side of the plane to avoid putting weight on his injured leg.

Other than scrubs of juniper, the field appeared fallow. He couldn't see a farmhouse or any sign of life nearby. He dragged himself and his rucksack up a small knoll to wooded cover where he hoped he'd be safe. Exhausted, he drank stale water from his canteen and fell asleep in the woods.

At first light Willy awoke to a weapon pointed in his face. His heart pounded and his leg throbbed, the makeshift bandage now blood-soaked. He was dizzy, hungry, but most of all scared to death. He stared at his captor who looked to be as frightened as he. Regardless, the soldier kept his gun trained at Willy's head. The bearer was not much older than Willy, and wore a disheveled uniform, French . . . the enemy. Willy raised his hands in surrender, but the soldier lowered his weapon to the ground and shoved it away. He set about pulling medical supplies from his own pack.

He spoke rapid French using hand gestures. He unwrapped the blood-soaked bandage from Willy's leg; then carefully attempted to loosen the boot and raise the pant leg. Willy cried out in pain. There was shrapnel in the wound which had become quite swollen. The Frenchman poured water from his canteen to flush the wound, then applied a fresh bandage from his own pack. He pointed to the shrapnel and shook his head indicating he was afraid to try to remove it. Willy's breathing was labored. What happens now? Would he be taken as a prisoner of war?

His captor sat down and offered his canteen, nodding his head and speaking more French. Willy drank deeply, thanked him in German, and passed it back and the Frenchman drank also. His name was Renard and he, too, was a reconnaissance pilot. His plane had run out of fuel and gone down an embankment beyond the location of Willy's plane. Somehow he, too, had managed a survivable crash.

When Willy reached for his pack, Renard quickly grabbed his weapon, pointing it again at his enemy. Willy shook his head no and simply opened his pack completely to show Renard he was only looking for rations. He withdrew several tins of sardines, crackers, and a bit of chocolate, and they both ate. The sun was shining and they removed their heavy damp coats and laid them out on the ground to dry. In their respective languages with the sounds of war in the far distance, they tried to discuss what they should do about their circumstances.

Sleep was critical. The two moved deeper into the trees and slept most of the afternoon, shared rations again, after which Renard searched through the small woods for a suitable stick that Willy might use as a cane. They said good-bye at twilight and Renard headed away from the Somme to where he believed he could connect with his regiment. Willy remained in the copse near his plane, waiting expectantly for rescue which would come a day later.

He was admitted to the infirmary and doctors surgically removed the shrapnel from his leg where an infection had developed. He was in a great deal of pain and had difficulty sleeping and could barely put any pressure on his left leg. He experienced nightmares of falling out of the sky and searching for his camera. He had frightening hallucinations from the morphine which caused him to be disoriented when he awoke. He would call for help and ask repeatedly for his camera. He dreamt of his family, particularly his brother, Georg. They were playing ball on a summer day. His sleep was restless and he would awaken drenched in sweat, crying and shaking uncontrollably with tremors. Like many others, Willy was diagnosed with shell shock [3] and remained in the infirmary several weeks; he was exposed to the severely injured and to those who died from their wounds. He was subsequently returned to his unit and given a sedentary assignment. His flying days were over.

Two passenger Rumpler C. VII (photography WW I)

Single passenger Pfalz E.1 1916 (photography) WW I

---

[3] The World War I name for what is known today as post-traumatic stress disorder or PTSD, this is a psychological disorder that develops in some individuals who have had major traumatic experiences (and, for example, have been in a serious accident or through a war).

When the Armistice was signed November 11, 1919, the soldiers were systematically mustered out and sent home. Willy's family, particularly his mother, was heartbroken over the poor condition of her youngest son. He was thin and gaunt and he seldom smiled or relaxed. His nightmares continued and she took him from doctor to doctor to find out what could be done. She didn't understand the ramifications of shell shock and why it just didn't go away. He was moody and reclusive, preferring solitude. He spoke very little of his experiences in the war. He was convinced that he was a failure and a disgrace to his family, particularly to his father and brothers.

Weeks turned into months and Willy continued to withdraw to the point of locking himself in his bedroom. No one could help him. He refused to see anyone, not even his mother. She sat outside his room hoping he would just say her name, but he never did. She would leave a tray of food with a small vase of pretty flowers and a sketch pad and pencils for him. He ate what she provided and occupied his time with sketching and sleeping. One day, he just came out of his room and rejoined the family. Although he was much improved, he was never quite the same.

The economy in Germany was abysmal and much of Dresden was in shambles. Willy's father still held his job at the famous Lindt-Sprungli Chocolate Factory. He had plenty of work there, constantly maintaining the machinery to keep it functional. But like everyone else, he brought home little money. It was often commented that it took a wheelbarrow of Deutschmarks to buy a loaf of bread. This was never a joke to the German people. Returning soldiers could find no work and often left the country seeking their fortunes elsewhere.

In the spring of 1920 Willy boarded a train for France. His family encouraged him to go, thinking a holiday would do him good. Little did they know, his plan was to search for

Renard. He hoped he had remembered the name of the town correctly, Vincennes, approximately six kilometers east of Paris, an easy walk from the train station.

In Vincennes, Willy found lodging and took a job waiting tables in a small café. He had asked how to go about finding his friend and with help from his employer, Willy obtained a street address, but when no one responded to his knocking, he left a note in the post box. A few days later, Renard took a seat at a small table outside the café and surprised his waiter, Willy. "So, I have heard you have been searching for me, yes?" asked Renard, standing and offering his hand.

"Yes," said Willy, smiling. They shook hands, embraced, then both started talking at the same time in bits of German and French. Renard invited Willy to his home and introduced him to his wife, Gabrielle, who was expecting their first child.

Renard worked as a woodcraftsman's apprentice making furniture and soon Willy was apprenticed also. He loved the feel of the wood and of the tools in his hands. Willy was a natural and learned to carve intricate designs and inlaid pieces which sold for quite a bit more than the furniture his employer usually made. Willy believed he had found a niche. He found peace and tranquility in woodworking. With the depressed economy in Germany, Willy continued to live in France plying his new trade during the day and studying fine art at night. Surprisingly, his mother was at peace with his decision. They kept in contact as much as possible considering the state of both countries after the war.

He returned to Dresden for his sister's wedding. He looked different to his family. He was more mature, relaxed, and healthy. He brought a special gift to his sister and her new husband, an intricately hand-carved wooden chest with a velvet lining, a gift she would treasure all her life. Although he thought about returning to France, another more promising opportunity was afforded him by a cousin who had recently immigrated to America.

AERIAL IMAGES OF DRESDEN

KINETOSCOPE

POST-WAR ARIAL IMAGES OF DRESDEN

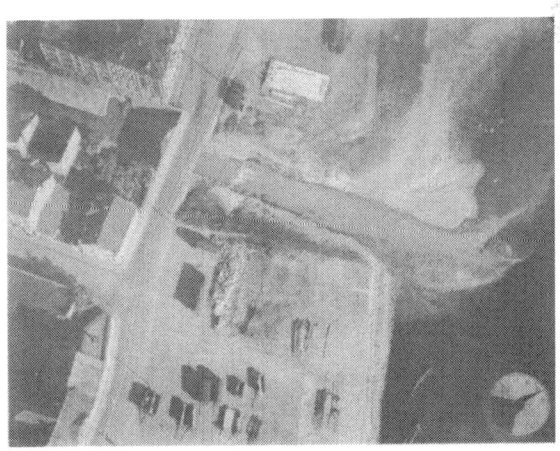

Celeste Yost

PRE-WAR PHOTOS OF DRESDEN

CHAPTER FOUR

Leaving Home 1923

Hugo Weissflog, a cousin on Willy's mother's side, had immigrated to America several years prior to the war. Hugo had secured a good job working for the Pennsylvania Railroad in Altoona, Pennsylvania. Knowing the tenuous state of the European economy after the war, and especially the dire straits of Germany, Hugo wrote a letter to Willy's parents offering him the opportunity to come to America. He would be Willy's legal sponsor if Willy's parents approved and gave their blessing. Hugo would obtain the necessary documents for entry into the United States and make the appropriate contacts in Germany to process them. Willy would need a passport and Hugo would arrange and pay for his passage. He made it clear to Willy and his mother that the terms of the sponsorship required that Willy have the promise of a job before he left Germany. Hugo would arrange for the job, and committed to house, clothe and feed Willy for one year. It was to be understood that if after a year Willy was not self-sufficient, the US government would deport him back to Germany.

On November 3, 1923, at age 24, passport and documentation in hand, Willy bade good-bye to his family, all of whom traveled to the Port of Bremen, Germany to see him off. His ship was the beautiful S.S. Muenchen bound for the Port of New York in America. Although his mother promised not to cry, when they looked into each other's eyes, they both had tears. His parents were getting up in years and were becoming frail and the thought struck him that this may be the last time he will see them. He hugged them tightly; then he boarded the ship.

He lingered on deck with many others waving goodbye to their families long after they were out of sight. Willy was exhausted from the excitement leading up to this moment. Once settled in his sleeping quarters, he went back up on deck to look out over the ocean. His beloved homeland was no longer in view. He saw only the wide expanse of the Atlantic and the chilling gray skies of November.

The Muenchen and many similar ships transported immigrants to America from all parts of Europe. Like every immigrant, Willy's sleeping quarters were in steerage and he shared facilities with many men of different nationalities his age and older. He was cautioned to be very careful about his passport and other documents and kept them always hidden on his person in a pouch his sister had sewn inside his clothing. He read and reread Hugo's letter describing his wife Delores and their new home on Crawford Avenue, Altoona, Pennsylvania. Hugo also described Willy's new job. He would be hired as a "Joiner" working for the Pennsylvania Railroad. Willy wasn't certain what a "Joiner" was or what the job entailed, but he knew he would be working with wood and that made him very happy.

On November 14, 1923 Willy and his new friends and traveling companions clamored to stand on deck as the Muenchen grandly entered the Port of New York. The sight of the famous Statue of Liberty was inspiring to all onboard and great cheering erupted among the immigrant passengers so excited to become part of America. Here in this place a brand new life with exciting opportunities in a young country was offered to all. He knew he was blessed to be here and was eager to meet his cousins who had made this possible.

After waiting hours in long lines, the overwhelmed, exhausted, and somewhat frightened immigrants of many nationalities were individually processed at Ellis Island. Their names were officially entered into the United States Immigration Records. Everything was so new and confusing, but oh, so exciting. The new immigrants moved as one body toward another large room where they were to finally meet their sponsors.

The room was crowded with men and women holding their handmade signs and calling out names. Willy scanned the crowd for his cousin, Hugo. Which man in this crowd was he? Some signs had the name "Willy" printed on them, but the surname was not Lippert. It was then he realized for the first time that he had not seen his cousin in years and only had an old photograph to help him. What if he wasn't here? His heart pounding, he scanned the crowd once more. Then, to his great relief, he heard a voice shouting "Willy Lippert!"

Willy waved his arms high in the air as he looked about. A big burly man holding a handmade sign threaded through the crowd to where Willy stood. His arms enfolded Willy and he hugged him so tightly. Then, he pulled back and looked Willy all over; then, he squeezed him again. Hugo's tears ran down not only his own cheeks, but Willy's too. Then Willy cried. He couldn't believe he was actually in America and was being hugged and squeezed in the arms of his cousin.

Willy was eager to write to his family and describe his adventure crossing the ocean and finally coming into the Port of New York. He was awestruck riding through New York City and gazing up the twenty-two stories of the Flatiron Building, one of the first skyscrapers in the United States. Willy and Hugo laughed and talked in their native tongue as Hugo answered Willy's myriad questions about American life -- the economy, his new job, and where they lived in Altoona. Willy could barely believe he was really here. If this were a dream, he never wanted it to end.

Celeste Yost

Willy's passport photo

Manifest Willy Lippert # 3

KINETOSCOPE

Continuation of Manifest #3 refers to Willy Lippert's sponsor, his cousin, Hugo Weissflog

Celeste Yost

CHAPTER FIVE

Snyder County, Pennsylvania 1900s

More than four thousand miles across the Atlantic in America, particularly in the Commonwealth of Pennsylvania, young Harry Martin Bathurst married Emma Eliza Varner on July 24, 1900. The young couple began their married life in Penns Creek, a tiny "census-designated place" in Snyder County. The village was originally called Weirickstown, named in 1896 after its founder, Lt. Col. George Weirick. The name was later changed to Centreville; then changed again to Penns Creek, due to a conflict with another village of Centreville in Crawford County.

Penns Creek is bordered on the north by its namesake creek and lies along PA Route 104 between Middleburg to the south and Mifflinburg to the north. The total land area is only 1.1 square miles; hence it is noted as a "census designated place" in the Snyder County records.

The Bathursts would raise eleven children, who in birth order were Leonard Henry, Pauline Elizabeth, Eleanor Ethel, Harry Malcolm, Gerald Franklin, Sheldon Joseph, Everett Paul, Berwin Eugene, Irma May, Bernadine Emma, and, lastly, Junette Alice, all born within a span of only twenty years.

Harry was an enterprising young man with the vision of owning his own business. Penns Creek offered few opportunities. Shortly after their marriage, the young couple relocated fifty miles west to the Borough of Bellefonte. Harry bought a dray and a few horses and started a business hauling furniture, barrels, grain, and just about anything else that could be hauled.

Three years later, in 1903 their first child, Leonard Henry, was born. Pauline Elizabeth, my mother, was born in 1905.

In 1849 Pennsylvania Railroad officials had established a new town they named Altoona. It nestled between Brush Mountain and the Allegheny Mountain range. Altoona, a shortened version of the Cherokee Indian word "Allatoona," meant "highlands of great worth."

Plans were developed for the construction of a rail car repair facility. Officials chose downtown Twelfth Street in the heart of the city as the perfect site for an eight-stall roundhouse, locomotive repair shop, machine shop, paint shop, woodwork shop, blacksmith shop, and foundry. Construction commenced immediately on the first building, and by the end of the year, construction was complete

Following the end of World War I in 1917, a second machine shop, which housed a tank shop, was built in the Juniata section of Altoona. This facility was for the construction and repair of locomotive tenders. Soldiers returning from the war were eager to come home to their families. Many good jobs were available with the PRR -- the area's largest employer.

In the spring of 1918 Emma gave birth to the couple's ninth child, Irma May. When Irma was only a few months old, Harry decided it would be worth driving fifty miles to Altoona to see what opportunities were available for a man who owned his own dray and several horses. He was willing to work anywhere that paid well, even if it meant uprooting his family. He had heard about the opportunities in Altoona and decided they'd move there during the summer. Emma was against the move and preferred staying in Bellefonte to be nearer her family in Penns Creek, because the distance from Altoona to her homestead was nearly a hundred miles.

Harry acquiesced to Emma's wishes, but on November 8, 1919, when their tenth child, Bernadine Emma, was born, Harry was finally able to talk Emma into moving to Altoona. Much to Emma's chagrin, the "Bathurst Brood" packed up and moved their large family fifty miles south to the up-and-coming PRR Mecca—the City of Altoona. They settled into a home on Crawford Avenue in the "Dutch Hill" section of town.

By 1922 the railroad shops and departments occupied fifty acres and were housed in hundreds of buildings in several locations in Altoona. The workforce employed nearly 16,000 workers in all capacities and trades. Harry now owned a large gasoline engine lorry which was capable of hauling just about anything heavy, including beer barrels and pianos. He knew that Altoona's growing population would provide plenty of work for him and his sons.

One late spring afternoon in 1923, at their mother's request, Pauline and her closest sister, Eleanor, who Pauline had nicknamed "Sy", took their three younger siblings to Highland Park for a picnic. Emma was now in the third trimester of pregnancy with her eleventh and last child. She shared with her daughters that she hadn't slept well the night before and asked them to "tend to the little ones" so she could rest. They were happy to comply. The girls packed a lunch and their father drove them to the park and said he'd return for them at 4:00 PM.

Pauline and Sy chatted and played in the sandbox with Irma and Bernadine while their youngest brother, Berwin, played ball with some other boys in the park. Sy had just remarked what a beautiful day it was when, while pushing Irma and Bernadine on the swings, the wooden crossbeam of the structure began to crack. At first no one who heard the cracking sound knew where it came from, but the swings suddenly shook and Pauline and Sy quickly got the girls off the swings out of harm's way.

Pauline had looked away to find Berwin when the heavy wooden crossbeam gave way and caught her shoulder knocking her to the ground. Her head and back struck the ground forcefully. A small secondary support also gave way and fell across her abdomen. Other parents and children in the park ran to render assistance and lifted the broken support from Pauline's midsection. She was dazed and could barely breathe. The back of her head was bleeding, and she had a bruise and gash on her forehead, as well as lacerations to the shoulder and upper arm.

"Don't move her! Don't move her!," someone shouted as another ran to a nearby house to call for an ambulance. With all the confusion, Irma and Bernadine began to cry and Eleanor tried to calm them through her own tears for her beloved sister who was pale and breathing shallowly. Only Berwin stood by silently biting his lip, trying to be brave and not cry. The ambulance arrived and carefully lifted Pauline onto a stretcher. Eleanor and the three little ones sat in the back with Pauline and a nurse who held Pauline's hand.

When the police were unable to reach the Bathurst home by phone, they dispatched a unit to the house. Emma quickly wrote a note for Harry and the boys; then, she went to the hospital in the police cruiser. Harry and the boys joined her a short time later. The entire Bathurst family was upset and were encouraged to sit in a private solarium while their eldest daughter was being examined.

The first few days of hospitalization, Pauline was heavily sedated and her body was weighted down with sand bags to keep her immobile. Her neck was only strained and would require a neck brace, but her spine was fractured which required surgery. Only Emma and Harry were permitted to see her. A small gash on her forehead had been sutured, and wounds to her shoulder and abdomen were dressed. Bruises and scrapes would heal, but serious internal injuries would not be discovered until years later.

Following surgery, Pauline remained bedfast. Sy came to the hospital every day to visit and help with bathing and personal care for her seventeen-year-old sister. She would often read to Pauline and sing to her. Sometimes she had to be admonished by the hospital staff when it was time to leave, and she reluctantly kissed her sister goodbye and went home. Pauline's midsection was casted to keep her spine straight and she wore a thick collar to protect her neck. She remained in the hospital several months.

Pauline's baby sister, Junette Alice, was born July 20, 1923. Before taking the baby home, the nursing staff allowed her mother to bring little Junette into Pauline's room so she could see her.

When Pauline was finally discharged and sent home to recuperate, her father hired home-care nurses to come twice a week to monitor her progress and help with medication, bathing, exercises, and teaching her techniques on how to "live" in the cast. The surgeon also made house calls periodically to check the cast. When the cast became loose, Pauline returned to the hospital to have the first cast cut off and a new one put on. The next step, months later, was a brace she was required to wear constantly. She was happy she was able to dress normally and wear the brace over her clothing. With the brace, she was able to sit up for longer periods of time, walk some without assistance, and take care of her own personal needs.

She could not attend classes because she was limited in her ability to sit upright for any length of time without sustaining pressure to her spine. Sy and Leonard helped with her studies at home and her father hired a tutor over the winter months, with the goal that his daughter would be able to return to school and graduate with her class in the spring of 1924. But that was not to be, the girl who had never missed a day of school for eleven years was unable to graduate with her class. She was deferred a year and, instead, graduated with the Altoona High School Class of

1925. It was a proud day for the Bathurst family to see her walk down the aisle unaided to receive her diploma.

Pauline Bathurst, Altoona High School Class of 1925

Following graduation, Pauline wanted to work and knew exactly where. She had always loved music and literature. Throughout school she participated in glee club, chorus, harmony, and played French horn in the orchestra, and accompanied the chorus on the piano. She walked downtown to Winter's Music Store and spoke with the owner, Arthur E. Winter, and he hired her immediately. Pauline was overjoyed. The popular store sold pianos and multiple instruments, offered music lessons, and stocked the latest in sheet music and choral and opera scores. Everyone who worked there loved their jobs, but most of all, everyone loved Arthur. Pauline was no exception.

When fall came, she volunteered two evenings each week to teach English at night school. With the large influx of Europeans seeking a better life in America after the war, the English classes were well attended and many teachers were needed. Pauline was an avid reader and thought helping others learn to read and speak English was worthwhile and something she could do that would not conflict with her job at Winter's.

Celeste Yost

CHAPTER SIX

In 1924 and 1925 the Juniata Shops of the PRR were expanded to include a fifty-stall erecting and machine shop at the eastern end of the existing shops, along with a three-story storehouse and a small flue shop. The purpose of the move and expansion was to relocate the locomotive works from the downtown Twelfth Street area to Juniata.

Willy worked in the machine shop during his first year in America. He lived with his cousins, Hugo and Delores on Crawford Avenue and began paying rent when he received his first paycheck. At Hugo's suggestion, Willy opened a savings account with the goal of saving enough money to eventually move into a place of his own.

Willy liked his job with the railroad working as a Joiner. He was meeting new friends from Germany, Poland and Italy. They all muddled through in their various languages as they learned a new trade. The downside was the taunting of immigrants that was almost constant. Ethnic slurs were rampant where he worked and every day you'd hear "hey you Polak" or "what's the matter with you, you dumb kraut?" or "you're a lazy wop" -- words that the immigrants just absorbed and tried never to show any emotion, fearful they'd lose their jobs which meant deportation. They all just tried to stay out of everyone's way, keep their heads down, and work hard.

When the noon whistle blew, the shops stopped working for a half-hour lunch. Willy went to his locker to retrieve his new lunchbox and found it missing. His heart sank. The lunchbox was a gift from Delores and Hugo. Delores had packed him a lunch early that morning and placed it carefully in the new lunchbox.

He heard laughter and crude comments from the chief perpetrator, an overweight, obnoxious old man everyone called "Bub." It seemed his goal was to entertain the whole shop by making loud derogatory comments at the immigrants' expense.

Willy saw his lunchbox in the middle of the table where the troublemakers always sat. When he got closer, he read the word "KRAUT" painted in bold white letters on his lunchbox. When he attempted to pick it up, the handle broke loose on one side. His new gift had been nailed to the table. This, of course, was the prank of Bub who sat at the table slapping his knee and laughing so hard he had tears in his eyes. Then he said to the whole table "Take your lunchbox you dumb Dutchman! Can't pick it up huh? Too heavy for ya'? Looks ta' me like someone nailed it down!"

Willy was furious but he had seen others be the brunt of Bub's jokes and knew he couldn't respond or he would make things worse. Bub would pick on him like he picked on his Irish friend, James. Willy never said a word, just opened it, removed his lunch, snapped it shut, and went to another table to sit with his friends. The ridicule died down.

When the three o'clock whistle blew, every worker checked out with the Shop Steward, but Willy hung back and asked if he might return to the lunchroom and get his lunchbox to repair it. Obviously, the Steward knew all about the prank; chuckled and told him to go ahead. Willy got his tools and pried the box off the table and reattached the handle. Then, he set to work cleaning the slur off the side. He didn't want his family to see it like this.

The Steward watched him a while then left the shop. Willy consequently missed his ride and had to walk home, which he rather enjoyed because the walk helped release the tension he felt, and cleared his head. The next morning, Willy's Steward wrote him up for staying in the shop after hours the day before, even though he had approved it. This action was disheartening and Willy was unsure what it meant and worried he would lose his job.

Willy didn't lose his job. Instead he received a small promotion which came with a pay raise, as did others in his shop. The extra wages made it possible for him to move out on his own. He found a small apartment located at 2205 Eighth Avenue, second floor, rear which was small but quite comfortable. He was nervous about telling Hugo and Delores about his plan to move out on his own for fear they would think him ungrateful for their many kindnesses. As it turned out, Hugo and Delores had something exciting to share with Willy. They were expecting their first baby! Hearing this news Willy had no problem telling them about his raise and his plans. The three of them laughed and talked about the perfect timing of these events. Willy would have his own place and they would turn the guest room into a nursery.

"We were so worried you would be upset and feel you had to move out," said Delores, "we did not know how to tell you the news!"

"This is a good news day!" laughed Hugo. "We should have a celebration!"

"Yes!" agreed Delores, "A special dinner to celebrate Willy's new home and our new baby!! I hope you are not moving too far from us, Willy . . . we want you to live close by."

"So we can keep an eye on you, Willy," joked Hugo.

Willy laughed and thanked them for their kindness, but he knew it was time for him to stand on his own two feet. He moved to his new home the following weekend. He offered to help Hugo paint the nursery, but he had a special surprise in mind for Delores. After the walls were painted, Willy came over in the evenings to paint Charles Perrault's "Mother Goose" characters on the nursery walls as his gift to the baby. "So the baby will learn all these beautiful stories," he said, pleased that he could do something special for them.

Willy's apartment was perfect for one and as he settled into his new life alone he found he rather liked it. He often came home and after dinner, read, wrote letters home, or sketched until bedtime. Life was good in America.

In1926 the PRR Altoona Works consisted of the Altoona Machine Shops, Altoona Car Shops, Juniata Shops, and the South Altoona Foundries. It was to the South Altoona Foundries, specifically the Pattern Shop, where Willy was transferred.

The Foundries cast wheels and other metal parts, and could produce a thousand cast iron wheels a day. The transfer included a promotion to Pattern Maker Apprentice. The Pattern Shop employees built the wooden molds or patterns for casting those wheels and the best part of his transfer was that the men he worked with were much different and friendlier than those in the Juniata Shops.

Within a few months, the Pattern Shop was assigned to build wooden patterns for the train axles. This was Willy's niche. His work was meticulous and the Shop Foreman often came by to compliment him on his work ethic and quality.

One day the Foreman saw him working on a drawing and asked about it. Willy showed him the design indicating how the pattern they were currently using could be improved. Management was interested in Willy's idea and with additional sketches, Willy showed how his modification to the mold would improve efficiency of the entire casting process. The horizontal pattern they were using often took many man-hours just to scrape off the slag that rose to the top after the axles were removed from the molds. Willy's upright perpendicular design provided ease in pouring and reduced the amount of slag which rose to the top of a much smaller area. The new mold would save time and effort in the finishing process. His superiors were pleased with his innovated pattern and it was then adopted and used exclusively by the PRR for many years thereafter.

Willy, far left front row, with his co-workers,
South Altoona PRR Pattern Shop 1926

Celeste Yost

CHAPTER SEVEN

One summer evening Willy stopped in to visit Hugo, Delores, and their beautiful new daughter, Christina. He had a small gift for them and was anxious to see their reaction. Delores undid the wrapping of a framed charcoal drawing Willy had made of the three of them. "Oh Willy," Delores began to cry and hugged him tightly, "this is a most beautiful treasure. When did you…"

"I have my sketch book always," Willy replied, "I remember your smile and that of Hugo and of Christina, of course." He showed them the sketches in his little book, "From this sketch, I make the drawing."

"This is a most thoughtful gift," Hugo said with a pat on Willy's back, "our first picture of the Hugo Weisflog family. Your Mutti raised you with kindness for others!"

They all laughed and Delores suggested they all sit on the front porch because there was something important she had to discuss with Willy. She explained that the Altoona High School was offering classes in the evenings for anyone desiring to learn English.

"That's a very good idea for you, Willy," said Hugo, "there is no cost to immigrants and the classes will help you in your studies to become a United States citizen. What do you think?"

Willy smiled and clapped his hands. "Will they teach me to read and also to write English?"

"Of course, and other things about America and its history, too," Delores chimed in, "you can use my Langenscheidt to help you." [4]

---

[4] Langenscheidt is the groundbreaking invention by the founder of the publishing house, Gustav Langenscheidt (1832-1895), who laid the foundations for future success. Together with his language teacher, Charles Touissant, in 1856 he developed an innovative phonetic system, the purpose of which was to make learning languages easier.

"Ha!" Willy said laughing, "Then I will know when they make sport of me at my work! Maybe I will keep a secret and surprise them when they think I don't know what they say! Yes, yes, I will do it! Now, you give a gift to Willy! The gift of knowledge!"

Willy's classes began in the Fall and the high school was not far from his new home. He was glad he arrived early and was able to take a seat in the back, as the class quickly became full. His teacher was a young woman named Miss Pauline. He liked the sound of her voice and she had a pretty smile. He often made sketches of her in his notebook so he could show them to his cousins.

"Ah...another good reason to learn English – meet an American girlfriend," Hugo said. "You need someone to dance with!" They both laughed.

Willy studied every evening using Delores' Langenscheidt which was a tremendous help to him. He had ready answers for Miss Pauline when called upon and she was pleased with his progress. His good looks and attentiveness were not lost on her either. He lingered behind one evening after class and she asked if he might have a question.

"Yes, a question...my question is to ask if I could walk home with you," said Willy. Totally unexpected, Pauline's heart skipped a beat, and she smiled and nodded yes. He carried her satchel and took her hand as they walked and talked about the weather and the changing colors of the leaves and what it is like in Germany at this time of year. They talked about their jobs and his family in Dresden and her family in Altoona.

Standing under the arc light on the sidewalk in front of the Bathurst's home, Pauline happened to see the parlor curtains open just slightly. She knew Sy was at the window peering out when Willy took her hand and kissed it. This was something new to her, none of the boys she knew ever did that! He returned her satchel, nodded, and said, "Guten Abend" and walked swiftly down the sidewalk, turning only once to call out "Goodnight, Miss Pauline!"

Pauline was barely in the door when Sy grabbed her and hugged her, "Alright, fess up! Who is he? Is he the one you said took a shine to you at the school? He's so cute, and so European! Tell ALL! He kissed your hand – how romantic!! And, most importantly, you and I could double date – and you could tell Daddy about your German beau and that I have a German beau too!"

"Oh no you don't. You must tell Daddy about Herman...don't make me your scapegoat!" The inseparable pair giggled and ran up the stairs to their bedroom talking and laughing until the second warning from their father, when they quieted down and went to sleep.

The next week while walking Pauline home after class, Willy asked if she would like to go to the cinema with him on Saturday. "*La Boheme* will be shown," Willy told her, "it's a beautiful love story, it is of Italy. I hope you will agree to come."

"I cannot, Willy," Pauline said, "I must work. The music store is very busy now before Christmas, and Mr. Winter needs me. I've heard about this new film and would love to see it, but I cannot go, I must work that day. I am so sorry."

"Yes, I am sorry too, Ich verstehen (I understand)," said Willy dejectedly, "another time, we can go. Yes?"

"Yes," Pauline replied and squeezed his hand, "another time."

Saturday morning Pauline was at the music store waiting on a customer when she heard "Humoresque" being played on the piano. She looked beyond the counter and was shocked (and delighted) to see Willy seated at one of the

Steinways. She was taken aback and could barely count the change correctly into the customer's hand.

"How clever of you, Arthur, to hire a handsome pianist to entice your customers to buy your pianos!" commented one of Arthur's close friends. Arthur Winter was delighted that someone would just sit down and begin to play. He walked over to speak with the young man. Pauline was a nervous wreck and called for an assistant to cover the counter. As Pauline approached, Willy was still playing while talking and laughing with Mr. Winter. When he saw Pauline, he beamed, stopped playing and stood up. Pauline introduced them.

"Oh, Pauline, we've already met," said Mr. Winter, "we met over my love for Dvorak! I understand you two are already acquainted, so now we must meet formally," and the two men shook hands. "It's indeed a pleasure to meet you, Willy, and I want you to come back to play whenever you like. Now if you will excuse me, I must go and sell pianos!"

"I hope this is not an offense," Willy said to Pauline quietly, "I wanted to see you today, so I came to your work and to ask if you must work tomorrow. I took a chance to play this beautiful piano…es ist Klavier auf Deutsch."

Pauline blushed, "Ahhh," said Pauline, "'Klavier' how interesting. Now about tomorrow, it's Sunday and no shops are open. I only have church in the morning."

"Then perhaps *La Boheme* tomorrow afternoon?"

"Yes, of course, *La Boheme* tomorrow afternoon. I would like that very much, and perhaps you would like to come to dinner at my house after the film and meet my family?"

"Oh yes," responded Willy quickly, overjoyed at the invitation, and a little concerned if he didn't respond immediately, she might withdraw the offer. "I accept the dinner. I would like it very much to meet your family and you to meet my German-American family also. I will ask my cousin to drive us to the cinema in his auto. We will come to your house for you. I must go now and will wait until the time to see you again tomorrow at one o'clock – that is how you say it, yes?"

"Yes, that is exactly how you say it," Pauline blushed.

"Until tomorrow, then," Willy said, squeezing her hand, then whistling a little tune, left the store. He glanced back only once. She was watching him and waved good-bye.

The following day Willy and Hugo arrived promptly at one o-clock. Willy brought flowers for Emma and a small bottle of scent for Pauline, as suggested by Delores. Both gifts were well received.

Willy and Pauline Circa 1926

After the cinema, Delores and the baby accompanied Hugo to the theater to retrieve the young couple. Delores wanted to meet this girl who had so captivated her nephew's heart. The moment they met, Delores knew she and Pauline would be friends, especially since Pauline immediately asked to hold the baby.

When they pulled up in front of the Bathurst home, Emma and Harry and all the children came out to meet Willy's family. It seemed they all approved of the Germans, with the exception of Harry Bathurst who was skeptical of all "foreigners."

Most surprising of all was that Sy's new beau, Herman Stetter, was there to meet Willy also. Sy was beaming and Herman was so happy to have a fellow countryman present. Herman had immigrated to America several years earlier and was a few years younger than Willy. Herman also worked for the Pennsylvania Railroad in the Car Repair Shop/Planing Mill housed in the main downtown facility.

At dinner, Emma and the family had questions for both Willy and Herman about life in Germany compared to life in America and what their families were like and did they have siblings, too? Harry, however, was a quiet observer and not very friendly to the German boys, even when nudged by Emma. He was not so sure about his daughters getting "mixed up with these foreigners." After all, one could not be too careful these days, and what do we really know about these strangers seated at our dinner table?

As time went on Willy and Herman became frequent guests at the Bathurst home. Sy married Herman and they moved into a small apartment across town. Pauline missed her sister greatly and the foursome tried to get together once a week to play pinochle and chat. Mr. Winter hired Pauline's father and brothers to deliver pianos. After a few weeks of debating the issue with himself, Harry approached Willy to work with his sons to help with the piano deliveries. Willy was pleased with Harry's offer, but did not realize that this was one of Harry's tests of Willy's mettle. The Bathurst boys were initially reserved about interaction with Willy, but came to respect his work ethic and soon the boys included him in conversations and jokes, but Harry remained aloof. Emma always welcomed Willy in their home, as did all the siblings. He enjoyed the noise and companionship which reminded him of his family in Dresden.

Apparently, Willy had passed Harry's test. On April 7, 1927 at the Saint James Lutheran Parsonage, Harry Bathurst reluctantly walked his eldest daughter down the aisle.

Harry kissed Pauline, then joined her hand with Willy's and stepped aside. As the couple said their vows to each other, Emma and all the Bathurst sisters were in tears. The nuptials were witnessed by all the Bathursts, Hugo, Delores and little Christina, and Arthur and Mrs. Winter. Even Harry admitted later to Emma that he shed a tear or two at the ceremony.

"I know," said Emma, "I saw you."

The newlyweds moved into Willy's apartment. Each evening they would sit together with large Webster dictionaries and Willy's Langenscheidt spread out and Pauline would help Willy with English. He was a quick learner and eager to impress his new bride, who was very pleased with his enthusiasm.

Emma and Pauline planted winter herbs in a small garden in the back yard and Emma began crocheting a layette for her eldest daughter's first baby. As the pregnancy progressed, it became apparent that the little apartment was too small and Pauline would have difficulty going up the stairs with the baby.

Only a month before Pauline's due date, they moved to 870 Thirty-seventh Street and, of course, all the Bathursts pitched in and helped with the move. Pauline and Sy had a wonderful time choosing fabrics and sewing curtains for the nursery and Willy and Pauline's brothers gave the apartment a fresh coat of paint.

Pauline continued to work at Winter's Music Store, but after the Christmas holidays, reluctantly gave her notice to Arthur at Willy's request. Arthur Ernst Lippert, named after his paternal uncle and grandfather, was born April 19, 1929. Willy and Pauline were thrilled with their beautiful son, as were the families on two continents.

Willy had steady work and they were saving their money to purchase a home of their own. Letters and photographs to and from Germany were a joy for each side of the family. They corresponded regularly by mail, always addressing Pauline by her middle name, "Elizabeth", but neither of them ever really knew why. Willy was the translator for both the Americans and the Germans and the fact that his family always wrote to 'Willy and Elizabeth' made them chuckle.

Willy also corresponded with his French friend, Renard, each sending photographs of their children and from their friendship, the two decided to keep in touch playing chess through the mail.

They played for years each drawing a new chessboard on a postcard with their respective moves. Neither family could ever afford to travel either to Europe or to America, but their friendship through cards and letters and photographs and the chess games meant a lot to each of them.

CHAPTER EIGHT

The era known as "The Roaring Twenties" evolved at the end of World War I at a time when the United States and Western Europe were war weary and longed for a respite. With the introduction of jazz music and the dramatic change in women's clothing that ushered in "the flapper era", societal mores changed. "Speak-easies" defied the Eighteenth Amendment which prohibited the sale of alcohol and spirits.

Cellar Clubs flourished where bathtub gin flowed freely and a good time was had by all, drinking and dancing to the upbeat jazz. Art Deco, electricity, telephones, radio, motion pictures, and the wide use of automobiles sparked major industrial growth, more consumer demand, and significant changes in lifestyle.

This was a time of wealth and excess and in that single decade the United States gained financial prominence in the world. Throughout the 1920s all the U.S. railroads combined employed more than two million workers. Just the car building shops of the Pennsylvania Railroad located in Altoona employed over 20,000 workers in various capacities. During those years, rural Americans left their farms behind and migrated to the cities in vast numbers with dreams of finding a more prosperous life in the ever-growing expansion of America's industrial sector.

The US railroad system had its ups and downs in the 1920s that began with a major labor strike in July 1922 when 400,000 workers in the shops and roundhouses across the country revolted against a 12 percent wage cut and walked off the job. U.S. President Warren G. Harding and his incredibly corrupt administration smashed the strike. At least ten workers were killed by the National Guard and private detectives.

Pennsylvania Railroad President Samuel Rea, like others of his ilk, thought little about safety for their employees. With skilled machinists striking, 71 percent of locomotives failed monthly inspections from August through September 1922. Instead of negotiating with union workers, Rea hired 16,000 gunmen to break the strike[5] of nearly 20,000 employees at the company's shops in Altoona, the largest car shop in the world. Although the railroad workers were finally defeated, their great struggle forced the capitalist government to pass the 1926 Railroad Labor Act.

While the American cities prospered, the over-production of agricultural produce created widespread financial despair among American farmers in the Heartland. The rising share prices encouraged more people to invest, believing the share prices would rise further. Many people borrowed money to invest and the speculation fueled further rises which created a false economic reality.

The same was true in Europe, particularly Germany. After its devastating defeat in World War I, pursuant to the Versailles Treaty, particularly the "War Guilt Clause" (Article 231), the blame for the war was placed upon Germany and the German Army was limited to only 100,000 men. Submarines and the Air Force were banned, and the German Navy could not consist of vessels weighing over 100,000 tons. Germany was also forced to hold war crime trials.

In addition, Germany was bound to pay reparations to Great Britain, Belgium, and France in addition to relinquishing thirteen percent of its land to France, Belgium, Denmark, Czechoslovakia and Poland. Germany initially tried to recover from the war by creating transportation projects and the modernization of gas works and power plants which were all used to battle the increasing unemployment rate. However, social spending for the

---

[5] "The great railroad strike of 1922" By **Stephen Millies** posted on February 20, 2014. Article in Workers World

country's citizenry had more than tripled from 20.5 marks per resident in 1913 to 65 marks per resident by 1925. By 1929 it had reached over 100 marks per resident and municipal officials and politicians were unable to restore order to their budgets.

As the income tax revenues decreased, the government began to depend more on state trade and property taxes. It also became dependent on profits made from municipal utilities. Germany struggled to produce and sell their goods to foreign countries in order to make the reparation payments required under the Treaty of Versailles, but foreign countries placed protective tariffs on Germany's goods which further depressed an already fragile economy. The government, in turn, printed more money until inflation was out of control.

Then came the unthinkable. On Tuesday, October 29, 1929 the stock market on Wall Street collapsed sending the worldwide financial markets into a tailspin with disastrous effects. The United States, which had loaned funds to Germany to help rebuild the German economy after the war, was calling in the debt. When those loans suddenly became due and when the world market of German exports dried up, the German industrial machine ground to a halt. The Deutschmark became worthless and there were no jobs and very little to purchase, even if you had money to spend.

In 1923 while Willy was learning his woodworking trade in Vincennes a year before he immigrated to America, an upstart named Adolf Hitler arose from virtually nowhere. He began his so-called "career" in politics as a street brawling revolutionary who persuaded others of his ilk to join him in an attempt to overthrow the young German democracy by force. But he lost.

Willy didn't know much about Hitler before he left Germany, but his sister, Flora's, letters kept him well informed about Hitler's rise in popularity. Hitler had changed his tactics and began courting the German industrialists and middle class societies. He was a persuasive speaker with an innate ability to know and proclaim what his audience wanted to hear. He was determined to overthrow the government, but this time legally by getting elected, not by force. At the same time, he had the vision of building a Nazi shadow government that would eventually replace the democracy.

In October 1929, just prior to the Wall Street crash, the outstanding German Foreign Minister Gustav Stresemann died. He was well-liked and respected and had spent years after the war working to restore the German economy. His plan was to stabilize the republic, but he died, having exhausted himself in the process. The world economy was in chaos and by mid-1930 the German democratic government began to fall apart. The time was ripe for Adolf Hitler.

Germany was in crisis and the German Parliament, known as the Reichstag, was politically divided into uncompromising squabbling groups. In March 1930 Heinrich Bruening became Chancellor. He, too, encountered stubborn opposition and as a last resort, went to President Hindenburg and asked him to dissolve the Reichstag, according to the parliamentary rules, and call for a new election.

Hindenburg agreed and the new elections were set six months later for September 14, 1930, thus giving Hitler and the Nazis the very opportunity they wanted. The German populace was tired of the politics in Berlin. They were tired of misery, suffering and weakness in their government and the country was desperate for leadership. The people were willing to listen to anyone, even Adolf Hitler.

Letters from Willy's family were few and far between now and those they did receive mentioned nothing of the political unrest, homelessness and starvation in Germany.

A brief, carefully-worded letter from Renard scarcely explained the economic status throughout Europe and barely a reference to political unrest in Germany. Indications were that 84-year-old President Paul von Hindenburg would not seek another term, for even if he could be persuaded to run, he would be 92-years-old at the end of his seven-year term. "The other" (not mentioned by name but referenced Adolf Hitler) loomed in the background and if Hindenburg died during his term, "the other" was the likely successor.

The terrible news in Renard's letter was unsettling to Willy. He hated Hitler and anything to do with him and the Nazis. He feared for his family and his beloved homeland. He was extremely anxious about his elderly parents since he and Pauline had received no mail from Flora in nearly two months. Pauline was very concerned about Willy's family and the hardships in Europe, especially Germany, which they read about in the Altoona Mirror.

"We need to help your family," Pauline stated, "they say there's a shortage of food and the currency is worthless...how will we ever know for sure what is happening other than what we learn from the "Die Welt von Heute"? Your family would never say this to us. It hurts me inside that they send gifts to Arthur while they are struggling."

Willy hugged her, "I am thinking the same. We just have to make a plan on how to do this effectively." Arthur was barely a year old when the young couple began sending US currency to the Lippert family in Dresden. When letters arrived from his sister Flora, who wrote on behalf of their mother, Flora never mentioned receiving any money. It was unlike the family not to comment on the letters or gifts they received. Flora's letters were also not so frequent now, perhaps overseas postage was "too dear", as Emma had suggested.

When one of Flora's letters appeared to have been opened then resealed, Willy suspected the mail was interrupted before it left Dresden. They wondered if their letters entering Germany had been opened as well. He was upset and moody worrying that the money they sent was confiscated by dishonest postal workers and never reached his family.

As the German economy disintegrated there was talk among Willy's co-workers that food was in short supply and that even fights were breaking out over bread or a few potatoes. Willy agonized over the situation and he and his fellow Germans who were also sending money to their homeland, were sure the money intended for their families was never received.

Willy's father was still working at the chocolate factory in Dresden which had sustained only minor damage in the war. His father maintained the boilers which was hard work, but he was used to it. Although in his seventies, Ernst Hugo Lippert was in good health and worked every day.

Willy was anxious about his family and would often take walks by himself. Pauline did not know what to do except to allow him his privacy. Sometimes he would have recurring nightmares about his service in the army, often thrashing about in his sleep. He would sweat profusely and cry out which would wake Pauline and the baby and all three of them would be exhausted by morning.

Willy never talked about his erratic nights, always dismissing Pauline's concern, but she knew he continued to suffer from shellshock and she didn't know what to do. Willy refused to see a doctor until he developed asthma, perhaps from the sawdust in the Pattern Shop. The doctor prescribed daily use of an atomizer. He also prescribed medication to calm Willy's nerves and suggested warm milk before bedtime.

Hugo and Delores understood Willy's increased anxiety and were helpful by rationally discussing what could be done to help his parents and theirs so far away. They, too, were aware of the handling of the mail and agreed with Willy that it was very likely the money in his letters had been confiscated.

Hugo had a trusted friend in the government who was able to intercept mail to and from the Weissflogs in Germany, thus, the mail and its contents were always received. This interception was done at great risk to their friend and his own family. Willy had no such contact and did not dare suggest Hugo's friend to help him and Pauline. That was too dangerous.

Hugo suggested that Willy might ask his French friend, Renard, if he would be willing to receive Willy's correspondence in France and hand-deliver it to Germany. Willy would pay Renard's train fare. It was much to ask, since the timing of the trip was uncertain due to the damage done to the railroads during the war and the slow reconstruction efforts. If the travel went well, the trip could take more than ten hours each way. Willy was reluctant to even suggest such an undertaking, but he knew he could trust Renard and that if it was impossible, Renard would say so.

Although France was still recovering from the war, its economy was better than Germany's. Renard had plenty of work and the business owner who had apprenticed Willy, liked Willy and understood his plight and agreed to allow Renard the time off so that he could make the courier trips to and from Dresden to Willy's family.

Willy continued to have steady work at the Pattern Shop and was making a good wage. He and Pauline budgeted a sum each payday to be accumulated and sent to Renard for delivery when possible. As their children grew older, Renard, Gabrielle and their children made an outing of the train ride to and from Dresden. At Gabrielle's suggestion Flora now had a code sentence she would write in her letters: "Please send more pictures of Arthur" which meant the money was received and Willy's family was grateful.

KINETOSCOPE

CHAPTER NINE

Even after the Stock Market Crash of 1929, the railroad industry continued to thrive in the Northeast while America's Heartland suffered through three major droughts in the ten-year period from 1930-1940. That timespan was dubbed "The Dust Bowl" or "The Dirty Thirties."

The usual practice of Midwest farmers the decade prior to "The Dust Bowl" was to plow the virgin topsoil deeper than 20" in order to conserve moisture in the soil. Due mainly to the farmers' insufficient understanding of the ecology in arid and semi-arid areas, the extensive plowing also displaced the deep-rooted native grasses that normally trapped the soil in order to retain moisture.

Consequently, without rain, the unanchored soil turned to dust which the prevailing winds blew away in great clouds that even blackened the sky. These "black blizzards" often traveled as far as New York City and Washington D.C. affecting a million acres of land on the panhandles of Texas and Oklahoma and even adjacent areas of New Mexico, Colorado, and Kansas. "The Dust Bowl" forced many farming families to abandon their farms and migrate further west to California, only to find that economic conditions there were much the same as those they left behind.

The industrialized East continued to hold its own, due mainly to the railroad industry expansion. The light manufacturing industries in the New England, Mid-Atlantic, and Southern states sustained only a slight decline because of the consistent demand for their textiles, clothing, and leather goods, especially footwear. Additionally, a new industrial group that was manufacturing chemicals, petroleum, tobacco products, and paper products, achieved impressive increases in production during the 1930s.

Conversely, heavier industries such as automobile

manufacturing, coal mining, and steelmaking, experienced a decline in demand for their more costly manufactured goods during this period of uncertainty.

The railroad was booming, and in Altoona in 1930 construction was completed on a Brass Foundry which expanded the South Altoona Shops. Employment was increased and so were wages. Willy saw an opportunity to save the entire amount of his salary increase every month in order to purchase a home. He had been talking to a friend at work about being a home owner, not a renter. His friend was buying his own home and Willy asked him to explain the procedure to make sure he understood all the ramifications of such an endeavor before broaching the subject with Pauline.

One warm evening after dinner, as usual when the weather was fair, the young couple took Arthur for a walk in his carriage.

"I'd like for us to live in a house with a yard, Pauline," Willy mentioned casually as they walked along, "you should have a garden and we should have trees for Arthur to climb." At that suggestion Pauline chuckled since Arthur was only a year old, but Willy continued, "Children need safe places to run and play and make friends. I've been saving my pay raise so we can buy our own house."

"Buy a house? Willy, that's a big step, there's a lot to know about buying a house. First of all we'd need to *find* a house, we'd need to borrow money and get a mortgage and...well, it's just not that easy. Maybe you should talk to Daddy about this. Do you have any particular house in mind? It seems like you do."

Pauline had learned early on that Willy pondered many things and worked out all the details before ever mentioning his ideas to her. This idea, though, was especially appealing.

"I have a good friend at work who is buying a house now and he has told me how it is done in America. He also told me about a house not so far from the shops…only a short walk to work for me and it is a house, not an apartment. It would be larger and not so confined for our son, you know. It has a yard."

"And you've seen it?"

"Oh no, Pauline, we will see it together. I've only heard about it." Willy pulled a slip of paper from his pocket, "The address is 3613 West Chestnut Avenue, do you know that street?"

"I think so, but we could find out for sure where it is and look at it. Maybe bring Daddy with us since he's bought houses before. Would that be helpful?"

"I think we want to see it first, and then ask your father to see it," Willy replied, "then this means you are interested?"

"I am interested. I'd also like to have more space and a nice yard with trees and flowers and maybe a little garden too," Pauline commented. "Do you know if it is available for rent too? I mean just in case….you know, if we can't get a mortgage. I don't know about your citizenship status, if you can buy a house or not till you are naturalized. But whether it's for rent or for sale I think we should look at it."

Willy was smiling, "I want us to *buy* a home, so I will speak to Gerhard at work. He said the house is only five years old and he thinks it could be available for rent for not so much money, but maybe available to buy. Once more, we share the same idea, eh, Pauline?" He leaned over and kissed her cheek and smiled at Arthur who smiled back and clapped his chubby hands, "Look our son thinks it's a good idea too!"

Pauline linked her arm in Willy's, "I think it's a wonderful idea if we like it and if we can afford it, but…." Pauline rolled her eyes and shook her head.

"Did I say something wrong or…but *what?...*"

"Oh no, Willy, that's not it! I'm just wondering if Daddy and my brothers will be willing to move us again!"

They both laughed and Willy held up crossed fingers on both hands, "First we see the house, then we discuss the future."

Pauline's family – even her father -- was actually excited to help move the young family into the lovely little house a few months later. They would rent for a year with the option to buy. Harry didn't like the idea of Pauline and his grandson being stuck in a second floor apartment in a busy part of the city where it was noisy most of the time. There were too many steps for Pauline to climb with the baby. A little house was a much better environment and he approved. He even boasted to his friends that his son-in-law had adapted well to American life and was a good provider and the caring father of the handsomest baby in the world – who, according to Harry, resembled his Grandfather Bathurst. Willy thought otherwise, that Arthur looked exactly like him, but he knew better than to even suggest that to Harry.

The little house was perfect and they moved a month later. They made new friends and settled in. Within a few months the flowers and herbs Pauline had planted were doing well. Willy set up a workshop in the basement for himself and began work on a little wagon for Arthur and drew up plans for a small sandbox out back.

Fridays were pinochle nights and they played every week, alternating host homes with Sy and Herman. Sy and Herman's daughter, Imogene, was three years older than her little sister Grenda, who was the same age as Arthur, and the children always came along. Imogene loved to read books to both babies who always nodded off to sleep and were put into a crib or playpen, then Imogene would curl up on the couch with her little blanket and fall asleep too.

Sy and Pauline were partners against the men and it was a bit much when the men started speaking German that the girls couldn't understand. However, in time, both Sy and Pauline began to figure out what they were saying and could sometimes anticipate their next play. The sisters always "played dumb" and if the men were any the wiser, they never let on. It was at one of these Friday night sessions that someone gave Willy the nickname "Count" – no one ever knew why, but the nickname stuck and he was called "Count" by family and close friends from then on.

In January 1932 the new Brass Finishing Shop began operation at the South Altoona Foundries and more workers were hired. In the spring of 1932 Pauline became ill and could barely care for her three-year-old son. She was nauseous and could not keep down much food. Willy called Emma to come over and find out what was wrong because Pauline refused to let the doctor come to the house and they had argued about it.

"Please come, Mother Bathurst, she won't let the doctor come and I'm worried she is very ill, and she cries all the time!" Emma still had her five youngest children at home. Harry drove her over one morning and she found Pauline crying while rocking Arthur who was also crying and could not be consoled. Emma took Arthur from his mother's arms and walked with him a bit, then laid him down in his little bed and read him a story, and he soon fell asleep. She then set about making broth and dry toast for "her" baby, Pauline.

"I think you are with child, Pauline," Emma said kindly as she spooned a little broth into Pauline's mouth.

"I don't think so, Mother, I wasn't sick like this with Arthur."

"Pauline, I've had eleven children and none of my pregnancy symptoms were the same with any of you. I'd like

Arthur Ernst Lippert circa 1932

you to allow me to make a doctor appointment for you, will you let me? If I'm correct, then you will know that this sickness will soon pass, and if it is something else, he will treat you for whatever ails you."

Pauline knew her mother was always right about everything. She was, indeed, expecting another baby and was assured by the doctor that this uncomfortable stage would pass soon enough. She was relieved and so excited she couldn't wait till Willy got home from work to share the news.

"A baby? Another baby? So you are not sick after all, just with a baby!! Maybe a sister for our little Arthur!" Willy was very happy and relieved that soon Pauline's symptoms would end. After dinner and when Arthur had been put to bed, Willy and Pauline sat together at the kitchen table and Willy drew sketches of different types of cradles for Pauline to choose for their expected new arrival.

In mid-April 1932 Willy brought home the "Berliner Tageszeitung", the Berlin Daily Newspaper, loaned to him by a fellow-worker. Willy was anxious for news about his homeland. He and Pauline sat on the porch together and Willy read line-by-line, translating everything into English for Pauline. The main article recapped the economic down-turn in Germany. Six million countrymen were unemployed, food was scarce, and thousands were homeless. The chaos in Berlin and the threat of Marxism created a very uncertain future for the divided country. The Nazis held thousands of rallies, gave out millions of pamphlets and copies of the Nazi newspapers. Many citizens now saw Hitler and the Nazis in a new light, as the wave of the future.

The presidential election was held March 13, 1932 wherein Hitler received 30% of the total votes cast and President Hindenburg received 49% -- not enough votes for the absolute majority Hindenburg needed. A run-off election was necessary and was held Sunday, April 10, 1932 which resulted in Hitler securing 36% of the popular vote to Hindenburg's 53%, which represented an increase of two million votes for Hitler and an increase of under a million for Hindenburg.

This time, the "Old Gentleman" Hindenburg, now 85 years old, was elected by an absolute majority to serve another seven-year term, but no one in the country was at ease. Hitler and the Nazis had shown massive popularity – disturbing news to Willy and his friends. They feared for the families they left behind when they emigrated.

A letter to their new address finally arrived from Flora. It had been sliced open and resealed, but when Willy opened it he saw that some words were blackened out or cut out with a razor blade so that many sentences were incomplete. He was fearful that Hitler was the cause of this. Often, Willy couldn't figure out the missing words.

A brief note from Renard advised Willy that travel to Dresden was banned because of the political climate between the two countries. Willy was disheartened initially, but understood, based on what he'd been reading in the German press, "Die Welt von Heute", The World of Today, that his German friend shared with him at work.

In August Sy and Herman invited Pauline, Willy and little three-year-old Arthur to accompany them and their daughters, Imogene now almost six and Grenda the same age as Arthur, to take a ride in their new car. As a surprise Herman chose to drive on the newly opened 6.8-mile-long macadam road recently completed by the PRR for access to the Horseshoe Curve located at Kittanning Point at the base of the Allegheny Mountains. Although they all knew about the Horseshoe Curve, none of them had ever seen it.

As they drove, Herman described how it was built and how long it took to build it. He explained the construction was done by hand by 450 mostly Irish workers who were paid twenty-five cents an hour for twelve-hour days. The three-track Horseshoe Curve was completed and opened on February 15, 1854. The purpose of this amazing engineering phenomenon of its time was to connect the cities of Philadelphia and Pittsburgh. Everyone enjoyed the ride in the Stetter's new car and the opportunity to actually see for themselves "The World Famous Horseshoe Curve".

That afternoon would be the last time they would see little Grenda, for only a few weeks later, she died in her sleep. The sadness was overwhelming for Sy, Herman, and especially, Imogene, who couldn't understand why her baby sister was gone. Sy was also expecting their third child and it was feared she would go into labor early because of the shock of losing Grenda. Pauline tried to be strong for her sister, but they both sobbed uncontrollably for weeks.

Little Arthur didn't understand where his playmate was now and kept asking for her. There was no answer for a three-year-old. Pauline was depressed and concerned about Sy's pregnancy, as well as her own, and heartbroken over her precious sister's terrible unexpected loss. Emma and Harry felt the loss deeply and Emma insisted Harry take her to each daughter's home every day so she could see for herself the health of her eldest daughters. She always brought soup and homemade rolls and Pennsylvania Dutch cookies for the grandchildren.

Ronald Herman Stetter, healthy and perfect, was born in the fall of 1932 much to the joy of his parents, Sy and Herman. His older sister, Imogene, wanted to hold him all the time and sing to him. She drew pictures of him and took them to school to show her teacher and classmates. Emma came to help Sy with Ronnie and sometimes kept Imogene overnight. She alternated between Eleanor's and Pauline's homes and Harry was always at her beck and call to do the driving back and forth.

Gretchen Ann Lippert was born December 19, 1932, just six days before Christmas. What a delightful Christmas gift for everyone on two continents! Arthur was so excited about the new baby that he lined up all his toys around the cradle, even his new Christmas ones. He spent a lot of time just gazing into the huge brown eyes of his new baby sister and she stared right back at him. Sy, Imogene, and Ronnie came to visit often and it was a comfort to Sy to chat with Pauline while they nursed and rocked their babies, Ronnie and Gretchen, while Arthur and Imogene played at their feet.

Willy had become somewhat detached when he came home from work. Now it seemed every morning, Werner, one of Willy's close co-workers in the Pattern Shop, brought "Die Welt von Heute" to work to share with Willy. As the days went on, Pauline noticed a tension about her husband but didn't necessarily connect it with what he was reading in the newspapers.

Werner was from Plauen in the Stadt of Sachsen near the Czechoslovakian and Bavarian borders. Sometimes while working, Werner and Willy would discuss the political climate in their homeland, particularly, the rise to power of Adolf Hitler. Today's newspaper announced on January 30, 1933, Adolf Hitler had been named Chancellor of Germany. They both despised him and what he stood for.

After dinner when the children were put to bed, Willy would translate to Pauline what the newspaper wrote about Hitler and what his being named Chancellor, could mean for the German people, particularly for the Jews.

"I have many Jewish friends, Pauline, and I fear for them. Hitler is a tyrant who only wants power. He sees himself as superior to all. He particularly sees the Jews as beneath him. He wants to annihilate the entire Jewish race. Look at this."

Willy showed Pauline a photograph of a temple in Dusseldorf that was defaced with a swastika and a message saying "Jude errecke." Pauline began to cry. Willy cradled her in his arms. "What do those words mean, Count?"

"The words mean "Jew perish" but the world will never allow this!" Willy said emphatically.

In April 1933 Willy read that a Weimar Constitutional Amendment gave the German Cabinet, in effect, Chancellor Adolf Hitler, the power to enact laws without the involvement of the German Parliament, known as the "Reichstag." His first order of business was the edict that no one is to purchase from the Jews, as the Jews were "Germany's misfortune". Within weeks, it was announced that the Jews were to be systematically transferred from their homes to concentration camps where, of course, they would be treated humanely.

The letters from Flora never mentioned the politics of their beloved homeland for fear of reprisal to their German family. There was no way Willy could learn anything more than what was published in "Die Welt von Heute".

By summer of 1933 Gretchen was crawling and pulling herself up in her playpen. By late fall, she could walk. She was a sweet little girl, but very quick and quite fearless. Unlike her quiet big brother who was more content to read books and dig in the sandbox, Gretchen would bear watching.

In the fall of 1933 the PRR furloughed 1,200 men in the Altoona Shops. Most of those furloughed found odd jobs to earn money to make ends meet. Willy repaired and refinished furniture in his basement workshop and also made wooden toys and sold them. The furloughed workers also received monthly "relief payments" and were eligible for surplus food commodities distributed by the railroad.

In Germany, by the end of 1933, ten thousand German Jews had been murdered, most while in police custody. Opposition of any kind would not be tolerated. The Third Reich had begun its rise.

In January 1934 the Nazis were ringing in the New Year celebrating the past year of success under the leadership of Adolf Hitler and Joseph Goebbels, his right-hand man. Under their continued leadership Germany would be the unshakeable force in uniting the entire world.

Only racially superior citizens were welcomed in Germany and in the New Year of 1934 they began engineering more of them. The Nazis prohibited undesirable people from breeding. They made propaganda films to encourage compliance with new laws dictating if you had any defect or genetic flaw, even having had a nervous breakdown, you could be and would be sterilized. Four hundred thousand Germans were sterilized for conditions such as Down Syndrome, blindness, epilepsy and other genetic flaws, as defined by the Nazis.

On February 25, 1934 the biggest "oath taking" in human history took place all over Germany. This was the mandatory Nazi greeting of "Heil Hitler!" which must be spoken with an outstretched right arm by every German citizen upon meeting one another. School children as young as kindergarten age, learned the greeting as well. Failure to abide by this edict could result in being sent to a concentration camp. Everyone was assumed to be a Nazi by that greeting in public. No letter, no telephone or word on the street was safe, for everyone was now suspicious of everyone else as being an informer.

The letters from the Lipperts in Dresden ceased altogether. Willy cried for his beloved family and his beloved homeland. In March 1934, the PRR recalled all 1,200 of the furloughed men for work on a special electrification project at the downtown Altoona Works. Fortunately, Willy and his friend Werner remained in the Pattern Shop in South Altoona.

Gretchen and her Daddy 1934

KINETOSCOPE

"Count is crazy over the kiddies as you notice.
That expression on his face and his friend, the pipe.
It shows a man's character. (these kiddies)"

Written by Pauline 1934

Celeste Yost

CHAPTER TEN

In the summer of 1934 Willy, Pauline, Artie and "Little Gretchie" were moving into a larger house at 5520 Roselawn Avenue in the Eldorado section of Altoona. The owners of the house on West Chestnut Avenue where they'd been living had changed their minds and no longer wished to sell. The young couple's disappointment, however, turned out to be a blessing in disguise because they found a larger house in a quieter neighborhood.

Unfortunately, Pauline's brothers were not available to help with the move. Now all six were either in the service or had married and no longer living in Altoona. A few weeks earlier Willy went to his in-laws to ask to borrow one of Harry's trucks to move their furniture. Harry was out but Emma spoke in Harry's absence and said that would be fine.

On moving day when Hugo dropped Willy off to pick up Harry's truck, he could hear Harry and Emma arguing as he came up the front walk of the Bathurst home. It was obvious Harry had been drinking, but Willy could also tell Emma was holding her own against his abusive language. Willy had barely knocked when Harry came out onto the porch, quickly closing the front door behind him. He gave Willy the keys and without a word, turned and went back inside, then slammed the front door so hard the glass rattled. The arguing began again in earnest. Willy knew Pauline would be upset if she knew that he had overheard her parents, so he decided to keep this to himself.

With the help of friends from the shops and Hugo and Herman, the men moved everything into the new house. Pauline, Delores, Sy and Junette, who was now eleven years old, wiped out closets, dusted floors, and hung curtains. All the younger children played in the fenced-in backyard, the older ones coming in often to see what was going on. As the furniture was placed and the beds put together, the girls put fresh linens on the beds and folded and put clothing away in the dressers, and the dishes and pots and pans were put away in the kitchen and pantry.

When most of the work was done, Pauline served hot dogs and cold drinks to everyone then asked Hugo, if on the way back from the house to return the truck, could they stop at Mr. Notopoulos's Confectionary for some ice lollies for the children? Hugo agreed and followed Willy to the Bathurst home to drop off the truck.

This time the house was silent as Willy walked to the porch and knocked. Emma answered the door, but stood behind it to shield her face. She merely held out her hand to accept the keys.

"Are you alright, Mother Bathurst?"

Emma mumbled she was fine, just tired, and that she'd come to see the house in a day or two. "I have to rest now, Willy, give my love to Pauline and the children, will you?"

"Yes, I will, but can I help you with anything? Do you need anything?"

"No. There's nothing anyone can do, but thank you," and she closed the door softly. Willy stood on the porch a few moments, then slowly came down the front steps. Hugo saw Willy's troubled look as he got into the car and while they were driving, he asked if there was a problem. Willy said Emma stood behind the door and he never saw her, she only told him she was tired and needed to rest. He was not invited in and she didn't give him cookies to take home to the children, which was something she always did.

"Well, maybe she's ill and doesn't want you or Pauline to worry," suggested Hugo.

"I don't think so," said Willy, " but I don't know."

Changing the subject, Hugo commented, "Well, that's a nice sturdy house you've got there Willy! You've done very well for yourself in America and we're all so proud of you. Pauline is a special woman and a good wife and mother.

You know, you and I are blessed to have good women and beautiful children!" Willy agreed and they both laughed. They stopped for the ice lollies then rode the rest of the way to the new home, chatting about how to set up Willy's workshop in the basement.

After everyone was gone Pauline and Willy bathed the children and put them to bed in their new bedrooms. Gretchen was overly tired and cranky so Willy sang German lullabies while he rocked her to sleep and Pauline read to Artie, who was asleep within minutes. Outside, Willy drew two chairs under the tree and he and Pauline sat and held hands.

"This was a good day, we've accomplished a lot and only have the small things to put away. I was surprised at how much help little Junette was for you, even playing games with the little ones and helping with the ice lollies," Willy remarked.

"Yes, little Junette…my poor little Junette…" then Pauline tearfully began to share what Sy had told her this morning about their parents.

"My mother is taking Irma and Bernadine and moving back to Penns Creek with Uncle Frank. Junette is going to live with Aunt June and Uncle George and their daughter, Jane, for a while till things get sorted out. That way she won't have to change schools."

Willy was stunned. "What things to be sorted out?" he asked.

"Sy told me how angry Mother was that Daddy started drinking again; in fact, he's been drinking for many months. I blame that on being around all the beer he's been delivering these past couple years. Sy said Herman told her when he helps Daddy with his deliveries, he's usually invited to sit a bit and have a beer and he always wants Herman to join him. Does he ask you to join him too, Count?"

Yes, sometimes, but I don't want to drink when I'm working and now he doesn't even ask anymore," said Willy.

"Sy said Herman might have one beer, but Daddy never refuses anyone who offers it, so then Herman wants to do the driving and Daddy gets hostile. One time they had words and Herman just got out of the truck and walked home."

"Herman told me," commented Willy, "I would have done the same."

Pauline began to cry harder now, "Sy said one evening she and Herman came by the house to take mother some fabric and they could hear mother and Daddy arguing as soon as they got out of the car. When they were coming up the steps, through the front window they saw Daddy pick mother off her feet and then push her against the dining room wall with his big hand around her little throat." Willy knelt down and wiped Pauline's tears with his handkerchief, then held his wife in his arms.

Pauline went on, "Herman intervened and they took mother and the girls home with them until Daddy sobered up and calmed down. Then Daddy banged on the door of their house demanding to be let in. He was crying and apologizing to mother and my sisters and said it would never happen again and he begged them all to let him come home. I don't understand why, but Sy never even told me about this till today," she burst into tears again, "what's going to happen to them now?"

In a few days Uncle Frank came with his truck to take his sister, Emma, and her daughters, Irma and Bernadine, to Penns Creek. Frank was a bachelor who continued living in the family home looking after his parents until they died, then he remained there alone. Frank and Emma were very close but, although their parents thought Harry would be a wonderful husband and father, Frank thought otherwise, believing Harry was never good enough for Emma. This was always a bone of contention between the two men. The truth was, that Frank never thought any of Emma's suitors were ever good enough for her, not just Harry.

Emma sought peace in her life and was happy for the opportunity to return to the old homestead. She had missed Frank and their walks together and when they sat on the front porch swing on summer evenings not saying much, just listening to the crickets and enjoying the solitude.

It was different with Emma's and Frank's parents gone and Emma was uncertain how it would be to share a home with her brother. The new surroundings would be a drastic change for Irma, now sixteen, and Bernadine, soon to be fifteen. The girls would be attending Black Run School in Union County which was a one-room school fifteen miles from Penns Creek. Frank would drive them back and forth and they'd take a lunch every day.

Surprisingly, the girls actually liked the school and made friends easily. It wasn't long until they each had friends their own ages and they each also had a new beau. Emma was happy they brought their new friends home. In the small room next to the parlor was a beautifully carved pump organ where the girls and their friends spent a lot of time taking turns playing it while the others sang and danced to the music.

Emma's spirits were lifted tremendously, as the kids kept the house lively with their singing and laughter. Everyone loved Uncle Frank too. He would stand by the coal stove in the kitchen melting bacon fat in a large cast iron skillet. He'd thinly slice potatoes from his garden and drop them into the hot fat. The delicious aroma of those potato chips brought back wonderful memories of Emma's childhood. Their father used to make them for Emma and Frank and their friends. g.

Kerosene lamps were used for lighting and Frank told them that trimming the wicks was a job only for him, so Emma and the girls were never to attempt it. Frank was fearful of a fire because of one that nearly burned down a neighboring house when they were youngsters. The girls didn't mind living without electricity.

The coal stove in the kitchen was for cooking and heating the house, and a well out back provided water with a pump at the kitchen sink. There was also a rain barrel that collected water for bathing. There was no bathroom, only an outhouse at the upper end of Frank's terraced garden. Frank strung a clothesline from the back porch to the outhouse so the three women could hang on to it and find their way back and forth from the house to the end of the yard in the dark.

The old smokehouse was still at the side of the backyard right where it was when they were little. Frank kept a pig named "Bacon" in a fenced-in area where years ago their parents had kept several pigs. Frank and Emma learned early on that their pigs were destined to be butchered for meat to feed them through the winter. Both Irma and Bernadine loved animals and enjoyed feeding and watching the antics of Bacon. They liked how he would wag his little tail and come to them nuzzling their hands for bits of apple or any other interesting tidbit.

In a small barn, Uncle Frank kept his little gray mule, "Coalie", who was "sometimes good and sometimes ornery" Uncle Frank said. That meant he would kick at the slats of the barn and bray loudly to get attention, but often he would just nicker a little which was almost his way of laughing.

Sometimes Uncle Frank would take Coalie for a walk and let the girls lead him. Coalie liked Frank better than when the girls held the rope, and would often just stand or sit in the middle of the road and bray until Frank took over.

The two girls shared an upstairs bedroom across the hall from Emma. Their bedroom had a huge bed they would share. There were no slats holding up the feather tick mattress, just ropes in diamond shapes for support which made the bed seem more like a hammock. Heavy goose down comforters sewn by Emma and her mother were still around and smelled like moth balls because Uncle Frank had put them away in a closet.

Each bedroom had a washstand with a pitcher and basin and fresh towels and wash cloths hanging on the towel bar. There was also a chamber pot in each bedroom and Emma explained that the girls would share the pot "for necessities" when it was too dark or too cold to go outside to the outhouse. Everyone's personal job was to take care of emptying and washing out their own wash basin and chamber pot each day. The girls shared the job but bickered over that task until Emma made a schedule for them to follow. That didn't end the bickering, but the task got done.

The front yard was smaller than Emma remembered, sweet-smelling honeysuckle was still trellised on one end of the front porch and the old porch swing was still there. The front yard sloped gracefully down to the street and when it rained, the big puddle Emma remembered playing in, still formed after a storm. The big shady maple tree was bigger now and Frank had planted hosta around its base and had planted many varieties of iris around the foundation of the house much to her delight.

Out back was the old cold cellar under the house where fruit and vegetables were kept year-round since there was no refrigeration, only a small ice box on the enclosed back porch. The cold cellar, accessible from the storm entrance out back, was the same as it had been since Emma was a child. They didn't use it anymore. She had fond memories of the crunchy apples nestled in straw that her parents kept there all winter, along with cabbages and potatoes.

One evening when there was a chill in the air, Emma told the girls that in the fall and winter her father would warm a brick in the coal stove oven, wrap it in flannel and bring it upstairs on a small shovel and place it at the foot of each child's bed to keep their feet warm all night. "You remember that Frank?"

"Oh yes," he said. "I might could find some bricks and some of that flannel and heat 'em up for the children tonight."

"Oh would you?" asked Irma, "wouldn't that just be the best thing ever, Bernie?" The girls giggled and hoped it would get cold soon so they could each have a hot brick to warm their feet.

"Don't worry," Emma said, "it will turn cold before you know it!"

"We have kerosene lamps here, and I'll be the one to keep 'em trimmed," Uncle Frank told everyone for the millionth time, "so don't you be worrying about no light. I take care of 'em regular-like. Now you come on to the kitchen and I'll make up your cups."

The girls had no idea what Uncle Frank meant, but they followed him downstairs to the kitchen. On the wall was a long strip of heavy wood holding several tin cups hung on thick pegs. Uncle Frank got out a roll of white adhesive tape and a pencil and each girl spelled her name while Frank wrote it on the tape. "I'll be callin' you 'Bern' on a counta' Bernadine is too long to put on the cup!" said Uncle Frank as he gave the strips of tape to each of his nieces and told them to stick them on where they thought best and to choose a peg to hang each cup.

"Here's your cup, Emma! I saved it all these years," Frank said with a grin and produced a blue speckled cup with a faded piece of tape with Emma's name barely discernible on it. They both had a good laugh and Frank said "Mine's long gone, had a hole, so it ain't no good for nothin' no more. I guess I could pick me another one, how 'bout it girls?"

"Yes, Uncle Frank," they chorused, "do pick another so we'll each have one!" He made a big show of choosing just the right cup from the assortment hanging on the pegs. He even counted the speckles on one of them just to make the girls laugh. He wrote his name on the tape and put it on his cup and hung it up proudly with the others.

The large dining room was adjacent to the kitchen and hanging on those walls were buck, moose and elk mounts—trophies from Leonard and Malc, given as gifts to their grandparents. "I kep' 'em around thinkin' maybe the boys would come around and want 'em back, but I guess not,." Frank said.

"No, I guess not," replied Emma, "they're all in the service or married now, Frank. I don't see them very much. I'll have to write and let them know about Harry and me, I suppose," she twisted her handkerchief and had tears in her eyes, "thirty-three years, Frank, thirty-three years and eleven children."

As for Harry, he was reluctant to let the Altoona house go, but he knew in his heart Emma was never coming back and in the end, it was the best decision. One fall day he delivered Emma's piano to Pauline. "You're the only one who'll want this, and you're the oldest girl, so it's yours," Harry told her, "I've got some strong boys to help bring it in, where do you want it?" Pauline and Willy looked at each other then started moving furniture to make a spot for the piano. It ended up in the dining room of the little house.

"And here's a box of music to go with it," Harry handed the box to Willy.

"Sit down, Daddy, and have some coffee and I made cream puffs, you'll have one won't you?" Harry agreed and stayed a while, but it would a very long time until Pauline saw her father again. Harry moved to Curtin Township "about sixty miles give or take" from Penns Creek where he and Emma began their married life on July 24, 1900.

CHAPTER ELEVEN

In October 1934, Willy and Pauline celebrated the birth of their third child, another little girl named Gertrude Elizabeth, but they called her "Trudy." Both Arthur and Gretchen were excited to have a new baby sister.

In late November a letter arrived from Germany, this time from Arthur. When Willy saw the stationery edged in black, a German custom that signified a death, he feared one of his parents had died. He sat down at the kitchen table and read the letter slowly to himself then asked Pauline to sit with him while he translated for her:

"Dresden November 3, 1934
Dear Willy, dear Elizabeth and children!
It is with a heavy heart, but it is my sad duty to write to you today. Thursday Oct. 25, early in the morning 7:30 our Father died very suddenly. The Sunday before we visited the parents and Father was pretty good, and when we left, he walked with us to the gate.

On Tuesday he had ordered 5 ton of coal and on Wed. early morning he shoveled those into the cellar. That was probably too much for him, too much stooping. But he wanted to do it.

He ate a good dinner, but at supper time he complained about stomach pain and had to vomit. He was in so much pain at 11 o'clock Herbert got the doctor. He gave him a tranquilizer. After a sleepless night he got up very early, had some oatmeal and a cup of black coffee. Then he decided to go back to bed. Mother hurried to the bedroom to make up the bed. Father made it to the door and said "Oh, what is wrong with me?"

He collapsed into Flora's arms and died. And so our dear father was gone forever from us.

Monday October 29 at 2 o'clock he was buried. We did what we could. For his funeral he got beautiful flowers and wreaths. He was laid out in our living room. Now he rests beside Olga and Oskar in our cemetery.

Dear Willy, now our Mother worries a lot about you and thinks maybe that you are in need or so because you do not write very much. She would like to send you Father's blue suit <u>if you write and tell her your size.</u> She also wants to mail a Christmas package to you, please let her know real soon.

How is everything with you? You let us know so little. Work here is not so good either. Everybody has to count with every cent.

Now, dear Willy, please take the time and write to Mother a few comforting words and don't let her wait so long. You never know what can happen. Mother is now 75 years old, and how quick you can lose a loved one, nobody knows.

In deep sorrow we send greetings to you and your family,

Arthur, Hedi and Karlernst, Mother and Flora.

(Aunt _____ wrote a letter the day Father died)"

Willy and Pauline were both weeping at the sad news as Pauline hurried to get Trudy before she woke Arthur and Gretchen with her crying.

"I did send a letter about the baby, Count, but it takes so long with the mail…"

"I know," Willy replied, "it didn't arrive yet. I must write to Mutti myself. Arthur knows it's been too long without a letter from me. It's you who always writes, now I must."

Willy was somber, "I'll take Trudy for some fresh air. A little walk will do us both good," he said as he took Trudy from her mother's arms and bundled her up in blankets. "I need time to think and to be alone, you understand, Pauline, don't you?" Pauline dried her eyes on her apron and nodded.

Gretchen and Arthur were awakened from their naps when the baby began to cry. Pauline took them both to the potty, gave them milk and a cookie for each hand, and poured a cup of tea for herself. They all sat at the kitchen table eating. Outside the air was crisp and she could see the smoke from the neighbors' chimneys against the graying skies.

"Artie, would you please get some blocks and books for you and your sister while I check the fire? Get a few toys, too, if you want." Artie liked books, especially now, because his mother was teaching him to read at home, since he started kindergarten.

Pauline held onto the bannister as she carefully navigated the basement steps. Having just delivered a baby a month ago, she was post-partum and before she reached the bottom step, she burst into tears. She was crying for Willy's sadness and her inability to say the correct words to make it all right. Because it wasn't all right. She couldn't imagine not seeing her family for ten years. That's how long it had been since Willy left home.

She opened the furnace door and added a small scoop of coal, then shook the grate just a bit. She wondered why Willy never mentioned returning to his homeland. She knew it was costly and probably out of the question, especially now that they had three children.

She dried her eyes and came back upstairs. Artie was helping Gretchen make a tower with her blocks. She smiled when she saw them playing together and couldn't imagine life without them.

Pauline and the children went to bed early but Willy stayed up late to write that letter to his mother. In the morning he told Pauline about his letter.

Letter Edged in Black from Arthur Lippert dated November 3, 1934
(Page 1 only)

"Next time you write to Germany, please remind me to add a few lines to your letters, Pauline. I need to be reminded. I am embarrassed that Flora had to point that out to me."

"How about when you're translating my letters into German? Pauline asked, "Wouldn't that be a good time for you to add a note?"

"Yes, of course, a perfect time, but please remind me anyway!" Willy smiled and pinched her cheek.

"We'll send a Christmas package right away," Willy said. "You and I should make a list of what we want to send.

Everything must look used because of the duty added onto any goods coming into Germany. It is costly for them to receive it from the dishonest government. I read this in the news every day, more and more what the corrupt government takes from the people."

Celeste Yost

CHAPTER TWELVE

Barely a year later Pauline's sister, Bernadine, and her boyfriend, Mickey Delappe, from the Black Run School, decided to get married. Bernadine was 16-1/2 years old and Mickey was only a few months older. They were a happy couple and everyone in the family loved Mickey and oh, how he loved "his Bernadine". She was always the life of the party wherever she went.

They were married and a few months later Bernadine became pregnant with their first child. She was sick and the doctor determined she had developed a bacterial or fungal infection. The doctor prescribed gentian violet to be used topically. She didn't really understand the instructions. Instead of applying the medication to the affected area, she drank it. Within hours, Bernadine became quite ill and Mickey took her to the Evangelical Hospital in Lewisburg. Drinking the medication compromised the intraperitoneal cavity which encases the stomach organs. There was nothing that could save her. She and her unborn baby died January 5, 1936. Mickey and the Bathurst and Delappe families were devastated.

Unbeknownst to Emma, her brother, Frank, went to see Harry in Curtin and told him about Bernadine and the baby. Frank asked Harry to please come to the funeral, which he did. Although most of the family ignored him, Emma and Frank stood by his side, together mourning their loss. Emma and Harry talked privately for a long while.

"I've wronged you, Emma," Harry said, "I don't blame you for leaving me. I want you to know I sold the Crawford Avenue house and paid off the mortgage. I have half the money we made on the sale with me right now to give to you. I miss ya', Emma, and I'm sorry. You deserved better."

He hung his head and pressed the envelope into her hand and kissed her forehead. She watched with fresh tears as he turned and walked away.

Irma returned to Altoona at Sy's insistence and moved in with Sy and Herman and their two children. Emma bade goodbye to her brother, Frank, and used part of the money Harry gave her to move to New York where her youngest son, Berwin, was living. He was seeking fame and fortune in the music business in New York City. Emma lived for a short while with him and his fellow musician friend, Merle Schrott, until she found a job.

Emma sewed beautifully and was offered a position with the Amalgamated Clothing Workers of America sewing "ready-made" clothing for men. Although the hours were long, she made a good wage. In addition to providing housing for their workers, the union also provided medical care. She often worked six days a week, but she loved her job and co-workers and they loved her. For the first time in her life, Emma opened a bank account in her own name. Also, for the first time in many years, she slept well and had peace in her life. She was comfortable living alone.

Berwin and Merle called themselves "The Smokey Mountain Boys" and played guitars and sang weekly on a very popular New York City radio program. Berwin loved music and wrote the music and lyrics to "Allegheny Mountain Mother" which he recorded and dedicated to Emma.

It wasn't long after Emma arrived in New York that Berwin married Helen Kotelnicki, the woman of his dreams who he'd been dating for nearly a year. The newlyweds moved to Baltimore, Maryland where the job opportunities were so much better. They both found jobs at Bethlehem Steel Shipbuilding, located at Sparrows Point, Maryland. The company was the largest steel mill, and one of the most active shipbuilders in the country. Helen worked as a data coil recorder and Berwin worked as a welder.

On Saturdays Berwin sang and played guitar and harmonica on his own popular Baltimore radio show, "The Happy Go Lucky Cowboy." Berwin and Helen urged Irma to come live with them in Maryland where a young girl had more job opportunities. Irma was delighted at the prospect of moving to Baltimore. She and Berwin were very close growing up and she was happy to come live with them. Irma worked two jobs. She worked in a bakery early mornings. In the afternoons she worked as a hair stylist.

Irma and Berwin each played guitars and entertained at USO block party events in their neighborhood. It was at one of these parties that Berwin introduced his sister to Paul Merciai, who also worked for Bethlehem Steel at the Sparrows Point Shipyard. Paul and Irma dated and eventually married. Irma conceived only one child, a daughter, who was stillborn. Not long afterward the couple divorced and Irma returned to Altoona.

In the spring of 1937, now with three children and after walking home from work in the rain twice in the same week, Willy decided it was time for the Lippert family to purchase a car. Herman was very knowledgeable about cars since he had owned several; so Willy asked him to help him look. Car sales were down during the depression years and the two Germans were seeking a bargain. Willy found a used truck at a good price, but it needed work and Herman quickly discouraged that idea.

"You need a car with enough room for five people. Your children won't stay little very long," Herman said. "A truck is good to have too, but a car would be better for children."

"Maybe a truck next time, eh, Herman?" Willy laughed.

"One step at a time, Count, it's a lot different driving a car than Harry's big drays, you know!" They both laughed because Harry was such a stickler about not allowing "any Tom, Dick and Harry," to drive his vehicles. That was funny to them because *his* name was Harry.

Willy ended up bartering on a 1931 Chevrolet sedan at a local dealership, but walked away when the salesman failed to budge on the price.

"Just wait a week," Herman advised, "then we'll come back and try again. Give him some time to think it over, that maybe taking your offer is better than not making a sale at all." Willy agreed and suggested they wait two weeks, but they did drive by several times during those two weeks to make sure the Chevy was still not sold. After the deal was made, Willy drove home in his new purchase and broke the news to Pauline.

She peeked at it from the front window and said, "Can we afford this car? We're a family of five now – five mouths to feed!" In her heart she knew Willy would never even suggest such a purchase if they could not afford it. She was very pleased to have a car of their own. While Willy still enjoyed walking to work when the weather was fair, he was very happy he had a car to drive in inclement weather.

Willy had gotten his own subscription to the Berliner Tageszeitung, the Berlin Daily Newspaper. The news was from Berlin but it was published in Harrisburg and delivered to the house daily. The articles were in greater depth and detail than Die Welt von Heute, The World of Today. However, he continued reading that newspaper, as well. Each evening after the children were bathed and in bed, he sat with Pauline and read both newspapers and translated for her.

The German news was not good and seemed to get worse as time went on. Often Willy would become somber and even combative when he read what was happening in his beloved homeland.

On September 15, 1935 the "Nazi Faithful" once again congregated in Nuremberg for the Annual Nazi Party Rally. The newest edict titled "The Nuremberg Laws" announced the exclusion of German Jews from Reich citizenship. Additional edicts prohibited Jews from marrying or having sexual relations with persons of "German or related blood".

Further, the laws stipulated that a Jew would no longer be defined as someone with particular religious beliefs. Instead, anyone who had three or four Jewish grandparents was now defined as a Jew regardless of whether that individual identified himself as a Jew or belonged to the Jewish religious community. Now, even non-practicing German Jews became enmeshed in the grip of Nazi terror, and those who had converted to Christianity having Jewish grandparents, were also defined as Jews. The reading of the new law was followed by cheers and applause, according to the article.

In 1936 the Olympic Games were held in Berlin and for weeks prior to the event, the Nazi Brownshirts, the SA, had removed "Jews Unwelcome" signage from public places to tone down its anti-Jewish attacks. Red banners bearing a white circle and a black swastika emblazoned with "11th Olympic Games" were seen everywhere in Berlin. Hitler put on a show for two weeks in August encouraging visitors to visit and see the Nazi Renaissance for themselves.

Outside the stadium, hotels and restaurants were encouraged to treat foreigners with extreme tolerance, and athletes commented they were never treated so well at home. Foreign tourists and Olympians carried home the impression of a happy prosperous nation and touted Hitler as the greatest political leader in the world. The delusion was that Germans are peaceful people who deserve the best the world can give them.

Eighty-nine medals were won by the German athletes and fifty-nine by Americans. Of course, German Jewish athletes were forbidden to participate in the Olympics in any capacity. After the Games ended, the Nazis resumed their persecution of the Jews.

The "Hitler Youth," comprised of Aryan boys and girls ages 10 and over, was established. Joining this group was absolutely mandatory and the participants were "given" to Hitler as a gift in celebration of his 48th birthday. Within two years, eight million children took the oath of allegiance to the Third Reich. Eight hundred girls came home from Nuremberg pregnant at the end of 1937. These young girls were called "Hitler's Brides".

Everyone in Germany was required to carry identification cards, but a red "J" was stamped on the Jews' cards. For those who did not possess recognizable Jewish first names, the Reich added middle names of "Sara" for females and "Israel" for males to the cards. This identification made sure the police could easily identify who was Jewish and who was not.

Willy had not heard from Flora in months. He longed for news from his family, particularly, how his mother was bearing up after the death of his father. However, his letters to Dresden remained unanswered, and none had been returned.

His disdain for Hitler and the Nazis grew stronger and sometimes he'd stay up late at night to read, then fall asleep in his chair. But Willy's sleep did not come peacefully, and Pauline would awaken to his calling out which brought on extreme coughing. She would come downstairs with his atomizer and calm his breathing, then make a cup of warm milk with honey to help him sleep, but he was difficult to console.

Willy was angry and heartbroken at the same time. He would always tell her she had no idea what life in Germany is like now. He often got angry at Pauline as if she wasn't she paying attention when he would read both American and German newspapers. He easily got upset describing what was happening in the world. Pauline was sympathetic but Willy's harsh words brought her to tears. Afterward, he would hug her closely, apologize, and say much he loved her.

At times he could not get beyond the guilt he felt for leaving his homeland and, particularly, his mother. Willy felt he should be there caring for her since his siblings were well up in years. Playing the piano soothed him and the children loved the music and would bring their toys over to play near his feet. Often Willy would hold Trudy on his lap and Gretchen and Arthur would sit on either side of him on the piano bench. Gretchen would put both hands on the keyboard and play along, but Arthur was more reticent and would sit very close to his father, but rarely touched the keys. Sometimes Pauline would play the piano and Willy would take out his violin and they'd play together. She read music and Willy played "by ear" and the children heard them talk about that. Arthur said Daddy was "sawing" the violin and Gretchen said "Daddy plays the piano with his ears" and they'd all chuckle.

One evening after dinner, the couple sat outside while the children played ball in the yard. "Why don't you think about joining the Frohshinn Club?" Pauline asked. "It's a men's singing group and most of them are of German heritage. I think you'd like that, Count. It would be good for you to make some new friends who like to sing like you do."

"Herman says we should join the Unter Uns," Willy replied. "We have many German friends there, men that I work with and you could meet their wives."

"Eleanor has mentioned the Unter Uns which is for families, but the Frohshinn is only for men who want to sing together. Joining that would be something just for you," Pauline commented.

"I'll think about both," said Willy, "but right now, let's catch fireflies with our children!"

CHAPTER THIRTEEN

"Trudy! Trudy, where are you? Trudy!" Pauline stood in the middle of her back yard calling her youngest. Where *is* that child? She was in the sandbox two minutes ago.

Pauline was nearly in tears when a window from St. Rose of Lima Parish next door slid up and Father Joseph leaned out the window and called, "She's here with me, Pauline, she's just watching me shave. I'll bring her over in a minute."

"That child will be the death of me," Pauline thought to herself, but didn't say the words. Soon Father Joseph swung open the back gate with Trudy in his arms munching a cookie.

"She's fine, Pauline. I'm really not sure how she opened your gate, or my door for that matter, she's really little. I apologize for leaving my door unlatched," said Father Joseph. "Perhaps if my door had been latched, we'd be scouring the neighborhood right now, wouldn't we, Trudy?" he tousled her hair.

"Oh, that child will be the death of me!" Pauline blurted out loud and they both laughed. Trudy finished her cookie and wriggled out of Father Joseph's arms to get down. "Thank you Father, she's a handful."

"I understand," Father Joseph smiled, "Arthur and Gretchen should be home in a bit. Good-bye, 'little one', and you, too, Pauline."

St. Rose of Lima School and Parish was about thirty feet away from the Lippert back yard which made it safe and convenient for the children to walk to school by themselves. Trudy wanted to go to school, too, but she wasn't old enough until next year.

Arthur and Gretchen came through the gate a few minutes later and they all went inside. The children showed their mother what they did in school that day. Arthur had spelling homework, but Gretchen's homework was only to take something tomorrow for "show and tell" to share with the class. Artie sat down with his spelling book and Gretchen went to her room to choose something interesting she thought the class might like.

During dinner Pauline told Willy about a house nearby that she heard would be listed for sale within the next few weeks. "The people who own it are moving to Ohio. I think we should look into purchasing a home of our own, Count.

We've moved more in the past eight years than both our families put together have moved in a lifetime. With your pay raise, couldn't we qualify for a mortgage? What do you think? Would you like to see the house? It's not far -- we could all take a nice walk after dinner and take a look. If you want to, that is."

"Well, yes, I suppose we could do that. How far from here is it?"

"The address is 557 Fifty-fourth Street. It's only a couple blocks away. It's a darling house with a nice yard and a basement. It's close to the Parish so the children will go to the same school. Highland Park is nearby and you'd still be close to the shops if you wanted to walk to work. There are lots of children on that block, too, and . . ."

"Yes, yes . . . that's enough, let me get cleaned up. After dinner let's go and take a look, how's that?" Willy proposed.

"Oh, I hope you like it," Pauline said. "It has three bedrooms. The one is really small. I think it's a sewing room now, but it could be a nursery. There's an attic that could be made into a large bedroom.

I think you'll like the large basement where the present owner has a workshop. Oh, and there are porches front and back with good lighting for your painting, and..."

"Let me get out of my work clothes and we'll have our dinner, then we'll go," said Willy as he headed upstairs to bathe, "and by the way, I'm hungry and it smells delicious!"

After dinner Pauline put sweaters on the children and draped one around her own shoulders.

"Let's go! Come on 'Little Lipperts, your Mama wants us to see something special at 557 Fifty-fourth Street", Willy said as he perched Trudy on his shoulders. Pauline took Artie's and Gretchen's hands. As they walked, Gretchen kept repeating to herself "Five-five-seven Fifty-fourth Street, five-five-seven Fifty-fourth street" and Willy quizzed Artie on his spelling words. He correctly spelled them all and remarked to his parents, "I like doing my homework while we walk. I'm a good speller, aren't I?"

"Oh, indeed," said his father, "you are the *best* speller!"

To Gretchen Willy asked, "Are you memorizing what you hope will be your new address, Gretchie?"

Gretchen just giggled, looked up at him with her big brown eyes and said, "Five-five-seven Fifty-fourth Street!" Willy and Pauline just grinned at each other.

The Lippert family of five obtained a mortgage. For the first time they purchased a home of their own, just before school began in the Fall of 1937.

Although Willy had written about the new house to his mother and family in Dresden and to Renard in Vincennes, he had received no answer from anyone. Willy was concerned about the changing times in Germany causing the citizens much grief. He believed that mail from America may have been confiscated by the German government and likewise, any mail addressed to America, may have been confiscated, as well.

According to both the "Berliner Tageszeitung" and "Die Welt von Heute", on November 5, 1937 Adolf Hitler held a secret meeting in the Reich Chancellery which came to be known as the Hossbach Conference or Hossbach Memorandum.[6]

The first order of business was to swear all the attendees to secrecy. Hitler's sole purpose for the meeting was to outline strategies to seize Czechoslovakia and Austria by military means. This action would be taken in order to protect Germany's eastern and southern flanks. That Germany was entitled to acquire "greater living space than in the case of other peoples..." was Hitler's opinion, and he planned to act upon it before the end of 1945 at the latest. The questions of how to do this and when, remained unanswered.

"We must write letters to your mother, my mother, and Renard letting them know our new address," Willy said. "It has been a long while since we've heard from any of them. Flora always writes, but it's been over a year without any news. I haven't heard anything from my brothers.

"It is strange we have not received even a Christmas card to the children. Also, we don't know if they have received our packages. Mutti is not like that, she would have Flora write. It makes me think they can no longer receive mail from America. That could happen, you know."

Pauline replied, "Count, I don't hear much from my mother either since she's moved back to Penns Creek to help Uncle Frank. I do miss her so and she's not even seen little Trudy yet and how big Artie and Gretchen are.

---

[6] Following World War II the Hossbach Memorandum was used in the Nuremburg war crimes trials as evidence of conspiracy to wage war, specifically targeting Goering. The memorandum also served to expose the ruthless cynicism of Hitler who repeatedly proclaimed a desire for peace in public, while laying out plans for war in Europe.

"I miss Uncle Frank, too. You would like him, Count, he's so very kind. Shall I write to her and ask when we could come? I wish they'd get a telephone. Uncle Frank refuses to allow one in the house. He's afraid of electricity and wires catching fire."

"If they still have kerosene lamps, Pauline, I would worry more about having a fire from open flames than from electricity and wires," Willy commented. "But yes, we can go for a visit sometime soon. Write to your mother!"

"What's 'kerosene lamps' mean, Daddy?" Artie asked. Willy launched into a way too complicated answer for his young son, but Artie listened intently with his little sober face, taking it all in.

Grandma Bathurst, Aunt Goldie
& Paulin Penns Creek, PA

Artie, Gretchen (with her dolly) and Trudy Circa 1937

Artie and his friend Circa 1937

At the new house, Artie and Gretchen had friends to play with who lived next door and across the street. The Lippert kids were happy they were finally allowed to get a dog. Willy and Artie got busy measuring and assessing what materials would be necessary to build a dog house.

"Could we get a cat, too?" asked Gretchen, "A cat would be fun and it could play with the dog and with us," she continued. Her father shook his head 'no' because of his asthmatic condition.

Gretchen was a bit sulky, but later whispered to him as he tucked her into bed, "I understand about your condition, Daddy, and a dog will be just fine."

In March 1938, after Hitler succeeded in annexing Austria into Germany, he was looking at the Sudeten area of Czechoslovakia where nearly three million people of German origin were living.

By May it became known that Hitler and his generals were in the process of drawing up a plan for the occupation of Czechoslovakia. The Czechs had an alliance with the French and were, therefore, counting on military assistance from France. The Soviet Union also had a treaty with the Czechs and indicated its willingness to cooperate with France and Great Britain in defending Czechoslovakia against the Germans.

As Hitler continued to demand that the Germans in Czechoslovakia be reunited with their homeland, war seemed imminent. However, neither France nor Great Britain felt prepared to undertake the defense of Czechoslovakia. Both countries were anxious to avoid military confrontation with Germany at any cost. The offering of the potential services of the Soviet Union was ignored.

On September 30, 1938, the Munich Agreement, a written plan among the European powers of Germany, Britain, France, and Italy, was introduced by Mussolini. The Agreement stipulated the Sudetenland section of western Czechoslovakia would be annexed to Germany.

Instead of fighting, the European powers gave in to Hitler, which was seen by the Third Reich as a major victory without a battle.

Industry was doing well and so was the economy in Germany. There was regular work and state-subsidized vacations, opulence for all, music, dancing, new films, and lectures.

Before this era, only the rich could live like this; now everyone could. The world, and even the Germans, were amazed by the unprecedented growth in the German economy and dubbed it "The German Miracle".

Hitler was praised as the reason for the prosperity. This "miracle" was being financed, in part, by land and raw material stolen from other countries, but that fact was never mentioned.

However, not everyone in Germany experienced the "Miracle". On November 9, 1938, the Nazis unleashed a torrent of atrocities against the Jews. Krystalnacht "Night of Broken Glass" was a night of horror when synagogues and homes were set on fire. The firemen worked to save only the Aryan homes and let 1,200 synagogues burn. The next day fellow passengers on the trains going to work could not bear to look out the windows to see the still-burning houses of worship. Three hundred thousand German Jews applied for American visas.

Willy continued to read both German newspapers each evening and translated for Pauline. His intense hatred of Hitler haunted him. Hitler now had advanced further into Czechoslovakia, disregarding the Munich Agreement he had signed in September of 1938.

Additionally, Hitler now eyed Poland as his next conquest.

CHAPTER FOURTEEN

On February 12, 1939, Girard Thomas Lippert was born, sharing his birthday with Abraham Lincoln. Girard was the fourth child and second son of Pauline and Willy. The children were excited to have a new baby in the house.

Artie was particularly happy to have a new baby brother, "We're even now, two boys and two girls," Artie told everyone at school.

"I'm thinking little Girard should be our last baby. After all, there's ten years difference between our two boys – that's a big span," Pauline remarked to Willy one evening. "We're not getting any younger, you know!"

"Well, you're probably right, Pauline. Like Artie said, we're even now with two boys and two girls. There's no question we're both getting too old for more babies, especially me," said Willy and they both laughed.

"You know, Count, I've seen the baby turn his little head from side-to-side like maybe his ears bother him, have you noticed? He doesn't seem sick, though, but the way he turns his head makes me wonder."

"Yes, I noticed that too when I rocked him to sleep last night," said Willy. "You must call the doctor tomorrow and ask him to come by. Maybe Girard *is* getting sick. You know with the other three in school now, they can pick up germs from the other children and bring them home."

"I'll call Dr. Bloom in the morning. Oh, and I forgot to tell you Artie told me a little girl in his class was sent home yesterday with measles. The Board of Health posted a quarantine notice on their front door. All the children made cards for her, he told me. Oh, I hope the baby isn't coming down with measles."

Girard cried intermittently through the night and no one got much sleep. Willy was already downstairs when Pauline awoke. He had banked the fire, made coffee, and eaten his breakfast. He was giving Girard his first bottle when his wife came wearily into the kitchen. Willy placed the baby in Pauline's arms and she burped him and commenced feeding him the remainder of the bottle. Willy poured her a cup of coffee and made her toast.

"He seems a little better this morning, but I still would like the doctor to see him," said Willy. "Look at his ears; they're a little red and feel warm to the touch. Maybe he's getting sick and has an ear infection.

Poor little 'Tyke', we don't want that to get worse, now do we?" Willy cooed to his son whose little eyes were now struggling to stay open. "Oh, so *now* you want to sleep, do you? I wish your little eyes would have been closed like this all night!" Willy joked

He kissed his wife and his little son, grabbed his lunchbox, and left for work. The nickname "Tyke" would stick to Girard for years, especially from his mother and older sisters. His mother always said, and her sister, Sy, agreed, the nickname 'Tyke' suited him perfectly!

Dr. Bloom arrived late-morning and remarked about the delicious aroma of baking bread. He told Pauline that there was a lot of sickness right now. Dr. Bloom also agreed that the other Lippert kids might be bringing germs home from school.

"Have the children wash their hands a lot," Dr. Bloom instructed. "Oh, and Pauline, measles are going around, too, and I've got two stops to make here in St. Rose's Parish, when I leave your house – both for measles."

Dr. Bloom took Girard from her arms while Pauline went to the kitchen to check the oven.

"Girard looks nice and healthy, Pauline," Dr. Bloom called into the kitchen, " but he's got a low-grade fever and I suspect an ear infection. I want you to put warm compresses against his ears, not too hot, but warm enough to comfort. Do this several times today and through the night if he fusses.

"I'll give you some ear drops, too, but use them sparingly, just at bedtime, because he's so young. You can continue the compresses if he needs them, but again, use the drops sparingly. Make sure he wears a snug cap when you take him outside. That'll help." He kissed the baby's forehead and gave him back to his mother.

"Thank you for coming so soon, Dr. Bloom, I know you're so busy," Pauline said, and gave him a paper bag full of rolls. "These are for you to take home with you," said Pauline and she watched as he opened the bag and peeked inside.

"Mmmmm, what a treat! I love these rolls, Pauline, and I thank you for your kindness. They might not make it home to Mrs. Bloom, though," he laughed, "it all depends on my schedule today. I might have to eat them for lunch!

"Now do as I say and use warm compresses from time to time, and the ear drops before bed at night. Call me if you need me!"

The Lippert kids didn't get measles – at least not that year. As winter turned to spring, Tyke's ears were a little better but sometimes, even on warm days, his mother made sure he wore a little cap to protect them.

Several letters from Dresden bearing different postmark dates arrived in the same week. Willy was convinced the German government was intercepting the mail going in and coming out of Germany.

As usual, in recent months, it was obvious the mail had been tampered with, but different postmarked pieces arriving together indicated time was needed by the new German regime to peruse the mail.

Willy was delighted to hear from Flora, and was relieved that the contents were casual and mentioned nothing political. Any untoward comments could put his family in danger. He was certain Arthur and Georg had warned his Mother and sisters to be very careful what they wrote.

Besides news from his mother and his brother, Arthur, one letter was from an old neighborhood friend Willy had grown up with. He invited Willy and his wife and family to come to Dresden for a visit. He requested Wily to please write and let them know when they would come.

Willy folded the letter and set it aside. Later, he translated it for Pauline and said, "My homeland is now America with you and our children. I have no desire to return to Germany. Not now since the war. I want to remember Dresden as I knew it."

Willy read the April 20, 1939 edition of the Berliner Tageszeitung out loud to Pauline. The edition reported details of Hitler's 50th birthday. The country had celebrated with a huge parade and the moronic roar of "Heil Hitler". The newspaper commented everyone was seemingly in a trance over this occasion.

"It's as if they're all insane," Willy remarked. He shook his head angrily that the German people didn't stand up for themselves and defend their Jewish friends against the Brownshirts. Instead, they allowed Hitler to continue his abuse against them.

Willy was glad this newspaper was published in America. It gave a more objective world-view of what was really happening in Germany. There was no censoring of the real news here. His only comment was "Germany, as I remember it, will never be the same again."

Each evening Pauline and Willy read the Altoona Mirror together. On April 30, 1939 the New York World's Fair opened for its two-year run. Spectacularly conceived for the

Flushing Meadows trash dump made famous by F. Scott Fitzgerald in Queens, New York, the Fair was quite elaborate. The Fair, in fact, was so elaborate, it was often credited with showing the world the United States had recovered from the ten-year Depression, and that prosperity was in its future. Fifty-two nations and eleven colonies participated in this spectacular event which drew forty-five million paid visitors.

During the same year, a competing fair in San Francisco, known as the Golden Gate International Exposition, was held in the middle of San Francisco Bay. Over fifteen million visitors attended, which became a second example of a spectacular World's Fair. Both were indicators that the Depression Era was in America's past.

In May 1939, the Cruise Line Saint Louis sailed from Germany with one thousand Jewish refugees. Three weeks later, they were turned away by Cuba, the United States, and Canada. The Saint Louis returned to Europe and within a year most of its passengers would, once again, be under Nazi rule.

By summer, the "Hitler Youth" or "Jungendbund" were 7.7 million strong, They were comprised of three groups, boys 10-14, boys 14-18, and girls 10-18. Parents were compelled to have their children "join" the Jungendbund.

A Hitler Youth Bike Trip to the Polish Border was planned that summer. Everyone in the Hitler Youth was looking forward to the Annual Party Rally, themed the "Rally of Peace", an oxymoron.

Hitler canceled the Bike Trip and the so-called "Rally of Peace" and, instead, declared war on Poland September 1, 1939. This meant there would be war with England and France – a Second World War -- but Hitler believed there was no other choice but to protect German honor.

Celeste Yost

CHAPTER FIFTEEN

World War II lasted from 1939-1945, and was the most widespread global war in history. It was fought in nearly every part of the world on every continent except Antarctica. Until its conclusion it would involve more than fifty countries and the entire world would feel its effects. Major battlefields included Europe, Asia, North Africa, both the Atlantic and Pacific Oceans, and the Mediterranean Sea. Although conflicts existed prior to the actual war years, two great military powers eventually emerged, the Axis Powers and the Allied Powers.

The Empire of Japan was already enmeshed in conflict with the Republic of China for the dominance of Asia and the Pacific which started in 1937. However, WW II historically began September 1, 1939 with Nazi Germany's invasion of Poland.

On September 4, the third day of Nazi Germany's assault on Poland, the citizens throughout Germany awoke to an enemy threatening their own backyards.

Sometime in the night British bombers flew into German airspace and dropped thirteen tons of propaganda leaflets on the German people. The leaflets read: "Warning from England to the German People: The truth has been withheld from you. You cannot win this war. We will not relent. Pass this leaflet on."

On November 8, 1939 Adolf Hitler was scheduled to speak at Munich's Bugerbraukeller Brewery. An unknown struggling German communist carpenter, Georg Elser, was busy making a bomb with a 144-hour timer.

When his weapon was complete, Elser moved to Munich and began sneaking into the Bugerbraukeller each night to hollow out a cavity in a stone pillar behind the speaker's platform.

After several weeks of painstaking clandestine labor, Elser successfully installed his bomb. He set it to explode on November 8, 1939 at 9:20 PM, roughly midway through Hitler's speech.

Although Elser had planned his bombing perfectly, WW II began two months earlier. Hitler had moved his speech back an hour so he could return to Berlin the same night. By 9:07 PM Hitler's speech was concluded and by 9:12 PM he had left the building. Only eight minutes later, Elser's bomb went off. The pillar containing the bomb was levelled. That caused a large section of the roof to collapse and crash down on the speaker's podium. Eight attendees were killed and dozens more injured, but Hitler was not among them.

Elser was captured the same night trying to cross the border into Switzerland. After authorities found his bomb plans, he confessed. He spent the next several years in Nazi concentration camps. In later years when the Nazi regime crumbled, Elser was executed by the SS.

Meanwhile, German bombs were leveling entire cities in Poland. Photographers were filming the onslaught which lasted eighteen days until Poland finally surrendered. The beautiful capitol city of Warsaw was decimated. Had Poland surrendered eighteen days earlier, the devastation would not have occurred. When asked why Germany was inflicting such pain and torture on the Polish people, the German reply was "We must!" Three thousand Poles died every day under German rule.

Willy became more and more agitated as he continued reading the German daily newspapers. Germany was doomed with the advancement of Nazism. After work each day and on weekends he spent much of his time in his basement workshop. He was making wooden toys for the children for Christmas. He craved the solitude of woodworking that took his mind off Europe. He considered asking Dr. Bloom for some medication.

"Count," Pauline called as she started down the basement steps, "I've brought coffee and some crullers for you. I just made them."

"I'm still working, Pauline, I need to get these patterns cut so I can finish the toys in time for Christmas. I want to send two to Germany for little Kurt and Anne Marie."

Pauline set the coffee and dessert down and perched herself on a small stool looking at Willy's patterns laid out on his work bench. One was a pull-toy elephant with moveable ears and trunk. Four unbalanced wheels would make the elephant lumber along like a real elephant. Another was a bunny pulling a little cart that had a wheel of bunny feet that revolved when you pulled it along.

"This wheel of bunny feet will make a clicking sound," Willy commented, "children like that." Pauline just smiled, pleased at her husband's cleverness.

He had also drawn a pattern of an inlaid chessboard for his brothers. He was so talented and Pauline knew all the children would love these toys. She knew also his brothers would be thrilled with the chessboard.

"These are wonderful, Count, you have such good ideas," Pauline commented, "is the coffee good? Please try a cruller and see if it's like your Mother makes. I used her recipe that you translated, do you remember?"

Willy reached out and kissed her hand then hugged her, "You always think of me, thank you. I'm finished for tonight and we can put the children to bed together. So you like the patterns so far, do you?"

"I do."

"Then the children will like them, too," Willy continued, "maybe a desk for Artie. What do you think – maybe for his birthday? And a big toy box for the girls, and a little bookcase and some blocks and a little wagon for Tyke."

Then Willy's face grew solemn, "Maybe sending a package to Germany this Christmas is not a good idea. It may never even reach the family, there's so much corruption. I've been thinking a lot about Dresden. There's seldom any mention of it in the papers.

"Maybe it will escape the peril of the other cities," then he whispered almost to himself, "if that is even possible."

The next day Pauline called Sy and they talked privately about Willy's worsening anxiety.

"Often he doesn't sleep well, and he gets so upset reading the news," Pauline shared.

"He should stop reading those German newspapers," Sy replied. "Count and Herman were talking last week at the Unter Uns and Herman said Count was really agitated about what he's been reading about Hitler. He hates all that's going on over there. He even got confrontational with some of Herman's friends from Bavaria who think Hitler is no threat."

"I didn't know that, Sy", Pauline said, "and I hope Herman wasn't upset about it. I don't know what to do or say these days.

"After dinner every night Count reads the paper then goes to the basement to work on toys for Christmas. I know he hates Hitler and he fears for Germany. He also fears for Altoona because the Railroad is centered here. Working with wood takes his mind away from the news.

"You don't think America will take part in a war overseas do you? I just can't imagine it, not again!

"I'm sorry, Sy, I have to go now, Tyke's awake and I need to bathe him. Please pray for us."

Pauline hung up the phone and tended to the baby.

She gave him his bottle and as she rocked him, she prayed for Willy and his family in Germany. She prayed especially for her husband to share his anxiety with her. He was so reclusive.

Most of all, she prayed he would cancel his subscription to the German newspapers. They served no good purpose and only upset him. There was nothing anyone could do about a war.

Celeste Yost

CHAPTER SIXTEEN

One evening in mid-summer 1940 the children were all outside catching lightning bugs. Tyke toddled around barefoot in the grass, waving his little hands trying to catch just one elusive lightning bug. He didn't have a jar of his own, so he hung after Trudy who would catch one for him. Then she'd carefully put it his hands and let him add it to her jar. Trudy and Tyke were closest in age, to quote Pauline, "Tyke thinks Trudy hung the moon!"

"Why don't you look at Gretchie's lightning bugs?" Trudy finally asked Tyke. "She caught the most tonight." Tyke looked at her with his hazel eyes and sweet smile and toddled off to Gretchen. He only wanted to be with the "big kids" and, of course, his mother.

He was content to stack blocks and knock them down and to bang on Pauline's pots and pans with a wooden spoon. He stuck close to his mother, playing nearly under her feet regardless of whether she was doing housework, cooking or sewing. But it was different when the kids were outdoors; he wanted only to be with them.

Willy with Girard, Trudy foreground
Gretchen background

Celeste Yost

Pauline with Girard Circa 1942

Artie Gretchen

Trudy Oct. 1938

CHILDHOOD PHOTOS OF THE THREE ELDEST LIPPERT KIDS
ELDORADO, ALTOONA, PA

When the mosquitos came out, Willy and Pauline brought all the children inside for their baths. Most summer nights after bath time Pauline played the piano and Count played his violin. Gretchen and Trudy danced around in their nighties pretending they were sugar plum fairies. Artie joined in on the trumpet Mr. Winter had given him for his birthday a few months earlier.

Sometimes their next-door-neighbors, who were sitting out on their porches, would applaud at the performance the Lippert kids put on. Realizing they had an audience, the children would hurry up the stairs to bed.

"He's not so good on that trumpet," commented Count quietly to his wife, "he could use a few lessons, don't you think?"

"Well, he's trying to learn on his own and I think he likes it," whispered Pauline, "I've heard of a Mr. Krivsky who plays with the Altoona Symphony. I understand he teaches trumpet and has a nice way with youngsters. I'll try to contact him. Speaking of lessons, Sy and I were talking about dancing lessons for the girls. What do you think?"

"I would like our children to appreciate music and learn to play an instrument," replied Willy. "If you want the girls to learn to dance, too, that would help develop grace and standing straight and tall...what you would call..."

"Good posture," replied Pauline.

"Yes, good posture...and learn how to be young ladies with good manners."

"I'll contact Mr. Krivsky, I'm sure Arthur Winter would have his number. I'll also see about Miss Barnes' School of Dance for the girls. Don't mention this; I'd like it to be a surprise."

"I think that would be a good surprise," commented Willy.

"There's something else I want to discuss with you, Count," Pauline added. "There's a new shop opening downtown, it's called "The Spinning Wheel" and they sell fabrics and notions. They need seamstresses to sew custom-made draperies and slipcovers. I would love to do that!

The money I earn could pay for Arthur's music lessons and the girls' dancing lessons. It's only a part-time job, just a couple hours on Saturday mornings. Sy told me about the ad in the paper and she's thinking about applying there, too."

Pauline could see by the look on his face, Count didn't care for the idea at all. She continued cautiously, "I know this is sudden, but I would enjoy working outside the house a little bit. I would like to have a little extra money of my own. I could buy things for the house and pay for the children's lessons. But if you are really against it, it's all right, I just…"

Count looked her in the eyes and said, "Of course this is another one of Eleanor's ideas! I'm the head of our house and it's my responsibility to take care of all of us. You don't need to work. We have four children to take care of. You out working is not in my plan. I make enough money for us. If you want your own money, just tell me and I'll give it to you."

"It's not the same," Pauline replied with a downcast look on her face.

"Our money is our money together," Willy said. Then he realized this wasn't about the money.

"It's not just the money, is it?" he asked, his voice softening, "I think you must need a little time to yourself to be with ladies your age, don't you?" Pauline nodded. Willy continued, "If this is important to you, go ahead and talk to the owner about the job."

Pauline's face brightened immediately, "Yes it is Sy's idea," she confessed, "but I really would like to learn how to sew draperies and slipcovers like a professional. Thank you, Count."

So it came to be that Pauline went to work at The Spinning Wheel learning to sew like a professional. Several other ladies worked with her, but not her sister, Sy. Instead Sy found another job she found more appealing. She took a job as a salesperson. She was selling Sunbeam appliances across the street from The Spinning Wheel at Gable's Department Store.

Pauline enjoyed the comradery of her new friends at the fabric shop. Her employers were kind and she valued learning more of the basics of sewing draperies and slipcovers. Having her own money and being able to help out with the extras, like trumpet and dancing lessons, pleased her immensely. Count got used to the idea and immediately saw the pleasure it gave Pauline to open her own savings account with her own money.

When school began in the fall Gretchen, age 10, and Trudy, age 8, began dancing school at the Ruth Barnes School of Dance in downtown Altoona. Miss Barnes was pleasant, thin and statuesque. She was also very strict about posture and precise ballet positions. No one wanted to be corrected in front of the class, so each child paid close attention to everything she said.

At home Gretchen began walking with a book balanced on her head, as Miss Barnes had suggested. Gretchen particularly wanted to conquer climbing the stairs without dropping the book. Trudy had no interest in that at all. She just wanted to tap-dance. Miss Barnes' sister, Miss Kitty, played the piano for the classes and the girls took a half hour of ballet followed by a half hour of tap after school one afternoon a week. There were seventeen girls and three boys in the class.

Miss Kitty had the opposite personality of her sister, Ruth. She was a little on the chubby side, always smiling, jolly, and lots of fun. If any of the children arrived a little early for class, she would play spritely music. The children loved it and would make up their own little dance routines, much to Miss Kitty's delight.

Gretchen and Trudy both loved tap a lot more than ballet, but ballet always came first – that's where "the essentials" are learned. Pauline would sit outside in the hall with the other mothers during the lessons and listen to what was being played. Pauline would then order the sheet music from Winter's Music Store so she could play the pieces for the girls to practice at home.

Willy continued his subscription to the Berliner Tageszeitung. He read about the war as it raged on in Europe, particularly Germany. Now forcing their way into the Ukraine, the Nazis oversaw the extermination of three to four thousand Jews.

Outside Latvia, Jewish men, women, and children were led to a trench, shot by a firing squad, and their bodies fell into the trench they had just dug. The killings continued until the trench was full, then another was dug. By the end of 1941 several hundred thousand Jews were murdered in this manner.

The Nazis documented triumph after triumph as they continued to march toward the City of Stalingrad. It was expected that Russia would surrender in less than five months. Instead, the Third Reich began to unravel. The Battle of Stalingrad would mark Nazi Germany's first major loss in this war. It also marked the end of Germany's advances into Eastern Europe and Russia.

On Sunday morning December 7, 1941 in a surprise attack that had been planned for nearly a year, the Japanese bombed the U.S. Naval Base at Pearl Harbor, Hawaii. The attack consisted of two waves of Japanese bomber planes flying approximately forty-five minutes apart in a barrage that lasted only 110 minutes, in total, from 7:55 AM to 9:45 AM.

KINETOSCOPE

The U.S. aircraft carriers were the main targets initially, but since all three carriers were out to sea the U.S. battleships in the harbor became the targets instead.

Seven of the eight battleships were lined up in what was dubbed "Battleship Row". During the attack, the "Nevada" left its berth attempting to reach the Harbor entrance, but it was bombed incessantly and beached itself.

The "Arizona" exploded when a bomb breached its forward ammunition room and 1,100 servicemen died on board.

The "Oklahoma", being repeatedly torpedoed, listed so badly, that it capsized.

All eight U.S. battleships were either sunk or damaged during the attack and all but two, the "Arizona" and the "Oklahoma", were eventually able to return to active duty. A total of 2,335 U.S. servicemen were killed and 1,143 were wounded. The civilian death toll was 68 and 35 civilians were wounded.

The Japanese hoped to also destroy the U.S. planes on the ground to minimize any counter-attack. They struck eight airfields. The U.S. planes were lined up along the airstrips wingtip-to-wingtip in order to avoid sabotage. This made the entire fleet very easy targets for the Japanese.

Japanese Commander Mitsuo Fuchida called out "Tora! Tora! Tora!" (meaning "Tiger! Tiger! Tiger!") upon flying over Pearl Harbor. That was a message to the entire Japanese Navy letting them know they had successfully caught the Americans by surprise. This plan was meant solely to dishearten the American people and, therefore, prevent the United States from entering World War II. Instead, it had the opposite effect.

In his message to a joint session of Congress, President Franklin D. Roosevelt gave a speech which summoned the nation to war. His speech would become part of the most iconic in American history.

Most famous was his line describing the outrageous attack the prior day:

"Yesterday, December 7, 1941 – a date which will live in infamy – the United States of America was suddenly and deliberately attacked by naval and air forces of the Empire of Japan." On December 8, 1941 the United States and Britain declared war on Japan. Thus the United States entered into World War II with the other Allied Powers.

THE ALLIED POWERS	**THE AXIS POWERS**
Great Britain	Germany
France	Italy
Australia	Japan
Canada	Soviet Union
New Zealand	Hungary
India	Romania
Canada	Bulgaria
China	Thailand
Soviet Union [7]	Yugoslavia
United States [8]	

WORLD WAR II EUROPEAN TIMELINE 1941-1942

December 7, 1941 Japanese attack on Pearl Harbor
December 8, 1941 United States enters into WW I
December 11, 1941 Hitler declares war on the U.S.
December 19, 1941 Hitler controls German Army

---

[7] The Soviet Union changed sides from the Axis Powers and joined the Allied Powers in June 1941.

[8] The United States joined the Allied Powers on December 7, 1941 after the Japanese bombing of Pearl Harbor.[8] The United States joined the Allied Powers on December 7, 1941 after the Japanese bombing of Pearl Harbor.

January 26, 1942 First American forces in Great Britain
April 23, 1942 Nazi air raids against cathedral cities GB
May 30, 1942 First Thousand-bomber British air raid against Cologne
June 1942 Auschwitz mass murder of Jews by gassing
July 22, 1942 Deportations begin from Warsaw Ghetto to concentration camps; Treblinka extermination camp opens
August 12, 1942 Stalin & Churchill meet in Moscow
September 13, 1942 Battle of Stalingrad begins
October 18, 1942 Hitler orders execution of all captured British commandos
December 17, 1942 British Foreign Secretary Eden tells British House of Commons of mass executions of Jews by Nazis; US declares those crimes will be avenged.

Celeste Yost

CHAPTER SEVENTEEN

No recent news had come from Germany other than what Willy read in the German newspapers. These days one had to wonder if the news was real or just Nazi propaganda.

Willy's weekly chorus practice at the Froshinn became less singing and more discussions of the war and, in particular, a quest for any news from their homeland. Most of Willy's friends also had family living in villages and cities being systematically destroyed.

Without contact from the Fatherland, there was much anxiety about loved ones now enmeshed in a Second World War, just twenty-one years after the First World War ended.

When America entered the War following the Japanese bombing of Pearl Harbor, the struggling U.S. economy quickly converted to the most productive manufacturer of war materials in the world.

Detroit auto makers retooled their plants in order to produce 10% of the nation's warplanes, 75% of its aircraft engines, 47% of its machine guns, and 87% of its aircraft bombs. Working long shifts and hiring many women to take the place of men who had gone to war, 2.6 million military trucks, more than 600,000 jeeps, and northward of 49,000 tanks were produced. Detroit became affectionately known as "The Arsenal of Democracy."

Surrounded by large deposits of anthracite and bituminous coal located at the junction of three navigable rivers, Pittsburgh, Pennsylvania was an ideal location for steelmaking.

Factories there were re-tooled to manufacture a variety of weapons, vehicles, aircraft and parts, battleships and tanks, torpedoes and bombs. The Sun Shipbuilding Company in Chester, Pennsylvania constructed 281 T-2 tanker oil carriers. This amounted to nearly 40% of all the tankers built during the war.

The Dravo Corporation built a new class of attack landing craft that made possible the successful Allied invasions in Italy and Normandy. The Pittsburgh Grease Plant manufactured the waterproof grease vital for amphibious operations in France, as well as in the Pacific.

The Keystone State was recognized as a manufacturing hub for parachutes, armor plate for warships, reconnaissance aircraft, compasses, radio crystals, and the mass production of penicillin that saved millions of lives.

More than forty military bases were now in Pennsylvania, ranging from the Philadelphia Navy Yard and Carlisle Barracks to hastily constructed bases, such as Camp Reynolds. Altoona became one of the largest hubs for transporting millions of soldiers across the State via the Pennsylvania Railroad. During the War the PRR facilities, including the Altoona Shops, were on target lists of German saboteurs, which, fortunately, were caught before they could complete their missions.

On May 31, 1942 all hell broke loose in Germany. Air raids and a thousand British bombers laid siege to Cologne, producing the largest devastation in Germany since the war began. The German regime outlawed any documentation of this occurrence. But this was just the beginning. For days following the Cologne bombing, tens of thousands of warning leaflets were dropped across Germany stating "We are bombing Germany city-by-city. We are coming by day and by night." None of this was permitted to be reported in the German newspapers, including the Berliner Tageszeitung.

In June 1942, Operation Pastorius, a German plot, to blow up the Horseshoe Curve which carried soldiers and war materials to strategic wartime facilities, was uncovered. The would-be saboteurs were apprehended by the FBI. The Curve remained closed for several years thereafter.

In the Fall of 1942, the same week Nazis were caring for people in a refugee camp, the world learned about other so-called "camps" in Eastern Germany of a much different nature, where hundreds of thousands of Jews were being exterminated. The Nazis continued their march toward Stalingrad, confident that in their 10th year of the glorious Reich, they would defeat their enemies and capture that great city.

By Christmas rations for German troops were replaced with imitation foods made with wood pulp and potato meal. For the troops in the East, it was much worse. Due to blizzard conditions, the troops butchered and ate their horses to survive. The Soviets surrounded the German troops and severed their supply lines. On January 31, 1943 the battle ended. Ninety-two thousand Nazis surrendered, eighty-six thousand died.

Despite this devastating defeat, in the Spring of 1943 the Nazis put out a propaganda film celebrating the Third Reich at its height of dominance in Europe. The film showed sculling teams, diving, athletics, tightrope walkers, dancing and parties. Only the bombing of the Berlin Zoo was shown, nothing else. Even though sirens and anti-aircraft guns, gas, murder, mud, and ice, and human beings burned alive was the reality. Germans are told only of the Reich's golden future and victory.

Six hundred miles away, the largest invasion in the history of the world was underway. On June 6, 1944, 156,000 Allied soldiers stormed a handful of beaches along the coast of Normandy, France. Germany was about to find out that not all of its enemies would be merciful. The Allies gained a crucial foothold that day, even though German resistance and choppy seas prevented them from fully meeting their objective.

On August 28, 1944 Paris was liberated and it appeared that the Allied troops were prevailing in Europe and that there could soon be an end to the war.

On the home-front, Pauline and Sy both left their part-time jobs to join other women volunteering to sew survival rafts for the US Navy. There were signs everywhere in Altoona announcing paper drives, rubber and scrap metal drives, and any other usable items that could be processed for use in making war materials to be sent overseas.

Willy, Herman, and Willy's cousin Hugo helped in that effort. In July 1944, the Altoona Works of the PRR, for the first time in its history, hired 1,070 women.

By 1945 the Altoona Works had become one of the largest repair and construction facilities for locomotives and railroad cars in the world.

On February 4-11, 1945 a second wartime meeting was held in Yalta, among Soviet Premier Josef Stalin, British Prime Minister Winston Churchill, and U.S. President, Franklin Roosevelt. Yalta was a neutral Ukrainian resort city on the south coast of the Crimean Peninsula surrounded by the Black Sea. The three leaders agreed to demand Germany's unconditional surrender and discussed plans for a post-war world.

On the night of February 13, 1945 hundreds of Royal Air Force bombers descended on Willy's beloved City of Dresden, often referred to as "The Florence of the Elbe". By the next morning more than 1,400 tons of high-explosive bombs and more than 1,100 tons of incendiaries were dropped on Dresden, creating a great firestorm that destroyed most of the city and killed numerous civilians.

As survivors attempted to leave the smouldering city, more than 300 U.S. bombers began decimating Dresden's railways, bridges, and transportation facilities, killing thousands more. On February 15, another 200 U.S. bombers continued their assault on Dresden's infrastructure. The U.S. Eighth Air Force dropped more than 950 tons of high-explosive bombs and more than 290 tons of incendiaries on Dresden. Later, they would drop an additional 2,800 tons of bombs on the City in three subsequent attacks before the war's end.

Because an unknown number of refugees had sought asylum in the City during the war, it was impossible to know the exact death toll. There was no shelter against a firestorm that spewed poisonous air heated to hundreds of degrees across the city. The death toll estimate was between 35,000 and 135,000.

In the City of Dresden most of the historic buildings, such as Zwinger Palace, Semper Opera House, and the Frauenkirche, the Women's Church, were gutted and nearly totally destroyed.

The Allies attempted to reconcile their bombing of Dresden by claiming the city was an important transportation hub and that the bombing was imperative to inhibit the use of vital lines of communication that would have hindered the Soviet Ally offensive. However, it was more commonly believed that the primary purpose was to attempt to force Germany to surrender by terrorizing the German population.

The mission was thought also to be in retaliation for the Nazi incendiary attack five years earlier, known as "Mondescheinsonate" or "Moonlight Sonata", against the historic British City of Coventry on November 14, 1940. In that attack the leading munitions center of England, which provided the RAF's aircraft for the War, was decimated. The famous historic Coventry Cathedral was also destroyed.

None of this devastating news was reported in the Berliner Tageszeitung.

On March 22, 1945 Hitler made his final appearance on film, coming out of his bomb-proof bunker to compel volunteers to die for "their Fuhrer".

The Nazi government surrendered unconditionally on May 7, 1945.

Following the Potsdam Declaration by the Allies on July 26, 1945, and the refusal of Japan to surrender under its terms, the United States dropped atomic bombs on the Japanese cities of Hiroshima and Nagasaki on August 6th and 9th, 1949, respectively.

With the possibility of additional atomic bombings and the Soviet Union's Declaration of War on Japan and the invasion of Manchuria, Japan agreed to an unconditional surrender on August 14, 1945. Thus, the war in Asia ended, cementing the total victory of the Allies of World War II.

Following the end of the War in 1945, representatives of fifty countries met in San Francisco at the United Nations Conference on International Organization, to draw up the United Nations Charter.

Fifty delegates deliberated on proposals worked out by representatives of China, the Soviet Union, the United Kingdom and the United States. The Charter was signed by the representatives of fifty countries on June 26, 1945.

Although not represented at the Conference, Poland later signed the document and became one of the original fifty-one Member Countries.

The United Nations officially came into existence on October 24, 1945 with the ratification of the Charter by China, France, the Soviet Union, the United Kingdom, and the United States, as well as a majority of other signatories.

A month later in Germany, November 20, 1945, the Nuremberg War Crimes trials began. Finally, the entire world could breathe a collective sigh of relief.

CHAPTER EIGHTEEN

Willy was relieved when Christmas cards and a package from Germany arrived early from his mother and siblings. He had finished making the toys and chessboard. He now wanted to hurry and get a package mailed to them. Pauline expressed concern that maybe there would be problems and the package wouldn't be received, but Willy thought since the War was over and Hitler's regime was no more, the situation in Germany would be better.

"We received this 'Paket" in good order, so we can send ours now, too," Willy commented. Flora's newsy letter was bright and happy. She explained she was writing every single word that Mutti wanted to say. In the cold weather Mutti's arthritis had worsened, so she asked Flora to write for her.

Willy read the letter to himself then began reading it to Pauline and the children.

"Read it again, Daddy!" said Tyke, "and could you read it to us in German this time?"

Asked to read in German made Willy very happy. After he read the letter in his native tongue, he began to sing some German Christmas carols and the children joined in, as Pauline played the piano. He'd been singing these songs to the children since they were babies and they knew most of the words by heart. "Stille Nacht", "Oh Tannenbaum," and the older children's favorite, "Ihr Kinderlein Kommt".

Willy then sang the little lullaby he always sang as he rocked them all to sleep when they were tiny babies. He and Pauline looked at each other, their children were growing up quickly. They each could hardly believe how quickly the years had flown by.

Willy looked around the table and marveled at his little family working on special Christmas cards for Oma Lippert and Grandma Bathurst. Gretchen took her time and glued paper doilies on hers and Tyke wanted his to be fancy too.

Artie was incensed, "You're a boy, don't put that stuff on your card! How about you draw a nice Christmas tree and glue little buttons on it like ornaments? And ask mother for some special gold stars like she puts on our "Helper List."

"Well, okay, but I thought the doilies were nice and both our Grandmas would like them," Tyke replied.

"Both Grandmas would like the doilies, Tyke, you just make your card your way, you don't have to listen to anybody. You just do what you like best," Trudy said as she gave Artie the "iron eye". Artie just looked away in disgust mumbling something that sounded like "bossy."

"I heard that!" Trudy shot back.

"That's enough, you two," Pauline sighed, "my that's a lovely card you've made, honey! Now how many Lippert children want marshmallows in their cocoa?"

In the middle of the night Pauline awoke and Count wasn't in bed beside her. He sometimes would awaken during the night and get up to check on the children, but he wasn't in either of their rooms. She smelled coffee and heard a light clinking downstairs and found Willy at the kitchen table, thoughtfully stirring his coffee. His Langenscheidt next to him, he was writing. She poured herself a cup of coffee, pulled out a chair and sat quietly beside him. She saw tears in his eyes and put her arm around him. He turned and kissed her.

"It's a letter to Mutti," he said softly, "I have not been a good son. My letters have been too few."

"Mutti will be very happy to receive your letter, she misses you so," Pauline said. Willy showed her the hand-painted Christmas cards he'd made for his family and also one for Renard, including a newly drawn postcard chessboard. Their chess matches had stopped during the war and they had lost contact. He hoped Renard still lived at the same address and that his family was safe. He missed their "over the ocean" chess games and hoped they could continue.

"I woke up and you weren't beside me or in the children's rooms. I thought maybe you had gone out for a walk in the snow, then I smelled the coffee. I'll go back to bed so you can finish this," Pauline squeezed his hand and he brought her hand to his lips with a soft kiss.

She went back to bed for a few hours. She heard Willy banking the fire before he came to bed just before dawn. The house was warm and toasty and the whole family slept late that Saturday morning.

During the Christmas holiday, Willy drove his family all over Altoona several evenings to look at the festive Christmas lights. These jaunts always ended up in the kitchen with hot cocoa and special Christmas cookies. Willy and the boys worked on setting up the trains on the Christmas tree platform and the girls strung cranberries and popcorn garlands. The homemade ornaments they had made in school were hung carefully by each child. They went sledding and had snowball battles and Artie tried to make an igloo, but Pauline insisted it become a "fort", not an igloo that could collapse on anyone.

Gretchen and Trudy entertained at local Christmas parties held at the Unter Uns, the Bavarian Hall, and the Venetian Gardens in downtown Altoona. Pauline made their costumes and Willy built two huge dice that they tap danced on. Pauline played the piano and the girls sang "All I want for Christmas is my two front teeth" and "Winter Wonderland" and other favorites that the party guests requested. Their shows were always a hit and the girls were very pleased when the various clubs paid them each five dollars and asked them to come back and dance again for other events.

One snowy evening after dinner, Willy drove his family through Llyswen to see the Christmas lights there. Most of the streets in the Llyswen section of Altoona are named for poets. They carefully drove down Halleck Place, a very steep hill that turned slightly to the right onto Browning Avenue, from there, Willy made a right turn onto Coleridge, drove over a narrow little bridge, another right turn onto Milton, then a left on Morningside, and the next left onto West Southey Avenue. The children enjoyed the ride and seeing the bright Christmas lights on most of the houses they'd passed. But Willy stopped the car in front of a dark house.

"I wanted to come by this house at night to see if anyone was still living here even though it's for sale," Willy began, "I now think it's probably empty. We'll come back tomorrow when we can see the "for sale" sign. It's too dark now. He pointed out Brumbaugh Body Works next-door where firetrucks were built. The business was enclosed by a high fence and within it were several firetrucks needing repair. On the other side of the house, was a large lot with snow-covered weeds and corn stalks.

"That house just looks so sad," said Gretchen, "it's the only one without Christmas lights or any decorations at all. I just think it's sad."

"Do you think the side yard next to the driveway belongs to the house?" asked Pauline.

"Yes, I think it does, but I don't think that weedy section is part of this property," Willy pointed to the area between the house they were looking at and the house on the other side of the weedy lot.

"It looks to me like maybe that part is a garden in the summer, or maybe it belongs to the people in that house over there," he said, pointing to a recently built house across the weedy lot.

"I don't like the weedy part, but I like the fire truck part," Girard chimed in.

"Well, I could ask some of my friends if they know anything about this house," Pauline said, "it's really not too far from Highland Park so maybe someone knows something about it. I'd like for us to see it in the daylight, Count. Where did you say you heard about it?"

"From Frank, who works with me. He was talking about it and how it would be a good investment for someone with a large family, and it's a nice quiet location and the children could walk to school. He said the "for sale" sign was just put up, but it's too dark and the snow's too deep to walk around tonight. I wanted us to see it for ourselves and look inside before we consider making an offer. Maybe tomorrow we'll come back.

After the children were snuggled in bed, Pauline and Willy sat at the kitchen table discussing the Southey Avenue house. "I'm concerned about yet another move and uprooting our entire lives again, Count," Pauline said, "especially since we'd have to sell this house in order to afford the other one and the children would have to change schools again."

"Oh Pauline," Count held her hand, "do not worry so, you know all those extra hours I worked at the shops? It was good for all of us – we got paid overtime for those hours and it was a lot of money. I didn't tell you before, but I opened a savings account with Reliance Savings & Loan downtown a couple months ago at Frank's suggestion. We could buy that house, don't you worry," he squeezed her hand and kissed her forehead.

"Why did you do that without even telling me, Count? That's what I want to know. I thought we shared everything, and now you tell me you have your own bank account!" Then she remembered she also had a bank account of her own.

"It's not my own, it's for us, for our family. I have a need to know we have emergency money set aside for troubled times. We could get our mortgage with them, too, since we already have an account. We can put our house up for sale and…"

Pauline interrupted him, "Not till we see this other house and we talk about our future plans and whether we want to invest in such a big house and property without having sold our house first. We could be 'house poor', Sy told me about that. She knows people who spend every penny on a house and then have no money to do anything because their mortgage payments are too high. I don't want to live like that! I like our little house."

"Maybe you will like this one better. Let's agree to at least look at it and let's go to bed now."

Willy kissed her hand and Pauline grinned, "You haven't kissed my hand in a while, you know."

"Uh huh…and now I kiss your lips without your parents and Sy watching us through the living room window!" They both laughed remembering their courting days, and went upstairs to bed.

After dinner the next evening Willy and the family took another ride to the Southey Avenue house. They parked in the partially shoveled driveway and walked around back. Just as Frank had said, the back yard was deep and there were many fruit trees and even a chicken coop.

"We could raise chickens and plant a vegetable garden and look, Pauline, there is a grape arbor right off the back porch. We could turn this whole yard into a beautiful garden. We could bottle grape juice and make our own wine, if we choose to do that. Of course, we would have to sell 'Five-Five-Seven Fifty-fourth Street,'" Willy mimicked Gretchen saying their address when she was little, and the whole family looked at Gretchen and chuckled.

"Well, that's not even funny, Daddy," Gretchen admonished.

"I dread another move, you know, Count," Pauline sighed.

Willy just looked at her as if a move with four children was even a problem. "We can do it. If the inside has all that Frank says it has, it will worth another move."

In the spring of 1946, 557 Fifty-fourth Street was put on the market and the Lipperts purchased 211 West Southey Avenue. Artie would still attend Altoona High School, but the other children would be changing schools. Pauline enrolled Gretchen in Roosevelt Jr. High, and Trudy and Girard in Baker Elementary for the fall term.

Lorene "Reenie" (Sy's youngest daughter), Gretchen & Trudy
Artie in foreground Alter Boy
St. John's Catholic Church, Lakemont, PA
Circa Summer 1946

Celeste Yost

Gretchen, Trudy and Girard on the back porch glider
Southey Avenue Circa Summer 1946

CHAPTER NINETEEN

Altoona, Pennsylvania, February 1947

The pair walked carefully down the rain-slicked sidewalk toward the streetcar stop on the corner. Pauline's heart was heavy and Tyke saw the sadness in her eyes so he focused on the sidewalk and was silent. She gave his hand a little squeeze and he looked up and she was smiling, but it quickly faded. He had just turned eight years old. She was forty-one.

"Look Mom, there it is! 'Mack's Sweet Shoppe – The *Sweetest* Spot in Town'", he excitedly read the brightly colored sign. "Could we go in? I read about it in the *Meer* (the colloquialism for the local newspaper, Altoona Mirror). They have a real soda fountain and they sell other stuff too, even comic books. Can we? There's time, isn't there?"

His enthusiasm about everything always lifted her spirits and her whole demeanor brightened, "There's time," she said resolutely. "We have a half-hour to wait till the streetcar comes. It'll be good for us to get out of the weather." He held the door for her as they entered the brand new confectionary. The interior just sparkled, from the glass cases of candies and nuts to the gleaming soda fountain fixtures. There were small tables and chairs near the window, but she knew her son would want to sit at the counter.

The waitress grabbed two menus and began her greeting, "Welcome to the Sweet Shoppe, the…" but before she could say it, Girard blurted out enthusiastically, "The sweetest place in town!" and the waitress, Pauline and everyone else in the place laughed.

Swiveling side-to-side in his seat, he perused the menu and after changing his mind several times, finally settled upon the popular root beer float. "That'll be two," Pauline said.

The waitress patiently answered Tyke's million questions about how the new fountain equipment worked and even brought him behind the counter to sneak a peek at all the connections underneath. She topped off their treats with whipped cream and a cherry and served them with a flourish, as one might present a treasure to royalty.

The rain turned to big flakes of wet snow as they left the Sweet Shoppe and crossed to the corner of Twelfth Avenue and Eleventh Street.

Pauline bit her lip and reached into her coat pocket and pulled out the white paper envelope of pills the doctor had just given her. Much to her son's surprise, she tore open a corner and shook out the contents and watched them disappear through the grate of the storm drain. She bent down and looked directly into his questioning eyes, "I'm not taking those pills, Tyke. I'm going to have a baby

CHAPTER TWENTY

Arthur 1947

One by one the Lippert children left the nest. Artie was the first to leave. His surprise announcement that he was quitting high school to join the Navy shocked his parents and his sisters. Needless to say, Willy and Pauline were not happy and tried to talk him out of it, urging him to at least complete his high school education.

"I hate school, Father, and I can complete this last year and graduate in the Navy. The recruiter said lots of guys do it. Please understand, I really want to do this. I'm eighteen now, so I can do it without your permission anyway," he looked away, then softly added, "but I'd like it better if you and Mother agreed that I could go."

Willy was torn over Artie's decision, but he remembered how eager he was to join the German Army at seventeen and how his mother disapproved of him leaving home also.

"It's not an easy path, Arthur," Willy cautioned his oldest son, "but I understand. I was younger than you when I joined the German Army, but I had completed my schooling. I didn't want to be placed somewhere I didn't want to be so I joined the Army before they called me up. That way I could choose what I wanted to do – fly airplanes."

The day Arthur left for Camp LeJeune, the whole family and his girlfriend, Shirley Lloyd, were there to see him off. As he got on the bus Pauline gave him a big tin of cookies to share with the other recruits. She began to cry as she hugged her eldest child who, in her mind, was still her baby, now getting on a bus bound for North Carolina.

He waved good-bye from the window and watched his entourage wave back and Shirley and his sisters blowing kisses to him. He opened the cookie tin and inside on top of waxed paper was a note from his mother. That brought tears to his eyes, too. He would miss them, but he was eager for his new adventure.

Willy and Pauline held off telling the children about the baby until Pauline could conceal her changing shape no longer. Tyke was happy that he'd not be the "baby of the family" anymore; conversely, Gretchen and Trudy were appalled at this scandalous news and kept it to themselves.

They babysat for the Unger, Powers, Hare, and Levine families in Llyswen and cringed when any of their employers would say "Tell your folks we said 'hello'." They continued dancing on special occasions at the Unter Uns, the Bavarian Hall, and The Venetian Gardens, but with Pauline's advancing pregnancy, she and Count no longer accompanied them on the piano and violin and the girls sang and danced to records or to various local bands.

On a hot July morning, Artie received a telephone call at the base from his father announcing the birth of his new baby sister. He was totally shocked and embarrassed to hear this news since his parents were so old and there were eighteen years between him and Celeste Marie. He kept that news to himself for a while, knowing full well his Navy buddies would have plenty to say about this turn of events.

Arthur Lippert Circa 1939

Celeste Marie Lippert & Mama 1947

Artie and Shirley were married in the Spring of 1949 at the Fourth Street Church of God in Altoona. Following their honeymoon, the newlyweds returned together to Camp LeJeune.

Artie often spoke of a major turning point in their lives. One of his Navy buddies had invited them to the First Baptist Church in Jacksonville, North Carolina where Artie accepted Christ as his Savior on March 18, 1951. When he phoned home to tell my mother all about his experience, she cried and so did Artie and Shirley. Artie grew up in the Catholic Church and had been an alter boy and even talked about the priesthood.

In November 1952, the young couple's first child, a beautiful baby girl, Pamela Ann Lippert, was born on the Navy base. They were transferred to San Diego, California and Artie was deployed. He served on the US Hornet CVA 12, an aircraft carrier, and the USS Prairie, a destroyer tender, deployed for six months in Sasabo, Japan. He was discharged in San Francisco on June 10, 1956, after serving in the Navy ten years.

He felt the Lord was calling him to the ministry and the little family moved to Winston-Salem, North Carolina where Artie enrolled in Wake-Forest University to study for the ministry. Their second child, Robert William "Robbie", named for both grandfathers, was born in 1958 and Pam was delighted to have a little brother.

Artie graduated from Wake-Forest in June 1960 and Girard drove us to North Carolina for commencement. We were all so proud of him, especially my parents. We had a wonderful visit with Artie and Shirley and my mother loved cuddling the grandchildren.

Artie never went into the ministry. He had been a dental technician in the Navy and was offered a job with Jelenko Industrial Gold. That job eventually took them from North Carolina to Memphis, Tennessee where their third child, Scott, was born in 1963.

The little family then moved to Suffern, New York for one year and finally settled in the south, moving to Lilburn, Georgia, on the outskirts of Atlanta, in 1972.

In Lilburn they found a beautiful wooded lot in a new development called Fox Forest Circle, and commenced building a large home for five.

Artie regaled us with what he called a "southern" story about a time when his New York colleague came to visit them in "Joe-jah". Shirley was making breakfast one morning.

"Do you like grits?" Shirley asked.

"Gee, I don't know," their friend commented, "but, I'll try one." Artie and Shirley smiled at each other then Artie reached into the box of grits and laid one tiny grit on his friend's plate.

"The look on your face is priceless!" Artie said. They all got a big laugh and his friend thoroughly enjoyed the grits and the joke. Artie said through the years his friend always reminded him of how he and Shirley set him up that morning. He also said he went back to New York and never had another "grit" the rest of his life.

Artie's graduation from Wake-Forest University 1960
Dad, Artie, Mother, Shirley, Pam, Celeste

Celeste Yost

CHAPTER TWENTY-ONE

July 1950, Altoona, Pennsylvania

Pauline gently passed her squiggling toddler to Bud, the streetcar conductor, and took his hand as he helped her down the steps to the trolley stop enclosure. 'Lakemont Park No Loitering' the sign read in bold white letters. Bud smiled and giving the little girl a soft kiss on her forehead, placed the child back into her mother's arms.

"Enjoy your outing, Pauline," Bud said and tipped his hat. The toddler waved good-bye and her mother put her down on the gravel walkway. I'm that toddler. It was a warm July morning and Pauline appreciated the leafy cover of the fragrant trees along the lakeside.

Today would be a day of reckoning. They were meeting Pauline's old school chum for lunch at the Park Restaurant. Pauline hadn't seen Cass Flaherty in several years, so "Lestie", as my parents and siblings had nicknamed me, would most certainly be a surprise. Pauline's stomach was in a knot, knowing full well Cass would commence a litany of admonishments and advice which Pauline clearly did not want to hear. It was a tad late for advice – three years too late to be exact. After their fourth child, Cass referred to Pauline as a "baby breeder" with no life of her own.

Having never had nor wanted children, Cass and her husband, Charlie, were free spirits with money to burn. Cass always dressed to the nines and bought at the finest shops. She and Charlie traveled extensively, a luxury Pauline and Count could never afford. Pauline sewed beautifully and made most of her own clothes and those of her two older daughters and now she had a little one for whom to sew.

"I just don't understand you Pauline, you could have been a highly paid seamstress in New York or Philadelphia,"

Cass sniped when they'd last been together. Pauline remembered that conversation as though it were yesterday.

"Why would anyone ever settle for less? You're so smart, you're so talented and what do you do? Go off with that foreigner!"

She and Cass had then gotten into a quarrel and Pauline had cried for days, trying to figure out what she could say or do to mend their friendship. Now it's been years, and it was at Cass's unexpected invitation that they were meeting for lunch at the new restaurant. Cass had offered to stop by for her, but Pauline thought a public place would be better for their first meeting with the baby – less chance of a fracas.

"Over here!" Cass stood and waved a gloved hand at Pauline. I walked obediently beside my mother and Cass only saw me for the first time when she stood to give my mother a big hug. "Well! What have we here, or should I say *who* have we here? This must be your granddaughter! Pauline, you never mentioned a word. You should have told me…my goodness…and how old *are* you, my dear?" Cass gushed as she bent down to take a better look. I held up three fingers then turned my face into my mother's side. They ordered lunch and I played with a small change purse of my mother's, opening and closing the little clips, while mother and Miss Cass talked.

"Surely this was just a frightful mistake. Pauline, you'll be forty-six in September! You're old enough to be a grandmother! What on earth *were* you thinking? Isn't Arthur in the Navy now? And doesn't he have that sweet little Lloyd girl for a girlfriend? The one who works at The Nut Shoppe? I thought surely this . . . this . . ." "This *what*, Cass? This blessing from the Lord?"

"Blessing? At *your age?* I just don't understand how you could have let this happen. What's wrong with that husband of yours anyway? He's a foreigner, they think little of women and want to keep them barefoot and pregnant. There *are* means of protection, you know, and of course, after the fact you could have . . ."

"Please stop, Cass." My mother got that icy look in her blue eyes that meant stop whatever you're doing. Even at my young age, I knew that look. "Having no children of your own, you just wouldn't understand. Count and I are happy about having another child. You should see how he dotes on her! It's . . .

"Say no more! What is she number five? Six? I've lost count. How old is Tyke now? You told me he was supposed to be the last one!"

"He's eleven, and he's so good with her, too. She's our fifth. He's a protector and spends a lot of time with her, we all do. The girls take her with them when they babysit, sometimes even on dates. She's a good baby, Cass, and even if she weren't, she's ours and we love her."

"Well," Cass huffed, "you don't have to make excuses for me, it's your business what you and that foreigner . . ."

It was then my mother stood and took my hand, "Enough Cass! We've been married twenty-three years. He's no foreigner, he's a United States Citizen, and I'd like you to once and for all stop this!" Suddenly the restaurant grew quiet. Yes, she had created a spectacle but my mother didn't care. She looked around and sat back down. I guess I continued opening and closing the little purse and my mother gave me a few pennies to put in it and take back out. The other patrons commenced eating and conversing; only Cass was clearly appalled.

"Well I only . . ."

"Don't. Only. Anything. Cass." Oh boy, did I learn quickly that parsed verbiage my mother used when she was clearly annoyed. She sighed and took a long drink of her iced tea.

"Well then," Cass began in a gentler sing-song tone, "How is Arthur? Is he still in the Navy?"

"He's in Saipan now, yes, still in the Navy. He and Shirley were married last April and she's living on base at Camp LeJeune in North Carolina until he returns stateside."

"Where on earth is Saipan?"

"It's in the Pacific, north of Guam, is all I know, but he says it's in the Mariana Islands, tropical and beautiful. He likes what he's doing and he's made First Class Petty Officer. We're very proud of him and we *love* Shirley."

"Yes, yes, of course," Cass muttered, now subdued.

After lunch, the three of us walked to the parking lot where Charlie was to meet Cass. He got out of the car and came over to say hello to my mother and gave my head a little pat, then opened the car door for his wife. Why do people always pat the heads of little kids?

"We must do this again sometime, Pauline. Now, you're sure you don't want a ride home?"

"I'm sure, Cass, but thank you and thank you, too, Charlie. It was nice seeing you again."

"Keep in touch. I miss the old times. Goodbye, dearie," Cass pressed a shiny bright penny into my hand, "add this shiny penny to your Mama's little purse for later. You could spend it in the Penny Arcade."

Pauline waved goodbye, not knowing then, that the next time she and Cass would meet, would be at Charlie's funeral only a few months later.

Mother took me on the Merry-Go-Round twice and bought a box of popcorn to feed the ducks. The park was crowded that day and no benches were available, so we sat on the edge of the bright blue cement fish pond in front of the open air casino. We watched the large goldfish dart about in the streams from the fountain. Noticing the pennies glistening on the bottom, I asked my mother if I might toss my pennies in there, too. "Of course, you may. Close your eyes and make a wish!" This was a Lakemont Park ritual for not only me, but all the other kids who came there.

'Thirty-first Annual Central Pennsylvania Bible Conference' advertised the gleaming white canvas sign hanging over the lattice entranceway to the casino. The speaker at the podium was barely audible, but once the singing began, Pauline recognized familiar hymns of her childhood. I guess it was hot and I was now running around the pond clapping my hands at the fish. My mother was seated on the edge of the little pond and she said her back ached.

Years later, when she told me this story, she'd thought *"I'd even sit in there just to be out of the sun." S*he was scanning the row of folding chairs for an empty one or even a bench inside, but the place was full. She said I was sweaty and becoming cranky so she picked me up and walked toward the entrance to get a better look inside. She saw a lone empty chair at the end of a long row and that made her smile.

She said she thought to herself *'Now isn't this just how God works?'* Carrying me, she went in and sat down. The hymns reminded her of her mother in Penns Creek whom she hadn't seen in nearly six months. She felt choked up about that. She was also choked up about Cass's critical words earlier. She was now on the verge of tears. My mother told me years later that thankfully I fell asleep on her lap, my head on her chest, and a leg on either side of her body.

For the first time in her life, Pauline heard a salvation message. She heard that Christ was the Son of God, born of virgin, and lived a sin-free life. He was crucified and died on a cross as atonement for the sins of the world. He rose from the dead on the third day and was on earth forty days before He returned to heaven to sit at the right hand of His Father,

God. He was alive and would return one day to take all His children home to heaven. Unbelievers would be cast into hell, a lake of fire – a real place, not just a state of mind as some believe. Most importantly she learned there was only one way to heaven: One Way Jesus, no other way, not by doing good deeds or living a good life or by believing on Mary, Jesus's mother, or the parish priest to be the intermediary to the Father. Simply, One Way Jesus.

A closing hymn was sung and people all around my mother were chatting and filing out. I was still asleep and she sat thinking about all she had just heard. She had so many questions and needed them answered. Two ladies in the back of the casino where placing drop cloths on tables of books and other items for sale and saw her with me. One of them, Sarah Shields, sat down beside her and introduced herself. My mother told her this was the most wonderful message and wanted to hear more.

"Just wait right here," Sarah said and quickly returned with a small book titled 'Sinners in the Hands of an Angry God.'

"You should read this," Sarah said, "it's a sermon written by Jonathan Edwards in 1741." Mother took the book and stared at the cover. "I've got to close up shop here, Pauline, but if you can wait a few minutes, I'll be back. Do you have a car here?"

"A car? No. I came here to meet a friend for lunch and we'll be taking the streetcar home."

"I don't drive," Sarah explained, "but my friend, Martha Yanke, does and I know she'd be glad to drive you and your little one home. We own The Gospel Book Store in downtown Altoona. Have you heard of us?" No, my mother had not, but she quickly became a regular customer by the end of that most memorable week in July, 1950.

My mother and I attended both the morning and afternoon sessions of the Central Pennsylvania Bible Conference the remainder of the week. We arrived by streetcar each morning, brought a lunch, as did Sarah and Martha, so together we made a picnic. After the afternoon service Martha drove us home.

By the end of the week, when the missionary gave an invitation, my mother, with me in tow by her side and flanked by our new friends, Sarah and Martha, walked forward and my mother accepted Christ as her Savior. That decision changed her life forever. It also changed the lives of our entire family.

Girard, Scoutie & Celeste 1950

CHAPTER TWENTY-TWO

November 1950

"Hya, hya, "my father sang to the tune of "Twinkle, Twinkle, Little Star," as he held me close and rocked me in a wooden rocker he had made years before. I was the fifth of his babies to be rocked by him. I was three-years-old.

My earliest recollection was of the day, he had carried me from the rocker to the stairway window in the foyer of the Southey Avenue house. There had been a heavy snowfall followed by icy rain during the Thanksgiving holiday. I later learned it was called by several names: "The Storm of the Century," "The Appalachian Storm" and "The Thanksgiving Storm of 1950," depending, of course, upon where you lived in America. The massive ice storm lasted three days raging through nineteen states.

I remember sparkling icicles hanging on the porch roofs and how my father breathed on that little stairway window then rubbed the glass with his handkerchief so we could see outside. We watched Brumbaugh's big trucks with heavy cranes working in our front and side yards. Then we went to the kitchen door to watch what was going on in the backyard. The kitchen was cozy and warm and smelled delightful because my mother was cooking and baking. We had a gas stove for cooking and a coal furnace for heating the house, but no electricity for lights because the power lines were down. My mother had put candles in every room so we could find our way when it got dark.

Brumbaugh's lifted and secured the maple trees out front which had been bent over from the weight of the ice. The workers used boards to brace the trees and large heavy straps to counter-balance the boards in the expectation the trees would survive. The backyard was more daunting. Two

Bartlett pear trees beyond our back porch were now propped by boards held by the stout straps. The upper yard McIntosh and Winesap apple trees, another Bartlett pear, and two sour cherry trees, were stabilized. Our Cortland apple tree was completely on the ground with part of the root ball exposed. My parents had hope that it would survive anyway.

When Brumbaugh's men finished, my father invited them all in for hot coffee and cinnamon buns fresh from the oven. They were my mother's specialty. I later learned during lean years before I was born, when my father was furloughed from the PRR, my siblings sold mother's cinnamon buns to our neighbors every Friday for extra household money. Thus, as I was growing up, Friday was always baking day.

In the spring of 1951, the fallen Cortland apple tree was thick with blossoms, as were all the fruit trees. We had one peach tree near a Concorde grape arbor just off the back porch. My mother had an herb garden across from the grape arbor. When I was little, my mother let me dig with her in that little garden. I planted succulents called hen and chicks that spread out in my own little spot and were fun to watch as the tiny new shoots piggy-backed on the larger ones like baby chicks on a mother hen.

My father built a sandbox in the back yard under one of the apple trees and he and mother planted iris around the foundation of the house with bulbs my Grandma Bathurst contributed. The iris had huge blooms and were beautiful. My parents also planted a willow tree in the back yard. My father kept it trimmed so that sitting underneath it was like being under a big umbrella, shady and cool. We had a rose garden, lilacs, mock orange, and various types of shrubbery as well.

My father made a big wooden front porch swing and ran lines of strong cord from the ground to the porch roof and planted honeysuckle vines which twined around the cord.

KINETOSCOPE

The honeysuckle grew quickly and shaded the end of the porch where the swing was hung. I have fond memories of that delicious honeysuckle fragrance and of watching the honey bees in the spring and summer gather nectar from the blossoms.

My parents kept bees and as I got older I watched when they would swarm and my father would use a "smoker" to get them all collected and shooed them back into the hive. The honey was so good and I liked to chew on the honeycomb my mother would add to each jar. We'd put it on toast and pancakes. It was the only food known to man that never spoiled, I found out later in school.

On the right side of our house as you faced it from the street, there was a lot owned by Mr. Savage, such a harsh name for such a kind man. He gardened there and also on a piece of ground that he owned on the other side of the Evans family's property next door. As he got older and couldn't keep up with the gardening, he offered to sell the land next to our house to my parents and they bought it.

This was before I was born and my parents and my siblings worked hard pulling weeds and clearing the land then planting grass. Together my parents designed a plan for the additional frontage that now with triple lots, was 220 feet. They planted a row of forsythia on the street side and a row of bridal wreath behind it so that year-round one or the other was in bloom. Together, the Evans and my parents planted a bayberry hedge between our house and theirs. My father made diagrams of gardens and had options as to which plants would be suitable in the various locations. My mother added her own touches, including a small tulip garden with a little white fence around it to keep out the bunnies.

They planted pampas grass tufts to divide the main part of the side yard from my father's vegetable garden, compost pile and bee hives in the back. He also dug a fire pit for wiener roasts when friends came over for parties, which was quite often.

Our side yard was the perfect venue from which to watch the Lakemont Park fireworks on the Fourth of July and my mother always invited friends and neighbors to come over for a wiener roast that evening. When I was older, my father spread lime making lines for a badminton court in the mid-section of that side yard and we played badminton just about every nice day.

We had a chicken coop at the end of the original back yard that my father repaired and in my younger years we raised chickens for the eggs and the occasional Sunday dinner (I later found out). I soon learned that coop was a bane to my father's existence because of predators, like weasels and rats, which would find a way inside and kill the chickens and eat the eggs.

I selected three chicks at the feed store for Easter one year and named them Thomas Jefferson, Nicodemus, and Mortimer Snerd. Thomas Jefferson was wild and scary and my mother tied his leg to one of the pear trees out back during the day because he wreaked havoc in the coop. Every time anyone ventured out the back door, he was in a rage leaping and flapping his wings and scared me and my little friends half to death.

By the time I went to Mrs. Hoffman's kindergarten in the basement of the "yellow brick church", meaning the Llyswen Methodist Church on the corner of Coleridge Avenue and Halleck Place, the chickens were no more and my father stored his yard tools and lawn mower in the chicken coop. My mother used part of it as a potting shed and I was allowed to use a section as a playhouse. My friends and I had lots of fun there, playing restaurant or having tea parties and playing with our dolls. It was also a great hiding place for hidey-go seek. But sometimes it got crowded with everyone hiding in the same spot. My parents would always chuckle at that.

The Lipperts always had pets, but never cats because my father had severe asthma and used an atomizer regularly. I remember the name of the medication was called Breathe Easy and he used a glass atomizer with a small cork in one end.

I think we had several dogs named "Scout". "Patter" was a tame bunny that lived in our house and my sisters would sit on the floor and feed him bits of apple while my mother played the piano. I had a bunny of my own named "Bunda" who lived in a little hutch outside.

My mother had a canary named "Toby" and we had some fish through the years that her good friend, Dot Brannen gave her.

Gretchen, Trudy, Girard & Artie Early 1940s

Celeste Yost

Girard and Gretchen Early 1940s

Mother & Celeste 1949

Daddy & Celeste 1949

Grandma Bathurst, Aunt Goldie & Pauline
Penns Creek, PA

Trudy bought her first car in the early fifties, a blue Buick Roadster convertible with running boards. I remember it well and she sometimes gave Girard the keys to drive it and sometimes he hot-wired it and just took it. That never went over well with Trudy or my parents. He often tormented her and hopped onto the running boards when she was trying to back out of the driveway. She took a dim view of that also.

When he was in high school he bought a small Harley Davidson motorcycle. He and Billy Hicks, our neighbor who lived on the other side of Brumbaugh Body Works, spent hours tinkering on their cycles and racing them at a racetrack in Bellwood, I think.

One night in late Fall Girard and Billy decided to ride their motorcycles to Pittsburgh and back. That's about 85 miles one-way. The evening got later and later and it was getting dark and snow flakes were starting to fall.

"They'll be fine, Pauline, they ride well, I've watched them both race, they'll be home soon," my father said.

My mother was anxious about the weather and the time they'd been gone. "I've been praying for them to get home, but now I'm getting nervous about this, Count, I mean it, where are they?" She called Billy's mom to see if she heard from the boys. Mrs. Hicks hadn't heard from the boys either and was anxious too, especially about the weather.

As the evening wore on my mother became more upset and finally my father called the State Police to report them missing. My mother was in tears.

It was late and I was still up when we heard the motorcycles rounding the bend onto Southey Avenue. Girard pulled in our driveway and Billy rode to his house at the end of the block. Daddy went outside to help Girard tie down the cover on the bike and to probably warn him my mother was 'as mad as a wet hen'. When he and Daddy lumbered up the back steps, my mother threw open the back door and grabbed Girard and hugged him. His face was bright red from the cold and mother opened the oven door to let more heat in the kitchen as Girard took off his coat and scarf. He sat on the kitchen chair and my parents each tugged off a heavy boot. My mother ran for a dishpan of warm water to thaw my brother's feet and a bucket for his hands.

Daddy gave him a cup of hot coffee, then rubbed his feet carefully in the warm water and wrapped them in warm towels. My mother rubbed his hands briskly and put them in a bucket of warm water.

She lamented, "Why would you do this to us? You have frostbite! You know you can lose appendages from frostbite? Do you know that? Well, do you? We've been worried sick, your father called the State Police!"

My brother groaned, "We're okay mom, we had dinner in Pittsburgh and started home right afterward, we didn't know about the snow. It wasn't getting heavy till we got to Bedford."

"Run upstairs and get the heating pad for your brother, Lestie, hurry!" I started up the steps and she continued, "Bring down a warm blanket for your brother, and a pair of his hunting socks!" I gathered all the items and came back to the kitchen.

My mother's rant continued, "Oh Tyke, when I think you two could have been killed, I just . . . well, you never should have gone for a ride so late in the year, it's so cold and look at you! You must be starving!"

"The coffee is fine, mom," Girard responded, "I'm not hungry. I just need to get warmed up is all."

Girard put on the hunting socks, wrapped himself in the warm quilt and lay down on the couch with the heating pad on his feet. He was soon fast asleep and the rest of us went up to bed.

In the morning, he thanked my parents for taking such good care of him. My mother was sweeping the kitchen floor and he grabbed her and started twirling her around the kitchen singing "Oh I have the most wonderful mother, she's just the prettiest mother!"

"Stop that, Tyke!" she giggled, "You had me worried to death and don't you EVER do that again, do you hear me?"

He just continued twirling her around the kitchen and only stopped when she laughed and threatened to hit him with her broom.

"Sit down and have some nice bacon and eggs, now, Tyke, you need strength, you've put your body through a lot, you know! That's a ninety-mile trip one way to Pittsburgh!

And why did you go there? What's Pittsburgh got that Altoona doesn't have?" Girard would just give up and chuckle and eat whatever mother put in front of him.

Through the years Girard would own several Harleys and sometimes he took me for rides on them. I would sit in front of him because my mother was scared I'd fall off the back and he'd never even know I was missing. She really worried about us, and for that we were all very grateful.

YESTERYEAR

Photograph submitted by Avanell K. Ruth of Altoona

Members of the sixth grade school patrol at Baker School in April 1951 included (from left): first row — Paul Winter, Richard Maximon, Melvin Engelman, Adair Stambaugh; second row — Gerald Lippert, Robert Drenning, David Ruth, whose mother submitted this photo, Edgar Bing, Peter DeIuliis; third row — Richard Kotzatoski, Neil Port, David Johnsonbaugh, William Hicks and Richard Werkmeister.

April 1951 Sixth Grade Baker School Patrol Boys
Girard is the boy in the middle row on the left with glasses.

KINETOSCOPE

Girard hoping to drive Trudy's roadster

Girard racing his motorcycle, Bellwood, PA

Celeste Yost

CHAPTER TWENTY-THREE
Gretchen

While in high school, Gretchen worked part-time as a cashier at the Acme Super Market on Plank Road and babysat for Llyswen families. In the late 1940s Gretchen met the love her life, Daniel McNeal Vickers, the son of a Baptist preacher. Neal had enlisted in the Army and was stationed at Ft. Dix, New Jersey. When he had leave he'd drive nearly 300 miles each way to come home for a weekend to see his girl. That weekend went much too quickly for both of them.

Gretchen and Neal

Neal's outfit was called up in 1950 to serve in the Korean Conflict where North and South Korea were battling each other over the right to govern the entire peninsula. Upon coming stateside, Neal was reassigned to Ft. Monmouth, New Jersey. He asked Gretchen to marry him.

Gretchen was the second Lippert child to leave the nest. My parents loved Neal and knew that he'd be a good husband and family man, but it was difficult for my mother to let go of her first daughter.

Neal and Gretchen were married December 30, 1951 in the Juniata Park Church of the Brethren, officiated by Neal's father, Pastor Dan Vickers. The newlyweds lived on base housing at Ft. Monmouth until Neal was discharged from the service.

Gretchen & Neal Vickers
December 30, 1951

I was five years old and remember their wedding. I think I helped them open their wedding presents. I was crushed when Neal took his new bride with him to New Jersey but it would not be very long until they'd come back.

Upon discharge from the Army, the newlyweds moved back to Altoona where Neal was hired in the Administrative Offices of the Pennsylvania Railroad in Juniata. They bought a bungalow on a large lot on Fifth Street, just about a mile from the PRR shops.

Gretchen & Neal's wedding reception
December 30, 1951

Mr. & Mrs. Neal Vickers, Ft. Monmouth, NJ
Yes, Gretchen put Neal's hair up in curlers too!

The house was small and had no foundation so Neal drew up plans to dig under the little house and raise it so that a foundation could be built beneath. The second phase would be to enlarge the house.

Girard was now a teenager working at the Plank Road Mobile Station and at Dodson's TV in Llyswen. Whenever he was not working, he was eager to help Neal with any and all projects, and the two became inseparable like brothers. Their friendship lasted a lifetime.

My father was building cabinets and shelves for their kitchen and Gretchen and my mother were busy choosing fabric and sewing curtains for every window.

On April 16, 1953 Gretchen and Neal welcomed their first beautiful baby girl, Kathleen Ann. My mother was thrilled to have two granddaughters born barely six months apart. To have at least one grandchild in the same town was my parent's delight. At almost six years old, I was an aunt to two nieces and felt very important. The new grandfather now had a new project: making toys for his beautiful granddaughters.

During those years, the Lakemont Park Roller Rink was a large part of our lives. My parents operated the concession stand for many years and Girard and I were skating at a very early age. I remember learning how to skate backward in the "little rink" a closed in section set apart from the larger rink where beginners could learn to skate. Railings were installed along the walls to hold onto till you got your balance. Don Rhodes' father was the rink manager and Don played the organ and everyone skated to his music. He and Trudy were dance step partners.

In 1953 the Lakemont Park Roller Rink produced Roller Rhapsody of '53 which was held at the Jaffa Mosque. Trudy and Don skated in that production and I skated, too, in the March of the Wooden Soldiers. Trudy made her costume and mine, as well as costumes for the other skaters. The costumes were beautiful.

On June 26, 1956 William Daniel "Billy" Vickers was born the day before my father's birthday. He was adorable and totally a mama's boy. He carried a little angora bunny tail that he called his "fuzzy" and always had his thumb in his mouth.

I enjoyed "babysitting" my nieces and nephews, which translated that I loved keeping them occupied when they came to visit. We had an old Victrola in a big cabinet that had a crank on the side to wind it up. My parents had a giant vinyl record collection of classical music and operas like "Hansel & Gretel" and "Peter and the Wolf". Pam and Kathy loved to dance to that music wearing my sisters' dance costumes. Even Billy, as he got older, liked to dance with a little doll baby while he wore his Davy Crockett coonskin hat.

In December 1960, Gretchen Nadeen Vickers was born just before Christmas. She was tiny and sweet and Kathy was so excited to now have a sister. Gretchen Nadeen was named after her mother and both mother and daughter had the same peaceful personality.

Like clockwork, every four years it seemed, the Vickers family welcomed a new baby and my parents were delighted with each new arrival.

Billy, Nadeen and Kathy – Easter 1964
Bonnie and Girard's home in the background

Their fourth child, Eileen Joy, was a total surprise and was born twelve years after Gretchen Nadeen on November 11, 1972. She was named after Eileen D'Andre, the wife of Pastor Richard D'Andre, Pastor of the Calvary Baptist Church on Ruskin Drive. Baby Eileen's middle name was "Joy" because her arrival brought great joy to her parents, grandparents, and siblings.

Neal's mother had passed away and several years earlier and his father remarried a lovely woman named Myrtle. She had no children of her own and quickly endeared herself to Neal and his sisters and to all the grandchildren. She was a gracious, loving grandmother and a friend to all who knew her.

KINETOSCOPE

Standing: Kathy, Neal, Gretchen & Billy
Seated: Eileen, Grandma Myrtle & Gretchen Nadeen

Celeste Yost

CHAPTER TWENTY-FOUR
Trudy

The third Lippert to leave the nest was Trudy. After graduation from Altoona High School, she got a job working as a Sales Representative for the Bell Telephone Company in downtown Altoona. There she met a handsome young man named Al Wendel who had just moved to Altoona from the Borough of Forty Fort adjacent to Wilkes-Barre, Pennsylvania.

There was an immediate attraction and as they got to know each other he found out that she roller skated, so he asked her to teach him how to skate. The rest is history.

They fell in love and on December 31, 1955 at the Altoona Bible Church, Trudy and Al were married by Pastor Henry Kulp. I was their flower girl. I was heartbroken when Gretchen got married and moved out of our house, I missed her so, but when Trudy got married and moved out too, I was really sad.

After those two weddings and my sisters each had homes of their own, I really missed them. I now had the bedroom they shared all to myself, but it was not the same. I remember how they took leisurely baths which caused my father to bang on the bathroom door in a feeble attempt to get them out of there. I watched as they put their hair up in bobbi-pins and wrapped their heads in bandanas before going to bed and the next morning they'd have curls. They both liked lipstick, perfume, and nail polish, and cutting each other's hair.

They definitely weren't happy when I got into their stuff in their absence, especially the scissors. There are several pictures around of me with very uneven, very short bangs – after I just "snipped off a little" like I watched my sisters do.

Celeste Yost

They both took me lots of places and made clothes for me. Trudy made my Brownie uniform and it was so pretty. She embroidered a little brownie on the pocket and I was the only one in the whole troop who had that special "brownie".

My sisters also often even took me along on their dates, shopping, or to the park. I learned years later that my mother had various medical issues often requiring hospitalization and a return home with bedrest. I was happily occupied with my sisters when I was little, but as I grew older, I never wanted to go to Girl Scout or Pioneer Girl camp or even to a sleepover. I was hesitant to be away from my mother. My father was also diagnosed as an insulin dependent diabetic, which required shots every day. That concerned me also.

Trudy, Gretchen & Celeste 1954

I missed my sisters terribly and wanted them both to come back home, but that was not to be. My mother suggested I accept that fact and enjoy having the bedroom all to myself now. She bought new frilly curtains for my room and a new bedspread. Turns out, as usual, my mother was right. I did enjoy having a big bed all to myself. Sometimes I pretended it was a trampoline and watched myself in the vanity mirror doing somersaults and other acrobatic tricks. My father was not very tolerant of that idea, and didn't mind hollering at me from the stairway landing. Of course, we all slid down the banister when we were kids.

1956 was certainly a baby banner year for our family. The Vickers and the Lipperts were ecstatic when Gretchen and Neal had their second child in June. William Daniel Vickers was named after both his grandfathers.

Only a few months later in September, Trudy and Al welcomed their first baby, a darling little girl they named Wendy Jean Wendel. She was a tiny "preemie" born a few weeks early. My parents and the Wendels were delighted.

Trudy & Al expecting their first baby 1956

Having two grandbabies in the same year was very exciting for my parents and for me. Trudy and Al rented an apartment from Shorty and Paul Blodgett, a middle-aged couple who had no children of their own. They became good friends and were overjoyed to watch how Wendy was growing so fast right before their eyes.

Al was offered another position at Bell Telephone in Reading, and the little family moved into a new development in Temple, Pennsylvania.

In January 1958, their first son, Alfred Louis Wendel III, "Alfie", was born. He was the third generation named after his paternal grandfather and his father.

Standing: Gretchen, Neal, Shirley, Artie, Al & Trudy
Seated: Celeste, Girard holding Kathy and Pam, Daddy holding Wendy and Mother holding Billy
Bathurst Family Reunion 1957

KINETOSCOPE

The entire Bathurst clan at a Bathurst Reunion 1957
Hosted by Aunt Eleanor & Uncle Herman

On April 7, 1965, the anniversary date of our parents, Trudy and Al's twin sons, Timothy Stephen and Stephen Timothy Wendel, were born.

The Wendel Boys
Alfie and twins, Tim and Steve
Born April 7, 1965

My mother died before the birth of Scott Lippert, Nadeen and Eileen Vickers, Tim and Steve Wendel, and April and Betsy Zapotoczny. She would have loved them all dearly. My father was especially pleased that the Wendel twins were born on April 7, my parents' wedding anniversary. My mother, too, would have been very pleased.

CHAPTER TWENTY-FIVE

My siblings and I grew up with parents who taught us to appreciate music, art, and reading. At some point in our lives, all five of us played an instrument of some sort. Artie played the trumpet, Gretchen played the piano, Trudy "sawed" along on a violin, and Girard played the harmonica and guitar. I took piano and cello lessons.

We had quite a collection of sheet music stuffed in the piano bench, mostly classical, show tunes, and popular music. I remember my mother playing "Mairzy Doats" and "In the Little Red School House". When my sisters rolled up the living room rug, they'd sing and dance up a storm as my mother played for them.

I took piano lessons for six years. My teacher was Alma Leighty, a short squatty irritating little woman who intimidated me and I dreaded my weekly lessons. Miss Leighty had a metronome that she set to keep time to the music. She also had a small baton that she tapped on her hand as she walked around the room.

Just like every other kid, I didn't like to practice. My parents encouraged me at home and I especially enjoyed playing duets with my mother. My father did not read music, but played beautifully "by ear" mostly on the black keys – I always thought that was a funny description, "how could you play the piano with your ear?"

In fifth grade I was offered a cello to play in the Baker School Orchestra. My mother was thrilled. She thought of the duets my father and I could play together, he on his violin and I, on my cello. It was not to be. My mother asked her friend, John Santone, a cellist in the Altoona Symphony if he would give me private lessons. She hoped that would pique my interest. It didn't. My friend, Cydney, played the cello and she was very good. I could not hold a candle to her.

I was so happy when Mr. Potter suggested that I give it up. "Hooray!" I thought, I would not have to drag an instrument taller than me six blocks to and from school every Tuesday. My mother was heartbroken.

My father was an artist and very creative in all aspects of drawing and painting and exceptional with woodworking. We always had art supplies and I liked to draw and paint but that, too, was not my forte. My father was a cabinetmaker and built our kitchen cabinets and a hutch for my mother and toys for all of us. He made two huge wooden dice for my sisters to dance on.

When the grandchildren came along he made toy boxes and wooden toys for each of them. I remember he made wooden stoves and ironing boards for the girls, including me, and wagons and blocks for the boys. Everyone had a pull-along elephant with off balance wheels which made the toy lumber along when you pulled it, and its ears and trunk moved, too.

My third grade teacher, Miss Clapper, taught our class how to knit and my mother encouraged me to knit. My mother taught me to crochet, embroider, and sew, all of which I enjoyed. I still have a small table cloth that I embroidered when I was about ten years old. I had ballet and tap lessons from Ruth Barnes for a short time. My lessons soon came to an end. My sisters were so good in both ballet and tap. I wasn't so fond of the regimen required for ballet, which was foundational. I really only loved those tap shoes!

In the early 1950s when the PRR furloughed thousands of workers, including those in the Pattern Shop, my father repaired and refinished furniture in his workshop in our basement for extra money. He was well sought after for his impeccable work. It was a godsend when my parents were offered the opportunity to reopen the snack bar at the Lakemont Park Roller-skating Rink.

The big snack bar was now gone and had been replaced with soda and candy machines. The new snack bar area was much smaller but easier for my mother. She was a great cook and loved everyone, especially kids. She enjoyed reopening and seeing how the skaters she remembered were now grown up and had children of their own.

My mother and I went to the rink on the bus Friday and Saturday nights and Saturday and Sunday afternoons. When the rink was rented out for special groups, we were there also. My father was at home either repairing or refinishing furniture. Sometimes he helped at the rink, but not very often.

My mother was spent at the end of the evening and had difficulty walking down the steep front steps of the rink. We would meet the bus at the bend of the road nearby which wasn't too far for her to walk. She often sent me on ahead to wait for the bus and flag it down till she could get to the stop. All the bus drivers got to know us and always waited for us.

At home I liked to go down to the basement with my father and help sweep up the curls of shaved wood. He made his own glue mixture and gave me some to glue scraps of wood together to make things. He made doll furniture for me and it was beautiful. He made a small table and chairs. The table had a Formica top with a tiny pattern. My mother provided fabric scraps for covering a sofa he made, and she sewed blankets and pillows for the little beds he had made for my dolls.

I remember my father and I walking from Llyswen to downtown Altoona pulling a wagon to pick up what were called "surplus commodities" for furloughed railroad employees. We had car fare for only one way. We'd walk down Broad Avenue to the New York Bakery and buy Brotchen (German rolls) to eat as we walked. My father was friends with the Bakery owner and he would give me a sugar cookie, also.

Downtown, we'd wait in line with the other furloughed railroad workers to receive "staple" items: flour, sugar, cornmeal, powdered eggs, powdered milk, canned meat, cheese, and butter. We'd put these in my little wagon and my father would lift it onto the trolley and we'd ride home.

My mother would say those were "lean" years and we were poor, but I don't remember being poor. I had a wonderful childhood, with lots of friends who were always welcome in our home. My mother really was a "soft touch" – I remember my friends and I playing "Missus" and clomping up and down Southey Avenue in my mother's high heels and hats and gloves and my sisters' dance costumes.

Mother had a stone marten stole, probably the only piece of fur she owned in her entire life. I remember sitting beside her in church working that little creature's jaws open and shut and clipping them to its tail. My mother never flinched – my father who bought it for her, probably did, but he never said a word.

I had a small toy printing machine and my friends and I decided to crank out a neighborhood newspaper. We went around and asked our friends if they had any news to share, then we wrote it all down, set the type, and ran off copies to circulate. My mother suggested we just publish puzzles, cartoon drawings, poems, or knock-knock jokes in our newspaper instead of any "newsy items" we might have overheard from our parents. In retrospect, that was a good idea, Mom!

In August 1955, the PRR ordered that all positions in Altoona not supporting the diesel locomotive program or car construction and repair would be abolished. All PRR workers from the 12th Street Works, Altoona Car Shops, and South Altoona Foundries where my father had worked in the Pattern Shop for thirty years, were reassigned to the Samuel Rea Shops in Hollidaysburg.

My father's job changed dramatically. He used to walk about two miles each way to and from the South Altoona Pattern Shop which he thoroughly enjoyed. He'd sometimes stop to visit Mr. Bushnell for a game of chess on his way home. He was always just as neatly dressed when he arrived home at the end of the day as he was when he arrived at work each morning.

The Samuel Rae Shops were different. There were no wood shops there. He and others from the Pattern Shop were assigned different jobs, mostly as laborers. His particular job was carrying buckets of greasy sponges to and from different locations in the huge facility. The work was dirty and the fumes from the shop greatly affected his asthma.

When my father left work, he was exhausted. He came in the cellar entrance and took his clothes off in the basement and put them aside to be washed in Fells Naptha soap. I remember helping my mother put his work pants on metal stretchers to hang on the clothesline to dry. My father liked a nice crease, even in his work clothes.

My mother had stepped off a curb the wrong way and fractured her foot that summer. She was in a cast and unable to go to the skating rink. My father and Girard worked at the concession stand. Girard had his driver's license and drove us to the rink and to various merchants to purchase supplies for the concession stand.

At sixteen, he was always at the ready to drive anywhere anytime. I went with them to United Home Dressed Meats to buy hotdogs and ground beef for hamburgers and sloppy joes. It was many years later I learned that United Home

Dressed Meats had cows corralled in a stockyard outside for other reasons than for children to be able to pet them.

We then went to Stroehmann's Bakery for rolls, and to Blair Candy for candy. Oh that heavenly sugar-laden scent inside Blair Candy! I remember it well. A young man named Luther delivered 7-Up directly to the rink, as did "the Nehi man" and "the Coca Cola man", as I called them, but someone had to be at the rink to let them in. My brother would work it out and have the car all to himself on those errands. Brownie's delivered potato chips and Benzel's delivered pretzels to our home.

My mother's foot healed slowly and she had to keep her leg elevated. I helped with the laundry using a Maytag wringer washer in our basement. I was short and stood on wooden "pop" cases to reach the wringer. I ran my fingers through the wringers more than once. My father gave me a dowel to use to start the laundry through the ringer instead of small fingers. I helped hang the clothes outside and my father would hang the sheets.

For me, he would loosen the tension in the clotheslines so I could reach them. We had lots of clothes props readily available for me to use once the clothes were pegged onto the drooping lines. When my father came home from work, we took down the clothes together and brought them into the house and my mother and I folded them.

Her foot healed eventually, but it didn't heal well and she had problems for years afterwards and especially had difficulty finding comfortable shoes.

In 1956 Girard brought home a small television set that someone had traded in at Dodson's TV where he was working. Girard was always taking apart radios, clocks and now televisions, with most of the parts stored underneath his bed. The Evans next-door had a television and my mother

KINETOSCOPE

and Helen Evans often watched the soapbox serial, "Kitty Foyle" together in the afternoons.

To have a television in our house, was wonderful. My mother ordered me "The Official Winky Dink Magic Screen" that you could stick to your tv screen. With the special magic crayons, you could complete the dot-to-dot picture at the end of each program. All my friends and I watched The Mickey Mouse Club, Captain Video, Howdy Doody, Soupy Sales, Edgar Bergan and Charlie McCarthy, and Captain Kangaroo. What a joy to be a kid in those days!

My mother faithfully watched the "The Today Show" with Dave Garroway each morning and marveled at how much news she had been missing all these years. She was enthralled in October 1957 when Russia launched the world's first satellite, "Sputnik". It was the size of a beach ball, weighed 183.9 pounds, and took ninety-eight minutes to orbit the earth.

My parents enjoyed the Champagne Music of Lawrence Welk and conversely, the "Gillette Friday Night Fights" boxing matches. My mother, believe, it or not, became a fan of "Studio Wrestling". She knew all the wrestlers by name. I can only remember a few, "Argentine Rocca", Bruno Sammartino, and my mother's favorite, "Gorgeous George". She was of the opinion that "studio wrestling" was the only legitimate sport left. She thought the Friday Night Fights were "fixed".

We also watched family programs together like "The Adventures of Ozzie and Harriet", "The Jackie Gleason Show" live from Miami, and "Leave it to Beaver". We watched "Your Hit Parade" and I loved to hear the Top Ten Hits of the Week. We watched "The Arthur Murray Dance Party" and I liked that one because I would try out their dance steps in my bedroom. Of course, I'd be wearing costumes my sisters wore in their dance performances.

Once again, that three-way mirror in my bedroom was great – I could watch myself dancing on my bed, sans the acrobatics, as I had been warned enough times and knew better.

Over the years as I was growing up my mother was gaining weight and became concerned about it. Sy thought perhaps it was the result of having a change-of-life baby. My mother started dieting and bought boxes of crackers called Rye-Krisp which tasted like dust. She once remarked, "they're a whole lot better with butter and peanut butter."

Before school every morning, I remember my mother gave me a tablespoon of Geritol. It had a funny taste but I sort of liked it. Its claim to fame was that it contained twice the iron of a pound of calf's liver. That's all my mother needed to hear and she bought it. She wanted me to be healthy and strong. After all, I was walking six blocks each way to and from school twice a day. When I was older I read the label and learned Geritol also contained 12% alcohol. No wonder I spent a lot of time in the school cloakroom for talking!

Metrecal came out in fourteen flavors in the 1960s. It was a diet "milkshake" sort of drink and my mother was a ready buyer. She would have it for lunch as the tv ads touted, but one can wasn't very much. I overheard her mention one time to a friend on the phone that "adding a scoop of ice cream made it so much better!"

Whatever product for dieting that came out, my mother would tell my father "Here's a new wrinkle…" and she'd give it a whirl. Ayds Reducing Plan was something my mother was sure would help her lose weight. Ayds were chocolate, butterscotch, creamy caramel and chocolate mint flavored caramels advertised as "appetite suppressants".

My mother (and I) tried all the flavors for months. My father was heard to say "the only people benefitting from Ayds was the Carley Company of Chicago."

Celeste Yost

CHAPTER TWENTY-SIX
Girard

Upon graduation from Altoona High School, Girard was next to leave the Lippert nest, leaving me "an only child."

Girard's Graduation from Altoona High 1957
Daddy, Girard, Mother, Celeste & Cuddles in the foreground

My brother joined the Navy and was bound for Great Lakes, Illinois for basic training. When he could come home on leave, he'd often bring friends along and my mother, "trooper" that she was, did their laundry and starched and ironed their uniforms. She fed them well, and of course, sent along a picnic for the road when they left.

One of his best buddies and our frequent guest was named "Sweeny" and he loved to joke with my parents about Girard at sea.

"Ya' see," Sweeny joked, "your son is not much of a sailor. He gets sick every time we put out to sea. One night we were to leave port and Jerry goes missing. I knew where he was – he was barfing in the head. So I go lookin' for him and he says to me 'I'll be okay soon, I just get sick when we first leave,' and I says to Jerry, 'Yeah? Well get up, our orders were scratched and we didn't leave the harbor! We all got a big laugh over that one!"

My brother punched his buddy in the arm and said "I'll get even with you, Sweeny, some day, somehow!" and everyone laughed harder.

Girard didn't come home on leave very often, but we had happy times when he did. In his absence on holidays, my mother always set a place for him at our table and displayed his framed graduation picture on his dinner plate so he'd at least be with us in spirit. Girard had a tender heart just like my mother.

He was in the active Navy from 1957-1959 and was a Sea Bee Construction Electrician 2d Class. He served aboard the USS Escape, a Diver-class rescue and salvage ship. She was originally commissioned by the US Navy for service in WW II, responsible for coming to the aid of stricken vessels.

In 1951 the Escape was recommissioned and home-ported at Norfolk, VA for salvage and towing services to the fleet along the east coast. From 1954 forward she spent alternate years in the Caribbean, based on San Juan, Puerto Rico. Girard spent the majority of his service time in San Juan, the Dominican Republic, Haiti, and Cuba.

U.S.S. Escape

One of the highlights of Girard's Naval career was a secret mission carried out on May 25, 1959 which began at the launching center in Cape Canaveral, Florida. On that date NASA launched two female monkeys, "Abel", a rhesus monkey and "Baker", a squirrel monkey, in a Jupiter nose-cone to test and evaluate the biomedical effects of space travel. The goal of the flight, which lasted more than fifteen minutes, traveling over a speed over 10,000 miles per hour, was to monitor the heart rate, body temperature, breathing rate, and muscular reaction of Abel and Baker in this extreme environment.

Both monkeys seemed to enjoy their ride and Baker almost fell asleep in their nine minutes of weightlessness. The capsule landed in the South Pacific and was recovered by the USS Escape. Abel died shortly thereafter, but Baker lived another twenty-four years. Both monkeys are preserved and on display in the Air and Space Museum of the Smithsonian Institute in Washington, DC.

Upon mustering out, Girard was hired as the Sales Manager of Town & Country, a new department store under construction in Llyswen. For the first several months of his job, he stayed overnight as a watchman until construction was completed and the store officially opened. He interviewed and hired the employees, one of whom was a young girl named Bonnie Buchanan, four years his junior. There was an attraction between the two and they began dating.

Neal and Girard repainted my parents' home on Southey Avenue which was in dire need of a coat of paint. My father was unable to help with the long-overdue painting and my parents thoroughly appreciated what their son and son-in-law did for them. Neal and Girard did a meticulous job and the house looked beautiful.

After much encouragement from "Sy", my mother decided to buy a car, go to driving school, and get her license. My parents bought a 1949 Buick Roadmaster Dynaflow. Let the lessons begin! My mother went to The Altoona Driving School during my school hours. The "Dynaflow" aspect of the car was simple. The driver was required to first use the clutch to put the car in drive or reverse. After that, every forward gear was automatic.

She got her license and she and Sy were so proud of that accomplishment. My father, who had given up driving for health reasons, was not so sure.

The Vickers Family in their new basement

Kathy and Billy 1960

Mother's 1949 Buick DynaFlow
211 W. Southey Avenue

Reverse was no problem for my mother, she could back out of the driveway with ease. It was the pulling into the driveway that became her nemesis. We had two tall maples in our front yard and the one closest to the driveway seemed always to be in the way of my mother's turn. She struck that poor tree multiple times, sometimes breaking the driver's side headlight. That old Buick was like a tank, though, and the body of it was usually unscathed. My father learned to keep an extra headlight in the basement for "next time." He was not one to throw caution to the wind.

I remember her driving me to Hollidaysburg to Dr. Haller's Oral Surgical Clinic to have teeth extracted before I got braces. On the way home, halfway up Park Hill from Lakemont into Altoona, the car stalled and started drifting backward. My mother and I prayed together that the Lord would keep us safe and give her mind clarity to remember the clutch procedure. There were no other cars even near us. We made it home safely and that was one of the few times mother didn't hit the maple.

My father put large stones at the entrance to the driveway and my job growing up was to keep them whitewashed with the lime, salt and warm water solution my father mixed. The bright white rocks helped my mother when pulling in and backing out of the driveway. At least that was the plan.

Mother's biggest accomplishment was when she and I drove almost a hundred miles each way, to and from Penns Creek to visit Grandma Bathurst and Uncle Frank. Aunt Goldie and my cousin, Frankie, lived six miles away on a farm and they came over to visit Grandma, too. We seldom saw Grandma and Uncle Frank and Aunt Goldie and Frankie. We had a lovely reunion that weekend. Frankie and I played games and had fun clanking away on the wonderful old pump organ in Grandma's parlor.

There was construction of a bridge not far from Grandma's house so Frankie and I took a stroll to see what was going on. Frankie told me all about the new bridge and road that would soon be completed.

When we got back Uncle Frank taught us how to make potato chips fried in bacon grease which were outstanding!

Uncle Frank let us help feed Coalie, the little mule, and the chubby pig, who I'm sure had a name, but I can't remember what it was. Grandma and our mothers enjoyed their time together chatting and catching up on family news.

A little girl with cerebral palsy lived next door to Grandma and Uncle Frank. I think her name was Clara or Clarissa. She couldn't walk or speak very well. Her bed was along a wall in their kitchen. Grandma packed some cookies in a "poke", as Uncle Frank called a little bag, and we took them over to her. Frankie and I talked to her and acted silly which made her laugh and clap her hands. She was always smiling and happy for visitors.

On our drive back home mother and I talked about that little girl and mother said she might not live very long. Mother said she might never be able to walk even if she did. We both cried.

That visit was the last one we made to Penns Creek, I'm sad to say. Being there was like living in the "olden days" when life was much simpler. A few years later Grandma and Uncle Frank sold the homestead and moved into an apartment on Second Avenue in Altoona where they were closer to the most of the family.

My mother and I visited Grandma and Uncle Frank in their apartment quite often. My cousins and I have precious memories of Grandma teaching us how to make ice water pie crusts. Grandma used lard and that made the crusts so flaky they melted in your mouth – no wonder, with all that lard! Her cranberry apple pie was my very favorite. We also baked Christmas cookies with her.

Grandma always wore a cobbler's apron and let all the grandkids each wear one when we baked with her. She was always interested in anything we wanted to chat about. Grandma had a little parakeet named "Pretty Boy" that she taught to talk. We tried to get him to say new words, but he usually only responded to Grandma. He'd say "Hello Grandma".

I have wonderful memories of Penns Creek and the apartment on Second Avenue with Grandma and Uncle Frank.

Celeste Yost

Pauline, Grandma wearing her cobbler apron, & Aunt Goldie
Celeste & Cousin Frankie 1959
Grandma Bathurst's home in Penns Creek, PA

CHAPTER TWENTY-SEVEN

Germany 1960s

Communication between America and Germany was difficult in the 1960s and my mother had lost contact with Annelies Funke, my father's niece. She was the daughter of his sister, Frieda. My mother had been sending food and clothing packages to Annelies to share with the rest of the family. After a while, correspondence ceased and my mother was concerned.

"I don't think they're getting our packages, Count," Pauline commented, "no acknowledgement is not like them. I always like to know that they've received them in good order"

"I'll talk to Hugo and see what is going on," Willy replied, "maybe he will know. I can't help thinking it is all political and they have to pay a tariff to pick up the packages. They probably don't have the money."

"Oh, I hope that is not so," Pauline said, but after my father spoke to his cousin Hugo, Willy's thoughts were confirmed.

Berlin became the dividing line between East and West Germany. Up until 1953 the borderlines from one side to the other could easily be crossed. Many East Germans took advantage of this route to escape. 4.1 million East Germans fled to West Germany by 1961, totaling about 20% of the East Germany population.

My father no longer read the Berliner Tageszeitung which was still being published. He had gotten to the point where he couldn't tolerate the twisted rhetoric coming out of his homeland. "I learn more on the television news than I would learn in our local newspaper or Germany's," Willy commented.

"Berlin is now completely divided like two separate countries. There is talk about a wall being built between the two. This will leave East Germany to the Soviet Union and life will change greatly. Khrushchev is a tyrant and cannot be trusted."

"The news, indeed, is disturbing and I worry about our family there," commented Pauline.

"We can do nothing from here, Pauline, nothing," was Willy's somber reply.

In early 1961 Walter Ulbricht, the First Secretary of the Socialist Unity Party and *Staatsrat* Chairman (Council of State Chairman), convinced the Soviets that only force could stop this movement.

The East German government began stockpiling building materials for the erection of the Berlin Wall. Although this activity was widely known, it was doubtful the East Germans were aware of the real purpose. The materials included enough barbed-wire to enclose the ninety-six mile circumference of West Berlin.

On June 15, 1961, just two months before construction of the Berlin Wall was to begin, Walter Ulbricht, addressing an international press conference, stated *"Niemand hat die Absicht, eine Mauer zu errichten!"* which translated means "No one has the intention to erect a wall!" This was the first time the word "Mauer" (translated: wall) was used in this context.

Two months later on Saturday, August 12, 1961 at a government garden party in Dollnsee, a wooded area north of East Berlin, Walter Ulbricht signed the Order to close the border and erect the wall, thus dividing the City of Berlin. At midnight, the police and multiple units of the East German army began to close the border.

By Sunday morning the border to West Berlin was totally closed. The streets were torn up alongside the barrier to make them impassable to most vehicles. Tangled barbed wire and fences were installed to divide the West from the East. 32,000 combat and engineer troops were employed for building the Wall, after which manning and improving the wall was tasked to the Border Police.

On August 30, 1961, the Soviets blatantly violated the provisions of the Pottsdam Conference of 1945, providing for allied personnel the ability to move freely in any sector of Berlin. In response, President Kennedy ordered 148,000 US Guardsmen and Reservists to active duty.

In subsequent months more Air National Guard units were mobilized and 216 aircraft from tactical fighter units flew to Europe in operation "Stair Step". This was the largest U.S. jet deployment in the history of the Air Guard.

In October 1961, the U.S. Chief of Mission in West Berlin, was stopped in his car while crossing at Checkpoint Charlie. He was enroute to a theatre in East Berlin.

Subsequently, Army General Lucius Clay, President Kennedy's Special Advisor in West Berlin, sent an American Diplomat, Albert Hemsing, to probe the border in a vehicle clearly identified as belonging to a member of the US Mission in Berlin.

Hemsing, too, was stopped by East German police asking to see his passport. Once his identity had become clear, the US Military Police rushed in to escort the diplomatic car as it drove into East Berlin, leaving the shocked German Democratic Police to get out of the way.

The scuffles continued with both sides standing their ground until U.S. Tanks faced Soviet Tanks at Checkpoint Charlie on October 27, 1961. Both sides realized that continuing this course of action brought no conclusion.

Khrushchev and Kennedy agreed to reduce tensions by withdrawing the tanks. Kennedy offered to go easy concerning Berlin in the future in return for the Soviets removing their tanks first. The Soviets agreed.

Concerning the Wall, Kennedy stated, "It's not a very nice solution, but a wall is a hell of a lot better than a war."

Communication from Willy's family was at an end. Letters Willy wrote to Germany came back opened and resealed and sometimes marked with black ink to block out the writing or even had sections of the letter contents cut out with a razor blade.

CHAPTER TWENTY-EIGHT

Altoona, PA 1960s

Girard and Neal talked a lot about Girard purchasing the lots next to the Vickers' property, and building a home of his own. Girard agreed and purchased several lots and made arrangements to have them cleared in the spring.

Bonnie's family lived in Hollidaysburg and invited our family to dinner at their house so we could all get to know one another. Bonnie had a little brother, Allen, and two sisters, Dorie and Judy. Her sisters and I had a lot of fun that evening dancing to records and laughing, I remember Bonnie's sister, Dorie, taught me how to dance the "mashed potato."

One Sunday evening, February 4, 1962 to be exact, Girard and Bonnie were watching "Bonanza" at the Buchanan's home. When they said good-night in the foyer, Girard asked Bonnie, "What color fireplace would you like, red brick or white brick?"

"Why would that make any difference to me?" Bonnie asked.

"Because you're going to live there," Girard replied. Bonnie told us later that she had made up her mind that if Girard didn't tell her he loved her by his birthday on February 12, she was not getting him a present! Apparently, he met the deadline and she bought him a birthday present.

At the end of March the couple drove to Juniata to look at the cleared lots. Girard proposed and put an engagement ring on the finger of his "bride to be". Both families were very happy for Bonnie and Girard. My mother just loved her.

The early months of 1962 had been a difficult year for my mother. She had several medical issues which kept her bedfast most of the time. She slept a lot and when awake, spent most of her time reading. My parents had given up the concession stand at the skating rink. My father was on the verge of retiring on disability. He could no longer endure the work of a laborer at the Samuel Rea Shops where the oil fumes aggravated his asthma.

In the fall I would start tenth grade at Altoona High School. My friends from Garden Heights, Patty and Linda, and I took the train to Harrisburg one Saturday in the Spring to shop for school clothes. All our fathers worked at the PRR in some capacity. One of their benefits provided free passes on the trains for them and their families. The three of us took the train and went shopping. Afterward we went to the movies to see "The Wonderful World of the Brothers Grimm" in Cinerama. It was shown in 3-D on a wide-screen, the first of its kind. We had never seen anything so amazing. The three of us had dinner on the train on the way home. My mother was pleased with my purchases and apologized for not taking me shopping herself or sewing for me.

We all thought it was great that all our parents allowed us to travel over a hundred miles each way by train for shopping and a movie. We really had a good time. We especially enjoyed being "on our own" in a big city!

In May Mother's health took a turn for the worse. She was taken to the hospital. Trudy came from Reading to take me back to her house. I stayed there only a week. I wanted to go home, but Trudy was hesitant to let me go. She finally agreed since my mother was being discharged and would need my help. I flew home from Reading to Martinsburg Municipal Airport.

My mother and I spent a lot of time talking after that. One particular conversation stands out in my memory and still makes me sad. My mother made a lot of my clothes over the years. She was always looking for new patterns and novel ideas.

She made a skirt for me when I started Roosevelt. Border prints and full skirts with lots of crinolines underneath were popular in the early 1960s. The fabric she chose for my skirt had a dark background with a "border print" around the hem that had wheels on it. I didn't like the skirt or the colors and told my mother I didn't.

"Why not?" my mother had asked.

"It's ugly and I hate it, that's why," I retorted, with no regard for her feelings. My comment made her cry. I felt terrible the moment the words were out of my mouth. She had enough going on health-wise without a smart-mouthed daughter to contend with. I said I was sorry and she hugged me. Thereafter, I wore that skirt quite often. Some of the kids made fun of it, but I wore it a lot because I felt I owed it to my mother for hurting her feelings.

My mother went into the hospital again. When she came home that time, she was tired and drawn looking. She slept a lot, ate very little, and was always thirsty. I opened the windows in her bedroom so she could hear the birds chirping and feel the warm breeze. The days were sunny and pleasant.

I lay down beside her in bed and we read the Bible and prayed together every day when I got home from school. I also read poetry to her and the classics that she liked, too. She often had tears in her eyes and so did I.

A few weeks later she saw the doctor again. He told her she required surgery to remove a tumor on her kidney. She was back in the hospital for the surgery in late May.

Once the operation commenced, the surgeon determined the tumor was too large for removal. From our understanding, there was no consultation with any other surgeon or the family. The operating surgeon removed the entire kidney. Within a few hours after the surgery, we were told my mother's remaining kidney appeared to be non-functioning.

Grandma Bathurst believed mother's kidney could have been damaged from years before when the swing set at Highland Park broke and the cross-beam fell on her, breaking her back. Grandma felt that because of the broken back, the doctors treating her at that time failed to check for internal injuries.

My mother was going to die of uremic poisoning and there was nothing to be done but to keep her comfortable, we were told. She was transferred from the recovery room to intensive care. She didn't live very long after that.

The night before she died I was able to visit her alone. She never complained. She was in an oxygen tent and asked me to put some ice chips in her mouth. She was not permitted to drink any liquids, just the bits of ice that would melt on her lips and tongue. Her lips were dry and sore and I put Vaseline on a q-tip and gently rubbed it onto her lips.

I remember our conversation and how softly she talked to me that night. Her voice was barely audible.

"When you grow up, you'll get married and have a family of your own," she said. "Buy a little house with a yard and plant lots of flowers. Have a place for your children to play. Always live alone; young families need to do that. It's so important."

I remember we cried together because we both knew she was dying, "Always keep Jesus in your heart," she told me, "pray to Him every day and read your Bible." We were holding hands through the zipper in the oxygen tent and her hands were so cold.

She told me she was tired and needed to rest, but that she needed to talk to Girard and Daddy before we went home. She told me to take care of my Daddy and to be sure to go to church in the morning. I couldn't reach through the oxygen tent zipper far enough to hug and kiss her. I held her soft hand to my lips and kissed it. "Sleep tight, Lestie," she said to me, "I love you. Please ask Tyke to come in, and then your Daddy."

I was sick inside and my brother went in to talk to my mother alone. When he came out, my father went in while Girard and I sat in the solarium. Neither of us spoke. There was really nothing to say.

I don't think any of us slept that night. We attended Altoona Bible Church the next morning and my father spoke privately with Pastor Kulp after the service. On the way home, as usual, we stopped at Sheetz's on Fifth Avenue and picked up chipped ham and fresh sesame seed rolls for lunch.

I remember asking if we should call the hospital and my father said my mother needed to rest and we'd go over later. By the time we got home, he had changed his mind and called the hospital as soon as we got in the door. The on-duty ICU nurse told my father we should come right away.

The Altoona Hospital was across town on Howard Avenue. The red brick building had a long porch across the front. There was a long row of green wooden rocking chairs for patients and visitors to sit in the sunshine. My father signed us in and we were directed to the Intensive Care Unit. Only family members were allowed, one-at-a-time. We waited in the hall because my Aunt Irma was visiting my mother.

Aunt Irma came out moments after we arrived and grabbed me by the shoulders. With wide-eyes and a bit of hysteria, cried to me "She's dead! She's dead! Your mother's dead!" I pulled away from her and ran down the hallway and down some steps to the main lobby, and then ran outside. Girard was on my heels and caught me as I opened the entrance to the hospital. He held me tightly and we both sat on the curb outside the hospital sobbing together. My mother had died. I felt empty inside, like my heart had been removed from my body.

"She's in heaven with Jesus now, you know," Girard said through his own tears. I knew that but I wanted her to live forever. The date was June 3, 1962. She was fifty-five years old and would have been fifty-six September 1.

I thought about starting high school and not having her guidance. I thought about Girard and Bonnie's wedding on September 22, 1962. My mother wouldn't be there, either, to celebrate. My father came outside and just stood near us silently looking up at the sun with his hands clasped behind his back. He had no words.

My sisters and I went to the mortuary the next morning to choose a funeral dress for my mother. Girard and my father chose the coffin. When we went back the next day to see our mother alone prior to the funeral, her hair was all wrong. Gretchen and Trudy asked for permission to style her hair the way she always wore it. Permission was granted and they restyled it as I sat watching them. Watching them was maudlin and sad.

The viewing lasted three days, afternoon and evening, at Mauk & Yates Funeral Home in Juniata. The final viewing and funeral service was at Altoona Bible Church. My mother loved flowers and the funeral home and the church had an abundance of them.

My father stood over my mother's coffin and told her he was so sorry. We never knew the why or wherefore of his pitiful apology. But we all remember how in those last few years together they quarreled quite a bit.

My mother was buried at Alto Reste Cemetery in the Garden of Prayer in our family plot my parents had purchased years before.

Roosevelt classes concluded that week and I wanted to go to school the last day, but at the same time I didn't want to go at all. How sad I was and my father said it was my choice what to do. Girard encouraged me to go, if only to keep some semblance of normalcy in my life.

I remember thinking about Dave Thompson who was in my class. His father was the football coach and had died earlier the same year. I wondered how his father's death had affected him, was he as heartbroken as me?

Our family celebrated my father's sixty-third birthday three weeks after my mother's funeral. I baked a birthday cake and we had a picnic in the backyard. We had a nice day, but my mother's absence was overwhelming to us all. Nothing was the same in any of our lives without our mother.

Willy and Pauline

My father's 63d birthday June 27, 1962

CHAPTER TWENTY-NINE

Just before school began in the Fall I got my braces off and my teeth were straight. I was sad because my mother never saw the result of straight teeth after two years of wearing braces. I also got contact lenses that summer.

That summer I got my first job at W.T. Grant Company in the Pleasant Valley Shopping Center. I was hired to be a salesclerk at 85 cents an hour. As time went on, I became a cashier and my hourly wage was $1. I had gotten work papers in order to be hired at the age of fourteen. I turned fifteen the end of July.

When I wasn't working I spent a lot of time in Garden Heights with Patty Rupert and Linda Fluke. Their friendship was a godsend to me after the death of my mother. We played a lot of tennis and had sleep-outs in Patty's yard and on Linda's front porch. Everyone had transistor radios and we walked around the neighborhood listening to The Four Seasons and Elvis and other popular singers of the day.

On sleep-out nights we often went to Ray's Diner on Plank Road because it was open 24 hours and we all liked their cold meatloaf sandwiches. We'd then go back to Patty's and make French fries to go with our sandwiches.

Linda's father, Harry, often took us to Lower Reese to spot deer in his old army jeep. Those times were so much fun. There was a swinging bridge near Linda's sister's house and we walked across that a time or two, but it was very scary for me.

Almost every evening after dinner, the Garden Heights kids congregated at Woodrow Wilson Elementary School playground. We'd sit on the picnic tables or the swings and just talk.

As I recall, we smoked a few cigarettes there too, a dozen kids sharing one pack of Luckys! I didn't care much for cigarettes and after a puff or two, one of the guys in the group was happy to take the remainder off my hands.

I was excited to go to Altoona High. The school was a huge old brownstone with a green tiled dome roof. On the dome was a big clock that had a face in each direction.

In the center of the interior of the school there was a light well and from the third floor you could see all the way down to the first floor. That light well was a great meeting place no matter which of the three floors you were on. It was so unique, as was the beautiful brownstone high school with the huge porch.

The students changed classes independently and I made a lot of new friends from the three sending schools, Roosevelt, Keith and Logan Area.

Across the street from the high school was a hang-out store called "Charlie's" and the boys who skipped class, or "hoods" as we called them, stood on Charlie's porch. There, they could smoke cigarettes and make cat calls to the girls.

Catty-corner from the school was Key Korner, a little store and restaurant. If you caught the early bus to school, that's where you'd go to have a nutritious breakfast of French fries and cokes before class. I remember the jukebox was loud and "Sherry" by the Four Seasons and "409" by the Beach boys played over-and-over and lingered in my head most of the day.

In the mornings, on arrival, all the students were required to sit in the High School auditorium till the bell rang. Sophomores were relegated to the main auditorium on the first floor. My homeroom was on the third. The year went by quickly. I didn't take any electives that year or join anything, not even the chorus, which I had been in for three years in Roosevelt.

My favorite class was Reading taught by Mrs. Schmidt, who was tiny and so cute. She had a gravelly voice and was stern and stood for no nonsense. She taught us well and my penchant for reading was so enhanced by her enthusiasm. I just loved her.

My worst class was Algebra II which was taught by Mr. McCall who never pronounced my first name correctly, and I gave up trying to correct him. My grades were awful even with my father's help at home.

Bonnie and Girard got married September 22, 1962 at Altoona Bible Church. It was a beautiful wedding officiated by the Assistant Pastor, Norm Mayer, a good friend of Girard's. Bonnie's parents hosted the reception at their home in Hollidaysburg and it was a lovely affair. The newlyweds spent their honeymoon at Niagara Falls. I thought that was so romantic.

Since their house in Juniata was not completely finished, they stayed with Daddy and me on Southey Avenue for a month or two, with the goal of being in their new home by Christmas 1962, and I they were.

When Girard and Bonnie moved into their new home our Southey Avenue house was so empty, just my father and me and Cuddles, who was quite old now. He was my father's shadow and followed him everywhere. The months following my mother's death were difficult for me and I'm sure my father felt the same emptiness. But in time, our hearts healed and we moved on.

I got a minus two on the Algebra final exam that year, which, to me, wasn't the end of the world. However, to my father, it might have been. "How can you get a grade two points below zero?" my father inquired.

Nevertheless, that was my grade. My final Algebra grade for the year was a two. In my father's world, barely passing was totally unacceptable. He shook his head in his hands and informed me that I disgraced our family.

Bonnie & Girard Lippert September 22, 1962
Our niece, Wendy Wendel, looking on

When school let out, I continued working at W.T. Grant in the Pleasant Valley Shopping Center. My father spent a lot of time at the Shopping Center and would often sit and chat with friends outside on a bench or have lunch at the Village Dairy.

He and I ate lunch there quite often. One day before I had to go to work we had lunch together. My father knew the menu by heart and ordered two "number fives" for us. As we were eating, I commented how delicious my sandwich was. He agreed saying, "This is the only place that makes a good tongue sandwich!"

On that note, and because it was time for my shift to begin, I gave my father a kiss, thanked him for lunch, and left for work. The only thing in the forefront of my mind the rest of that day was a vision of cow tongues.

CHAPTER THIRTY

In the fall of 1963 I got my learner's permit and Girard took me out driving in a 1956 Plymouth station wagon with push button gears. Almost always, by the time we got home, I was in tears, my brother was frazzled, and my father would just shake his head.

Bonnie intervened and taught me to drive and there were no issues between us and neither of us came home crying. I took my test in the winter and Girard let me drive their new Oldsmobile for my driving test. I had driven the Olds a time or two to get used to it and it certainly was plush and easier to drive compared to the Plymouth wagon, but it had disc brakes which were quite sensitive.

It snowed a little the day I was scheduled to take my test. As we drove out to the State Police Barracks in Hollidaysburg, I was a little nervous about driving their new car with the Trooper seated beside me in the front seat.

"Not to worry," my brother said. I hoped he was right.

I thought I was being cautious and also thought I did rather well, even the three-point turn, but when I pulled up and parallel parked in front of the barracks, I hit the brakes too hard and the cop lurched forward and grabbed his hat. He looked at me and said "Not today, honey," so I came back a few days later in the station wagon and became a licensed Pennsylvania driver.

In my Junior year at Altoona High my locker was on the second floor so I waited in the second floor balcony for the bell to ring each morning. One day I met a boy named Mike. He was originally from California and moved to Altoona a couple years earlier and had attended Keith Jr. High. We got to talking and we often sat in the same general area each morning. He and his friends, Dell, and another boy who lived near him, were silly and made me laugh and we talked about all sorts of things.

After the football games on Friday nights, everyone went to the high school dances held in the high school gym. My girlfriends and I went "stag" as they used to say.

I remember a quiet boy who came over and asked me to dance one night. He was very nice and we talked a little, but after we danced he mostly stood along the wall looking sad. For several Friday nights it was the same, one dance, a little conversation, then he would stand by the wall.

I later learned that he wasn't a current student, and had been in a serious accident and had a head injury. I don't even remember his name. I often wondered what became of him. He just sort of disappeared.

I had access to Girard's Plymouth station wagon and I picked up my friends to go to the Saturday night dances at St. Mary's. That was a "happening place" as we used to say, and my cousin, Tony Henck, was the D.J.

One Saturday night I was surprised to see Mike and his friends there, too, and he asked me to dance. Bobby Vinton's "Blue Velvet" had just been released and that might have been the first song we ever danced to. I think we danced several fast dances, the twist, the stroll, and the pony were popular and fun, and the music was great in that era.

When my friends and I got in my car to go home, I started it up and what a racket it made. I shut it right off and I was scared that something horrible happened to the engine. My friends found rides home with other friends and Mike and his friends followed me home with my car clanking loudly the whole way.

My brother started it up the next day and he wasn't happy. The engine was out of oil and had "thrown a rod" – whatever that means – but it wasn't good. I think it needed a new engine, but whatever it was Girard got it fixed and let me continue to use the car for a while until it finally conked out.

Mike and I began dating steadily and often triple dated with two other couples, Karen and Thom and Janice and Bill. When Dick D'Andre from WFBG TV started the Altoona Bandstand, the six of us went to the studio one night each week to tape the show which would be televised on the weekend.

We had so much fun at Bandstand. There were probably twenty of us altogether that went "on the road" to various venues with Dick, who was the DJ. Mr. and Mrs. DeLeo, parents of Camille, were our chaperones. We had lots of fun getting the crowd together for a shout circle to start off the evenings of dancing.

In the spring, Mike asked me to the Jr. Prom at the Penn Alto Hotel. We had a beautiful evening and afterward went with our friends to Taylor's Restaurant for a late dinner. I thought it was so romantic.

We had a great summer and one I'll always remember. Mike and I both worked during the day. Sometimes I had to work evenings and he would pick me up from work.

We frequented the drive-ins and the teen dances at the Lakemont Park Casino. We also went to the splash hops at Memorial Pool in Juniata, Lakemont Park, and Prospect Park Pool. Sometimes we got a group together to swim at the Tyrone quarries.

Girard had the Plymouth station wagon repaired and essentially gave it to me, for which I was grateful. When summer came, the station wagon was a great car for $1-A-Car-Night at the Altoona Drive-In. We could get about ten kids in that car and we all got in for just one dollar. That dollar for however many, entitled you to see a double feature, cartoons, and previews of coming attractions.

We'd park way in the back and put blankets on the steep bank at the end of the Mullin's back yard which abutted the drive-in parking lot. Girard grew up with the Mullin boys and their family didn't mind us sitting on the bank at the end of their property.

Mike and I broke up in late summer that year. After school began our senior year, I learned Mike had transferred from Altoona High School to Bishop Guilfoyle High School. I seldom heard from him after that and our paths seldom crossed. I could never forget him. He was my first love.

CHAPTER THIRTY-ONE

Bonnie and Girard played pinochle every Friday night with their friends, Frieda and Bob, and occasionally, if my father and I were at their house for dinner, the four of us would play. My father and I were partners against Bonnie and Girard. My father was a very good player and I struggled to remember all the rules and wherefores about the game. This frustrated my father no end. One night he stood up and put both hands on the table and said "That's it! You can't be my partner!"

Incredulous, I asked "Why not?"

He replied "Because you don't pay attention, you can't remember what was played, and you don't even know what the meld is."

Then he and Girard became partners and Bonnie and I were partners and she was much more understanding of my foibles. In addition to playing cards, we served snacks. She and I had a sort of rhythm and we held our own. For that, I was eternally grateful.

Bonnie and Girard adopted two beautiful baby girls, Lynne Renee, born April 4, 1968 and Dana Louise, born December 2, 1968. They certainly had their hands full with two toddlers and enjoyed every minute of it. Girard was a Material Manager for FL Smith Company at Wye Switches near Duncansville, and Bonnie retired from Sylvania, to stay home with her their new babies.

Bonnie was active in the Altoona Story League and was called upon frequently to visit libraries and school classrooms to tell stories to the children. She took Lynne and Dana along, much to the delight of the school children.

Girard began showing and selling properties for a friend at Raystown and he and Bonnie purchased a large lot at Shy Beaver overlooking Raystown Lake. They had the land cleared and a road made from the street to their lot at the top of the hill. There was a large gate at the street end.

Dana and Lynne 1973

Bonnie and Girard intended to clear the land, dig a well, and build a house on the property. Instead, they purchased a completely furnished double-wide mobile home and placed it on the lot. They built a large porch then planted flowers and shrubbery, put up tire swings for the kids and set up a badminton court.

Girard and Neal built a large picnic pavilion and called it "Shady Pines". The pavilion had all the amenities you could think of. Everyone enjoyed many delightful picnics there for years. In the evenings Girard made a bonfire in the fire pit and the grown-ups sat around and talked while the children were busy catching lightning bugs and toasting marshmallows.

The picnic pavilion at "Shady Pines"

Neal and Gretchen had also purchased a large property near Raystown Lake. Their lot included a pond and a frame house that had been built in the early 1920s. Neal drew up plans for the renovation. Neal and his son, Billy, and Girard and a few of Neal's friends came to help work on his house. It was a few miles away from Bonnie's and Girard's place, but close enough that they could be together often.

When Lynne and Dana started school, Bonnie went back to work at Hess's Department Store as Manager of the Lingerie Department and later was the Manager of the Hello Shop that sold cards and gifts in the Mall.

She retired in 1983 because she was going to have a baby! The girls were now teenagers and delighted when they found out they were going to have a baby brother. Jarret Thomas Lippert was born December 6, 1983. He was a tiny little baby as cute as a button with lots of black hair like his parents and beautiful mesmerizing eyes. He definitely was, and still is, quite the charmer!

I was living in Ocean City, NJ when Girard called to tell us about the new baby, a little boy they named Jarrett Thomas. He was a "preemie" and finally weighed five pounds so he could taken home from the hospital. I was thawing a chicken in my kitchen sink that weighed the same as my new baby nephew.

Jarrett was precious and everyone loved him, and I, for one, couldn't wait to get my hands on him!!

Girard, Bonnie & Jarrett 1986

Celeste Yost

CHAPTER THIRTY-TWO

One evening in the early Fall, I borrowed my friend, Nancy's, car while she was working second shift. My neighbor across the street, "Wolfie", came over and asked if I could drop him off at the Ancient Mariner and pick him up in a couple hours

The timing worked out for me so I dropped off Wolfie and picked him up at nine. He got in the car and said "Hey, let's go to Winky's, I'm hungry!" Winky's was one of the first fast food places in Altoona. It was on Sixth Avenue. Hamburgers were fifteen cents, fries and sodas were a dime.

Being a week night, Winky's wasn't crowded so I sat in the car while Wolfie got his food. When I turned the key in the ignition, nothing happened. I tried it a couple times more – nothing. I was really upset because it wasn't my car and I had to get it back to my girlfriend's job by 11:00 PM.

Wolfie got out and opened the hood and said everything looked okay to him and to try it again. I did and it still didn't start. I was sick inside.

Just then a black '57 Ford convertible with a white primered walk-off pulled into Winky's. "Hey, that's Zap, let me get him," said Wolfie, and he went over to talk to this kid named Zap.

Next thing I know, I'm introduced to Zap who looked under the hood and said everything looked okay, but he wanted to see what happens when he turned the key in the ignition. Well, what happened was the car started right up, of course!

"Turn it off and see if it will start up again," I suggested not taking any chances. Of course it started up again. I thanked him and told Wolfie we had to be going.

"Maybe I should follow you home," offered Zap, "in case it shuts off again so you won't be stranded someplace."

"No, that's okay," I said and started the car and he was still standing there, "thank you anyway." I backed out and started home.

Well, Zap did follow us home. I pulled into our driveway and Zap pulled in behind me, got out and asked if everything seemed okay with the car and I said yes. Wolfie went home across the street. Zap asked if I wanted to go for a ride in his car. I told him I had to study for a test and that I had to return the car to my girlfriend, Nancy, after that.

So we sat in our driveway in his car and just talked. About 10:30 he followed me to Nancy's job and waited with me till she came out. I gave her the keys and introduced her to Walt Zapotoczny which I could barely pronounce. Everyone called him Zap but he asked that we call him Walt.

Nancy went home in her car and Walt drove me home that evening. He was very shy and asked for my phone number and I gave it to him. We both had to get up early for school and work the next day. Walt worked at Force Electric and had to be at work by 7:00 AM. He walked me to the door and we said goodnight and I went inside to study for that test.

Walt called the next evening but I was at work and my father took a message. "Some boy called you," my father said, "and here is his phone number." I called but was told he wasn't there. It was a week until we connected and he asked if I wanted to take a ride "down the Kettle". The "Kettle" is part of Sinking Valley, a pretty area in a rural area in Altoona.

I agreed and he came and picked me up and met my father. Walt was very clean-cut, used a lot of Bryllcreem, and was neatly dressed and my father approved. He was also a "motor head" and his car had a big engine with a four-on-the-floor, a tachometer, a glass-pack muffler, and Baby Moon hubcaps.

Who knew there was a drag strip in Sinking Valley? Certainly not me and I was shocked to see so many "souped-up" cars down there that night. Of course we participated in the drag racing and it was so much fun, especially because Walt had a very fast car and beat most of the cars he raced. I met his brother, Tom, who had just gotten discharged from the Army. That night I learned they were from a family with ten kids. About a week later, Walt and I double-dated with Tom and Nancy and went to the drive-in.

There was an immediate attraction between those two and we double-dated a lot with them and they eventually got married.

I invited Walt to the Sr. Prom in the spring of my senior year and we had a very nice evening together.

Altoona High School Senior Prom 1965

Toward the end of the school year the top ten percent of the Business Ed. students were chosen to go out to various offices for two weeks of "work experience". I was one of them. I was assigned to work for Judge Samuel Jubelirer at the law office of Jubelirer & Carothers. Their office was located downtown on Twelfth Street above Simmons Dress Shop.

I remember being so nervous my first day, but everyone was very nice and helpful. The Judge's sons, Robert and James, and Richard Carothers, introduced themselves. I believe it was "Mr. James" who gave me my first assignment which was to go to Goldberg's Haberdashery and pick up a hat for the Judge to wear to a function that day.

I liked working in that busy office, the work was so diversified, and after two weeks I went back to school knowing that I wanted to work in the legal field.

Then came graduation held at the Jaffa Mosque. The class of 1965 was one of the largest classes to ever graduate from Altoona High School. I think we had 1,060 graduates in our class. My friend, Patty Rupert and I had our picture taken with my father. I think my father was happy to see the last of the Lippert kids graduate. I'm sad my mother wasn't there too.

Celeste, Daddy & Patty Rupert
AHS Class of 1965 Graduation Jaffa Mosque

When I told my sisters about my two-week stint at Jubelirer & Carothers, my sister, Trudy, suggested I call Mr. Hare's law office to inquire if they had any openings for a secretary. She and Gretchen babysat for the Hares for years. I spoke to Mr. Hare directly and he asked that I send him my resume. I was elated when he hired me to start work that summer. I would be working mainly for his associate, Attorney Ben Levine.

The office was on the fifth floor of the Altoona Trust Building at the corner of 12th Avenue and 12th Street in downtown Altoona. In those days, all the lawyers closed their offices on Thursday afternoons to play golf, so the secretaries were off also. However, we made up that Thursday afternoon by taking turns manning the office on Saturday mornings. Saturday was generally a quiet day which gave us time to catch up on odds and ends and get filing done without too many interruptions with the phones.

I had been taking the bus to and from work and my brother took me to look at a 1960 Ford Fairlane and I liked it. He co-signed for a $500 loan for me to buy it so I would have transportation to work. The Ford was a stick on the column and Walt taught me how to drive it. My car payment was $50 a month (more than I netted in a week), but do-able.

However, my brother had a different idea and insisted on doubling the payments to $100 a month. I think I cried, but that was the deal and I paid it off in five months instead of ten and was relieved. When I found out how much it cost to pay for parking in downtown Altoona, I continued taking the bus back and forth to work.

Hare & Hare did a lot of title work for the bank and I learned a lot about title searches, deed preparation and Estates in Mr. Hare's office. We also did matrimonial law. At that time in divorce matters, the court kept a rotating list of "Masters" assigned to hear divorce cases in their offices.

They would hear the case and make a determination on the outcome. Along with a Dictaphone recording, their secretaries took down the proceedings in shorthand.

I took my first divorce deposition shortly after I started to work for Mr. Levine, who was the designated Master. We had a Dictaphone machine. It had a "dictabelt" that fit on a cylinder and recorded the hearing. I was vaguely familiar with the Dictaphone because we had practice with them in my shorthand class. However, we were always taught in school to take everything down in shorthand, as well, just in case there were some problems with the Dictaphone. I was nervous and was glad when only the moving party in the divorce was there; the wife, who had filed for the divorce.

During the deposition she remarked that her husband had a power mower and she couldn't bear it any longer. That, being the main reason she filed for divorce. When I transcribed my notes later on, I had a question mark beside the words "power mower" and asked Mr. Levine about it. He got a funny look on his face and then started to laugh. He explained that the word was "paramour" and what exactly it meant. The woman's husband had a paramour – a girlfriend! Then I understood. I definitely had a lot to learn!

CHAPTER THIRTY-THREE

Altoona 1966

The last Lippert leaves the nest.

Walt asked me to marry him on Valentine's Day 1966 in Winky's parking lot where we had first met. By that time I had learned to spell Zapotoczny. Walt's brother, Tom, taught me to spell it using the phonetic alphabet: Zebra, Alpha, Papa, Oscar, Tango, Oscar, Charlie, Zebra, November, Yankee. Who could forget that?

Our engagement announcement

Shortly after our engagement, I learned that a local company, Sylvania, was hiring. Sylvania manufactured television and radio tubes. Starting employees were paid $2.17 an hour for assembly line work. Many of my friends were applying there because the pay was so lucrative.

I gave my notice to Hare & Hare and went to work as a "heater welder" at Sylvania which would almost double my salary. Walt and I were saving money for our wedding in August and paying for furniture we had put on lay-away.

I met Debbie Hite at Sylvania. We sat beside each other on "the line". She was also a recent hire and she was also getting married that summer. Debbie and her fiancé, Jim Smith, had their names on a waiting list for an apartment in a complex in Altoona. In the interim they were living in the downstairs apartment of 204 Jackson Street, in the Gaysport section of Hollidaysburg. They planned to live there until the Altoona apartment became available.

Debbie and Jim were married in June and we were married in August. Several weeks before our wedding, the Altoona apartment became available and Debbie and Jim moved in. They gave us the contact information for the owners of the Jackson Street house if we were interested in renting it. We were very interested and met the owners and signed a month-to-month lease. Another couple lived upstairs while they were building a new house.

Walt and I were married in a candlelight ceremony August 27, 1966 at the Garden Heights EUB Church. My father gave me away.

I continued working at Sylvania for another year. We paid off our furniture and were now saving for a house of our own. We started looking at ads in the real estate section of the Altoona Mirror. Girard and Neal were looking also for us.

L-R: Gretchen, Bonnie, Trudy, Daddy, Celeste, Walt, Neal Walt's Father ,Jim Smith &, Girard
Forefront: Nadeen & Walt's Mother

They found a small starter home just a few blocks down the hill from where they both lived in Juniata. The address was 509 Ninth Avenue, Juniata.

The four of us went to look at it. The vintage was 1920, which I loved. It had a big front porch and we all liked the neighborhood. The exterior was dark gray and it had a small back yard with hedges on either side of the yard. A picket fence closed in the yard from the alley. There was also a lovely rose garden. A one-car detached garage was a major feature for Walt.

Inside was a small kitchen, formal dining room with French doors leading into the living room. There were two bedrooms and a bath upstairs and a finished attic. The basement was cemented and had a new coal furnace. The entire interior was covered with very dated dark and dreary wallpaper.

We both liked the house and so did Girard and Neal. They believed it was well built and cared for. "This would be an excellent starter home," they both told us.

Walt and I applied for a $5,000 mortgage from Reliance Savings & Loan. We needed a twenty per-cent $1,000 down-payment. To us, it sounded like a million. Walt sold his car and we made settlement on the house in the summer of 1967. Our house payments were $100 a month which was thirty-five dollars more than our prior rent that had included utilities. We were on the edge financially.

When we returned from our honeymoon we started working on the Juniata house while we lived in Hollidaysburg for another month. Neal and Girard helped us with plumbing and wiring and tiled ceilings in the living room, dining room, and kitchen.

Every evening after work, we went straight to the house, changed into work clothes and scraped off wallpaper. The task was endless. We'd drag ourselves back to the apartment to sleep.

Mr. Buckel, the prior owner, was an elderly widower. He had remarried and moved across town to the home of his new wife. We had purchased a new refrigerator and stocked it with sandwich makings, fruit, drinks and ice cream. Stripping wallpaper was so dirty that we just wanted to fix something quick and easy before we started working.

One evening we arrived at the house and I opened the refrigerator to get cold drinks for us. The refrigerator was warm inside and ice cream was dripping from the freezer. We first thought something happened to our new refrigerator. Walt checked the main electric box and found the main switch in the off position. Knowing neither of us would ever do that, we realized the only other person who might still have a key to the house was Mr. Buckel.

Walt went out and bought new locks for all the doors and changed them that evening. We never mentioned the electricity situation to Mr. Buckel, but we did let him know the locks were now changed.

While installing new locks on the garage door, Walt noticed holes in the ground where the rose garden had been, and called my attention to it. Apparently, Mr. Buckel was digging up the roses and probably taking them to his new house.

We called him and asked that he kindly leave the remaining rose bushes for us. I don't think he understood, but he did leave a few of the roses for us and we bought and planted more. We never saw Mr. Buckel after that. We both felt sad for him because he and his first wife had built the house and planted the roses. He had memories there.

After sanding and washing down all the naked walls, we painted the inside of the house. Walt sanded and refinished the pegged wood floors in the living room and dining room. The kitchen was tiny and I put down peel-and-stick carpet tiles on the floor and wallpapered the breakfast area. We bought inexpensive linoleum rugs for the two bedrooms upstairs.

Neal and Girard helped Walt with upgrading the wiring and plumbing throughout the house. Girard also repaired an old washer and dryer for me and connected them both in the basement.

The following spring Walt and his friends painted the outside of the house white with red trim. We also had the coal furnace removed and a new gas furnace installed. We were so pleased with the results both inside and out. This was a cozy little house and we were so happy to own it.

Someone gave us a pool table and the only place suitable for it was the attic. Walt and his friends hoisted it up by ropes to the third floor and brought it in through an attic window. We cut the length of one cue to use when you had to make what we called a "chimney shot" since the chimney stood right in the middle of the attic. We had a lot of fun up there playing pool with our friends over the years.

I remember one night we had a bat in the attic and I became a "screaming mimi". Walt tried to catch it, but to no avail. Then he remembered that John Riley, the WFBG weather man and a friend of ours, claimed to be the "best bat catcher" around.

We called John. He came over wearing his "bat hat" and carrying a small narrow screen. Walt opened several windows in the attic and turned off the lights. John held up the screen to attract the bat. Amazingly, the bat flew onto John's screen and John held it out the window, gave the screen a shake, and the bat flew off into the night. I didn't witness the capture. I was downstairs somewhere safe.

On Memorial Day weekend 1967 Walt and I were driving to Hagerstown, Maryland for a car show. I was so sick in the car along the way, we had to keep stopping. I thought I was getting the flu. As it turned out, however, we were expecting our first baby.

In the late sixties, the Vietnam War was ramping up. The Altoona Mirror posted a weekly list of potential draftees for the military to serve in Vietnam. Walt's name appeared on that list shortly after my pregnancy was confirmed. When his appointment with the Draft Board was scheduled, Walt was told to bring proof that we were expecting our first child.

My obstetrician, Dr. Raub, confirmed the pregnancy with my due date of February 1968. Because of that, Walt was deferred from the military. His friend, Denny Spahn, was with him that day. Denny was drafted and served in Vietnam. Sadly, Denny never came home.

April Michele Zapotoczny was born in a blizzard at 2:10 AM on January 26, 1968. She was two weeks early. This cute baby was tiny and had dimples everywhere one could have dimples. She had black hair like her father and gray eyes.

Girard and Bonnie were so taken with her. They had been married six years and had no children. Being around April made them think seriously about adoption. It wasn't long until they adopted Lynne Renee who was born a few months after April.

My father was thrilled about his two new baby granddaughters. He set to work making each of them little bookcases with their names on them. He was also making toys. He made rolling pin holders and rolling pins and sewing boxes for each of us girls.

Gretchen, Bonnie and I took turns inviting my father to dinner. This insured he had a good meal every night with leftovers to take home. We also took turns cleaning the house on Southey Avenue, and doing Daddy's laundry. The big house was empty and lonely for him and he talked about selling it. He had heard Brumbaugh's was interested.

Lynne Renee Lippert and April Michele Zapotoczny 1968

My father enjoyed walking to the Pleasant Valley Shopping Center for lunch, and sometimes dinner, at The Village Dairy. He walked to Modern Cabinet on Frankstown Road to talk with his friends and buy handles and knobs for his various woodworking projects. He made beautiful wooden banks for my brothers and brothers-in-law and a beautiful corner cupboard for me.

He sold the Southey Avenue house to Brumbaugh's shortly after April was born and bought a mobile home with a pull-out living room section. The mobile home was delivered and set up in Gretchen and Neal's huge yard.

He enjoyed working with Gretchen in her garden, but he missed the shopping center and meeting his friends. There were no sidewalks where he now lived and there really was no safe place for him to walk. Each of us would take him wherever he wanted to go, whenever he wanted to go, and then bring him back home when he called us. But it was not the same for him.

Daddy told me once he felt like a prisoner. That made me cry. Moving nearer to all of us was not supposed to be that way. I'm sorry now that we didn't find an apartment for him in Llyswen or Garden Heights. He would have been free to go out when he wanted to go. He would be close to the shopping center and Modern Cabinet. All change is not good.

My friend, Peggy Fluke, gave me a vintage perambulator. My father would put April in it and we'd take walks around my neighborhood in Juniata where there were sidewalks. He enjoyed pushing the pram with the baby, but I knew he missed Llyswen.

Daddy liked the way the light was in his new home and began drawing and painting again. Gretchen often saw his light on late in the evenings. He had begun, once again reading his favorite mystery books. He had a huge collection of Ellery Queen, Perry Mason, Agatha Christie and Mickey Spillane novels. He would read far into the night, and fall asleep in his recliner.

My father also studied the scriptures and wrote poetry and comments on the Bible passages he was reading. Those writings are in my possession now. They touch my heart to know my father had also accepted Christ after my mother had died. What a blessing.

My father's health was declining. He was very frail and in the hospital. Within a week or so, he was transferred to Hillview Nursing Home. April was two-and-a-half years old and I would take her to see him. He liked to hold her and talk to her, but he often closed his eyes, and we'd quietly leave his room.

He died two weeks later in my sister Trudy's arms on September 3, 1970. All the siblings came for the funeral. My father was buried alongside my mother at Alto Reste. That day was very sad for all of us.

Celeste Yost

> You promised me oh Jesus; eternal life:
> My fear is gone, and darkness has come to light;
> My sins you washed away from me on Calvary; thy precious blood oh Jesus you shed for me.
>
> Abide with me oh Jesus, I need you so; I cannot go without Thee one step alone; Now guide me safely through untill you call me home; oh bless me Jesus; bless me I love you so.

A poem my father wrote about his love for Jesus

CHAPTER THIRTY-FOUR

After April was born I started writing greeting cards, miscellaneous articles for magazines and Christmas plays for children. I had a lot of my work published and I also had enough rejection slips to wallpaper a small room.

I was a stay-at-home mom until April was two-and-a-half. We enrolled her in Mrs. Smith's Happy Hours Day Care. Mrs. Smith was wonderful with the children. Her house was on Quail Avenue just around the corner from my childhood home.

I went to work for Bert Leopold, the youngest partner in the law firm of Scheeline & Leopold on Pleasant Valley Boulevard. I loved my job and everyone who worked there, especially Ruth Walter, who worked for Mr. Leopold. Tina Werts worked for Isaiah Scheeline. Bert was the Solicitor for Logan Township. My work was interesting and diversified.

April started dancing school at Ruth Barnes' School of Dance when she turned three. Her class was one afternoon a week, and Bert accommodated me in order to take her to her lessons.

The office was located in front of Riverside Market. One of us would go there almost every morning for chop suey rolls, bear claws or their wonderful sticky buns. We often brought back soup or sandwiches if we were too busy to go out. We took turns going out for lunch and one of us would stay to mind the phones.

Ruthie and I became good friends both in and out of the office. She was retiring after working forty-two years for Mr. Leopold. The plan was for Bert to hire another secretary. I learned that I was to be Ruthie's replacement and work for Mr. Leopold.

Replacing Ruthie was totally impossible. She was wonderful and very smart. She knew everything about everything in that office. She and I became lifelong friends.

One of my jobs was to keep the office books. Ruthie had done the books for forty-two years and I took her place. We had day sheets that were written by hand regarding accounts payable and accounts receivable. I made many trips to Ruthie's house on weekends or evenings to enlist her help balancing the books. I think she truly enjoyed working on them and I enjoyed the fact that *she* enjoyed helping me.

Ruthie reminded me so much of my mother. I came to refer to her as "my adopted mother" and she never questioned it. Ruthie was a dear friend and confidante and I miss her greatly. She was so much fun and she loved baseball. She loved listening to the World Series on the radio, especially when the Pittsburgh Pirates were playing.

One Saturday morning we drove to Pittsburgh for a double-header. What a pleasant surprise to meet Willie Stargel in the parking area. He even gave us his autograph. What a treat for each of us!

June 1971 Ruth Walter's Retirement Party
from Scheeline & Leopold
Isaiah Scheeline, Emanuel Leopold, Bert Leopold
Tina Wertz, Ruth Walter, Celeste Zapotoczny

In June 1971 Scheeline & Leopold threw a lovely retirement party for Ruth at the Penn Alto Hotel. Ruth's entire family was invited. They all came, even from as far away as South Bend, Indiana. The evening was just delightful.

I have a lot of stories about fun times with Ruthie. She was always happy and a joy to be around. My hair was long and she often was snipping away to make it straight across the back. This. of course, she did while I was typing. She made me laugh.

I remember buying a white London Fog raincoat one year when Betsy was a toddler. Ruthie told me "I'm taking your coat to my house, come and get it when you need it." When I asked why, Ruthie said "Because you can't wear anything white around THAT baby!" Betsy was into everything, which mostly went into her mouth.

After Ruth retired and after Betsy was born and I was staying at home with her, we often went out to lunch. One of our favorite "haunts" as Ruthie used to say, was The Red Barn on Union Avenue. Ruthie always brought her own silverware because she didn't care for plastic that they used there.

Afterward we'd go grocery shopping at Riverside and then to Sky Brothers for frozen food. We were especially fond of their apple dumplings!

Ruth's niece, Joyce, lived with Ruth from the time she was a girl and they were both dear friends. Joyce has been like a sister to me and I'm so grateful for her friendship through the years. We saw many concerts together at the Jaffa Mosque and celebrated each other's birthdays at Del Grosso's Restaurant in Bellemeade. They shared Christmas with us and we always had such a nice time.

I drove a Bronco sometimes and Ruthie and I would take it on trips. We went to Virginia one day for lunch at a special restaurant that had a renowned salad bar. The décor was unusual with lots of plants and waterfalls. I can't remember the name. We left early in the morning and were back home in the afternoon.

We drove up to Pete and Piggies Restaurant on Short Mountain one afternoon for their "sky high pie" – their famous trademark. We brought home pie for Joyce and Walt also and they couldn't believe we drove up that mountain just for pie!

Ruth was always "Grandma Ruthie" to my children who loved her as much as I did. We were so very blessed to have had her in our lives. I always find it interesting how God puts people in your life that you'd least expect and they come to mean so very much to you. Ruth and Joyce were those kind of people.

Grandma Ruthie holding baby Aaron, 3 months old
January 1993

This is one of the last photographs I have of Ruthie. She had been retired many years and was enjoying being at home. April's son, Aaron, was born November 1, 1992. April and I drove from New Jersey to Altoona on a very snowy day so that Ruthie could see him and hold him. She just cuddled him and loved and kissed him, and we all had a wonderful visit.

Sadly, that visit was the last time we saw her, I'm heartbroken to say. Ruthie passed away a few months later. I cared for my first grandson, April's son, Aaron, every day for four years while April worked. I was unable to visit Ruthie in the hospital before she died. I so regret that. She made a huge impression on my life and I'm so grateful for the joyous memories I have of our times together. I'm so blessed to have been part of her life. She was, indeed, a treasure.

Celeste Yost

CHAPTER THIRTY-FIVE

Walt was the Service Manager of Kelly Springfield Tires in downtown Altoona. After several years, he was offered a transfer to another Kelly Springfield store in Alexandria, Virginia. Walt accepted the position. We put the Juniata house on the market and moved to a new garden apartment complex called Southport. The location was convenient to the Beltway exit and also to Kelly Springfield.

April was three and a half years old and we enrolled her into Elf Land Pre-School which began in the Fall of 1971. We met the neighbors, one of whom was a single girl who worked in Washington D.C. I asked about jobs in the legal profession there. She told me they paid well and were plentiful. I answered an ad in the newspaper. The interview went well and I was hired by a law firm on Pennsylvania Avenue several blocks from the White House. I thought this would be so exciting to work in the hub of government.

There was no doubt about it, Washington was a fascinating city, but having to drive April to and from school each day became difficult. There were always traffic snarls getting in and out of town. I can say unequivocally I never went in and out of D.C. the same way twice. What a nightmare!

Six weeks later I left the D.C. law frim and started looking for jobs closer to our home and the preschool. I found one in Springfield, an exit or two away from the Franconia/Van Dorn exit off the Beltway where we lived. Traveling to work was so much easier. I quickly learned the back roads to Springfield. That saved so much time with the preschool and my job.

I worked for the firm of Scott, Blackburn & Clary. Almost all the attorneys there were high ranking military. At our

Christmas party, Colonel Blackburn performed magic. What a surprise that was to other new employees like me.

The firm was what was known in Virginia, as "green attorneys". That didn't mean they were "new and inexperienced," it meant they dealt mainly in real estate transactions, huge construction contracts, and all other related work. They earned a lot of money, hence the term "green lawyers".

My boss was John Thyden, a junior partner. He was smart and easy to work with. He made me laugh and we had a good working relationship. My first project was a huge development in Spotsylvania County. I can't remember the number, but I prepared more than a hundred deeds for that project. I liked the work and made a lot of friends from the office.

We had only one car when we moved, so Walt bought a 350 BSA motorcycle to ride to work. One Saturday we were invited to visit Walt's cousins' home in Waldorf, Maryland. It was a beautiful Fall day and we rode the BSA together about a half-hour each way on the Beltway. April had a play date with a friend who lived in our complex. Walt and I spent the day with his cousins, then left for home soon after dinner.

The traffic was getting heavier so we took an exit that put us on back roads when we got close to home. Coming off the ramp, the bike slid on shale and we went down. Walt and I each had a few scrapes, but neither of us was hurt. In those days helmets weren't required. After that experience, I thought of what might have been. We could have been severely injured by cars exiting the ramp that didn't see us. My days of riding motorcycles came to an end.

We lived in Virginia a year-and-a-half and Walt and I were both homesick for Altoona. The cost of living was very high anywhere around Washington and we missed our families and friends. Our Juniata house had been sold and we drove to Altoona one weekend to look at houses.

We found a house on Fourth Avenue in Columbia Park that needed work. Settlement was set for the summer of 1973 and we relocated back to Altoona. The house needed a lot of work, but we liked the house and the neighborhood. Columbia Park was a great neighborhood with lots of kids April's age.

That year brought a slow decline of foreign involvement in the war effort in South Vietnam. The United States, however, continued to participate in combat, primarily assisting the South Vietnamese Army with US air power. Negotiations were ongoing in Paris to put together a peace agreement including an exit strategy for the United States.

On the home front, five men were arrested on June 17, 1972 for breaking into the Democratic National Committee headquarters at the Watergate complex in Washington D.C. The FBI investigated and discovered a connection between cash found on the burglars and a slush fund used by the Committee for the Re-election of the President, the official organization of President Nixon's campaign. For months there was nothing but this scandal on news broadcasts.

Every day more details of the "Watergate Scandal" broke. The news became tedious and the whole country, it seemed, was calling for President Nixon to step down.

I, for one, was glad to have a project to keep my mind off the politics. Walt and I worked on the house inside and out, painting and having new carpeting installed. Walt tore off the old front porch and built a new one. The house really looked nice. The only thing missing was a garage.

In the Fall of 1973 we learned we were expecting our second baby. I wasn't sick at all with this pregnancy, I was happy to say. However, our baby always seemed to settle on my vagus nerve, which can, and did, often cause lightheadedness and fainting.

I carried this baby so differently from April so I thought for sure we were having a baby boy. To hedge all bets, however, we painted the nursery a pale yellow and I made yellow and white checked curtains for the windows. Walt added a half bath to the bedroom and we bought different colored shag carpet samples for the nursery floor. We were both pleased with the outcome.

Walt and I both worked on the attic to make a bedroom/playroom for April. He removed the hall door leading to the attic and we had the stairwell and attic floor carpeted. Walt repainted April's youth bed and dressers and I made a bed spread with curtains to match for the windows.

April just loved her room. She was so excited to have this huge area to play in. She was rather compulsive about her belongings. All her books were lined up according to the color of the binding. Little Golden Books were altogether, and the sizes and colors of other bindings were all organized.

She had a collection of little glass animals and they were set on her dresser in a certain pattern and no one could touch them.

She was the same way about Barbie Doll clothes. She would always share, but If any of her friends wanted their Barbie to wear one of April's Barbie's clothes, April insisted they put one away before taking another outfit. She had plenty of doll clothes and doll furniture that my father had made for me when I was little.

One day she said to her father that she wanted to go shopping for Barbie clothes. "Mommy won't take me and I only have one new "cloe" and I need some more." We looked at each other, he shrugged his shoulders, put their jackets on and off they went shopping for another Barbie "cloe" or two. He was such a light touch!

On June 23, 1974 Elizabeth Ann "Betsy" Zapotoczny was born in a "just made it to the hospital" delivery. From the time I registered when we arrived, until she was born, was about 20 minutes. My water broke as I signed in and they called for a litter to zoom me to the delivery room. Betsy was two weeks early. What a Godsend! Walt was permitted into the delivery room to cut the cord.

Betsy was tiny and I remember looking into her big gray eyes for the first time. I could feel in my heart a strong connection. She was an "Old Soul in a Young Body" our friend, James Roscher, often told us.

I remember when I delivered April, I was one of the youngest mothers in the hospital. Conversely, with Betsy I was one of the oldest. One nurse came in carrying Betsy and put her in my arms and said "Boy, you sure got a conehead!" I was shocked, then we both laughed. The nurse told me to just rub the top of my precious baby's head and it would become nice and round. She said she rubs Betsy's head and other "conehead babies heads" every time she holds them in the nursery.

After two relaxing days in the hospital, I was discharged with our new baby girl. This was so unlike my delivery six-and-a-half years earlier with April. New mothers back then were kept in the hospital for a whole week. We weren't allowed out of bed, let alone go home in two days. When we finally got discharged our legs were like jello. This arrangement was so much better.

The following day Ruthie and I went for lunch at Olivo's Restaurant and took April and Betsy with us. When the waitress commented on how tiny the baby was Ruthie proudly said, "Three days old!" Grandma Ruthie had a new baby to cuddle!

April was so happy to have a new baby sister. She went around the neighborhood inviting anyone who had an interest, to come and see the new baby. We had lots of little kids coming in wanting to see what a "new" baby looked like.

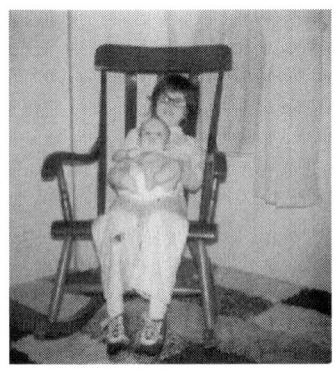

April and her new baby sister, Betsy, 1974

The congressional hearings droned on and on until finally, facing certain impeachment, President Richard Nixon resigned the presidency August 9, 1974. This action on his part prevented the House from impeaching him. Gerald Ford, his successor, pardoned him on September 8, 1974.

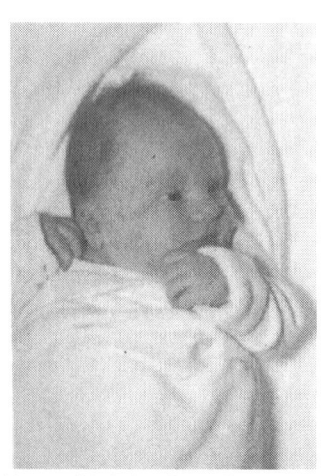

Happy Birthday Betsy! 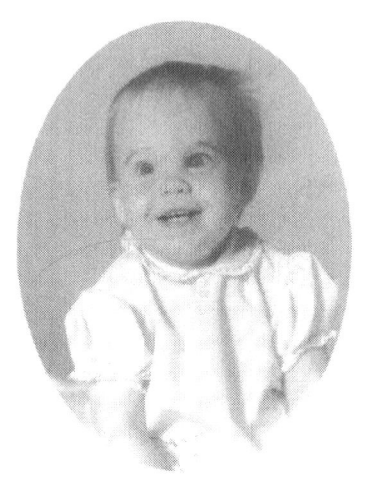   Happy First Birthday Betsy!

April started first grade at Adams School that Fall. Her teacher, Mrs. Moore, wrote her a lovely note to congratulate her on her new sister. April was so pleased the note was written to her. How very thoughtful of Mrs. Moore.

April walked to school every day with a little boy named Ralph who lived around the corner from us. She and Ralph were pokey, I soon learned. One day I followed them at a distance. It had rained and there were puddles and the two of them spent a lot of time jumping into the puddles as they made their way to school.

Go-go boots were THE thing and April had a pair of black crushed vinyl boots that she called her "clickity boots". Mrs. Moore called me one evening and asked if April could bring a different pair of shoes to school to change into. The clickity boots were a giant annoyance to everyone! I was glad to comply and everyone, including her parents, were happy when she outgrew them!

Adams School began a Story Time Program where mothers volunteered to read to the kindergarten and first grade classes. I volunteered and took Betsy with me once a week to read to the children. The little kids loved being around her. Betsy was a very happy baby that seemed to connect with everyone she encountered and she especially loved seeing little kids.

Celeste Yost

CHAPTER THIRTY-SIX

In the Spring of 1975 Walt and I put the Fourth Avenue house on the market and it sold almost immediately.

Our little family then looked at a house on Lark Avenue in Hileman Heights. The small neighborhood is two blocks wide and three blocks deep and is located off Pleasant Valley Boulevard. Each of the three streets have bird names, Lark, Quail, and Robin. There are grassy landscaped islands in the center of each street.

2605 Lark Avenue had a triple lot surrounded by a bayberry hedge and Norwegian pines along the back. To Walt's delight, it had a large three-car garage and a second smaller garage for storage. He was ecstatic about those garages and we both really liked the neighborhood.

When we rang the bell, I was totally surprised to see Mrs. Mary Brown answer the door. She was my sewing teacher in Roosevelt Jr. High. Mrs. Brown owned the home and was downsizing into something smaller. She said she remembered me from her classes and introduced us to her close friend, Harry Anslinger.

Harry was an interesting person. He was the first Commissioner of the U.S. Treasury Department's Federal Bureau of Narcotics. He had held that position for an unprecedented thirty-two years. He then held office two years as the US Representative to the United Nations Narcotics Commission.

Mrs. Brown showed us the downstairs first. The house had hardwood floors throughout. There was a living room, dining room and a large kitchen with a breakfast nook on the first floor. Upstairs were three bedrooms and a large bathroom. The attic was unfinished, but suitable for storage.

April asked if there were any kids her age in the neighborhood. Mrs. Brown laughed and told her there were lots of kids, and that the school bus stop was just around the corner.

Before we went down into the finished basement, Mr. Anslinger offered to hold Betsy. She went right into his arms. The basement was large and spacious with a tiled floor and a ping-pong table that Mrs. Brown said she would leave for the girls. There was a lot of storage area, a washer and dryer and utility sink.

Outside Mrs. Brown had spearmint planted around the foundation of the back porch. What a delightful fragrance. Walt, of course, was interested in the two garages, but especially the three-car garage. The smaller garage would be for storage of garden tools and a lawnmower. The yard was lovely. There were flowers and beautiful trees and, in particular, a wisteria in the front yard that was gorgeous.

When we came back into the house Betsy was holding onto Mr. Anslinger's fingers as he walked her around. When he sat down with her and bounced her on his knee, she looked at him and giggled. Mr. Anslinger said he had a grown son and that it had been a long time since he'd held a baby, and that he rather enjoyed it.

Peggy and Bob Peterman lived in the corner house next-door to us. They were a middle-aged couple who had never had children of their own. When Bob retired he came over every day at four o'clock to take Betsy to his house for "Happy Hour". They'd sit on his sunporch and talk and they'd have snacks. Bob would have a drink and Betsy would have a Shirley Temple with lots of cherries. She waited for him to come for her every afternoon.

One Christmas Bob dressed up like Santa to surprise the kids on Christmas Eve. He knocked at the back door and I opened it for him. When I saw Bob, I called the girls to come to the kitchen. Betsy looked up at him and was so excited. "It's Santa!" she cried, "Hi Bob!"

Bob laughed so hard that the elastic broke that was holding up his Santa pants which slid down to his ankles. He had on trousers and just calmly pulled up his Santa pants and asked if I had a pin.

Directly across the street lived Lucy and Eddie Gorman, an elderly couple with one grown son. Eddie had been Mrs. Brown's gardener and he'd often come over and offer to trim the roses. Walt and I took care of mowing the grass and trimming the bayberry hedge. Sometimes, Eddie even came over to help with that task.

Our new neighborhood was heaven for the girls with a plethora of kids April's age. She was so excited about meeting new friends and going to a new school. April spent the summer with the Fochler kids who had eight children in their family. They lived on Quail Avenue behind us.

Mrs. Fochler had a chore list and within a few months, April's name was added to the chore list at their house. They had a large above-ground pool and the neighborhood kids swam there. Hileman Heights had very little traffic and the kids rode their bikes all summer. They especially liked Robin Avenue because it was a big hill.

The Weidlich family lived right at the bus stop. Every morning the kids would congregate there to wait for the school bus. Buck and Earl and their sister, Cissy, were around April's age and she liked them all. Buck and Earl liked climbing trees and hanging around in the woods behind our neighborhood. Sometimes, they'd even allow the girls in the neighborhood to go with them.

April started third grade at Pleasant Valley Elementary. Her teacher was Mrs. Cathcart. She made new friends and I got involved with the PTO and made new friends with the mothers of Pleasant Valley Elementary School students. April's teacher was Libby Goulianis, who was a friend of mine. Her family owned Crist's Restaurant in downtown

Altoona across from where I worked at Hare & Hare. My work friends and I often went there for lunch.

Miss Goulianis was also the girls' basketball coach and she asked April to join the team. The PV Girls competed against all the other fifth/sixth grade teams in the city. The fiercest competition, without a doubt, was Wright School which was located across town. The girls from Wright Elementary didn't even wear sneakers. They wore platform shoes and beat the tar out of every other team in the league.

Pleasant Valley's best player was a girl named Michelle Conrad. She practiced basketball all the time and was really good at all sports. Basketball, however, was her forte. Michelle made more points every game than anyone else on the PV team.

I remember one game in particular when April got the ball. She was running and dribbling down the court as fast as she could go, the clock was running out, and we were cheering like crazy! "Go, April, Go!" She threw the ball and it bounced a bit on the rim, the buzzer rang, and then the ball dropped through the net. No points!

As it turned out, that was a Godsend. April was running the wrong way and had she made that basket, Pleasant Valley would have lost by two points. As it turned out, it was a tie. The buzzer had rung and the game was over.

By the time Betsy was two, I had to keep an eye on her every minute. We had kitchen cabinets under the sink and a set of drawers beside them. The bottom drawer was a metal-lined breadbox with a metal top that you flipped open.

. Betsy had been playing in the living room and I went to the basement to bring up the laundry. When I opened the basement door to the kitchen, I saw her walking on the narrow edge of the counter in front of the sink. I was scared to say a word for fear she'd fall.

KINETOSCOPE

I quietly set the laundry basket down, then raced over and grabbed her. I scared her and she started to cry. My heart was in my toes.

"Show me how you got up there!" I said in a voice reminiscent of MY mother. Not a problem, the drawers were already open. Betsy stepped on the lid of the breadbox, and I watched as she stepped into the next drawer, then pulled herself up onto the counter. When she reached the counter, she clapped her hands and giggled. She was so proud of herself.

"This is a no-no, I told her," and she looked at me with those enormous eyes as I lifted her off the countertop. We were able to latch all the kitchen doors and drawers, except, of course, the breadbox, which had that metal top, otherwise know as "Betsy's springboard". Betsy gave up that game because with locks on the higher drawers, it wasn't fun anymore.

When April was in sixth grade she took baton lessons from Nancy Siegel. Betsy, who was now five started Mrs. Walker's kindergarten. Mrs. Walker was so wonderful to the children. I remember Valentine's Day. Mrs. Walker instructed the kindergarteners to bring their valentines to school the next day and also a decorated box for the valentines they would receive. She said the next day she would draw a boys' name and a girls' name and whoever's names were drawn, they would be the King and Queen of the Valentine Party.

Betsy was a very optimistic child. She came home and told us all about it. She told us "Mrs. Walker said she would pick names out of a box for the Valentine King and the Valentine Queen, and that will be me."

I suggested that she just may NOT be the Valentine Queen and if so, she should be happy for the little girl whose name was chosen. The next day Betsy she came home with her box of valentines, a cardboard crown and a crepe paper cape. She was, indeed, the Valentine Queen.

Betsy took ballet and tap at Debra Anthony's School of Dance in Juniata. Just like her mother and her sister, April, Betsy loved tap dancing better than ballet. The school put on a recital every year. Betsy's group did a ballet number about a "ballet doll".

Betsy told us, "Miss Debra said whoever is the best dancer will be the leader, and that will be me." She was so optimistic. We reminded her that a lot of the little girls in the class were quite good and one of them could be chosen instead. Betsy didn't agree at all. When I took her to her lesson that week, Debra took me aside and told me Betsy would be the lead dancer in the Ballet Doll number.

In the Fall my sister-in-law, Bonnie, and I registered our kids, Lynne, Dana, and April for a Saturday morning bowling league at Holiday Bowl. We needed five kids on a team and invited Nancy and Jackie Claybaugh to join us. Betsy came too, but she was too young to be on the bowling team. She did roll a few balls before and after the games began and sat at the score table cheering.

The team had to have a name. After more discussion than that of nuclear reactors, the five girls finally settled on "The Born Losers" as their team name. They were pretty good bowlers and weren't losers very often, I'm happy to say.

Bonnie and I took turns doing the stats for the ten-team league and we showed the kids how to keep score. They had a good season and I think their team came out somewhere in the middle of the competition.

That December April's baton class participated in the annual Christmas Parade in downtown Altoona. That day was cold and lightly snowing when the parade began. Despite the cold and the snow, the whole group did quite well and Nancy Sigel was very proud of them. Afterward we bundled up our children and most of us went to the little café in Gable's basement to have hot chocolate and cookies with Santa.

In the Spring, Sigels put on their annual Recital at Jaffa Mosque. The twirlers, including April, started the evening off with "A Fifth of Beethoven", a very snappy version of Beethoven's Fifth Symphony. April's friends Nancy and Jackie Claybaugh took dancing from Sigels, and they danced in the program also.

L-R: Nancy Claybaugh, April, Jackie Claybaugh
Foreground: Betsy

Celeste Yost

April, Mrs. Walker's end of the year
Pre-School Program
1972

Betsy, Debra Anthony's Dancing School Recital 1979
Betsy was the "leader" in the front

CHAPTER THIRTY-SEVEN

Walt and I were married fourteen years. We have many good memories, but some were not-so-good. At one time I learned to ride an 80 cc Yamaha shortly after April was born, much to my father's chagrin. I liked to ride on back roads with little traffic. Sometimes I rode it to the Mansion Park tennis court, but not very often. My father was not happy about the motor bike and I practically gave it away. That made my father happy.

I took judo at the Altoona YMCA for a couple years. It was great exercise and I enjoyed everything but the competitions. I managed to earn three ranks, the final being a green belt. We have home movies of a few of the competitions which are reminders that I wasn't a shining star at judo.

One of my friends from judo class invited me to join her bowling league every Tuesday afternoon at Holiday Bowl. There were about twenty of us. All their husbands worked at the WFBG radio station. Our group was called the "Thursday Afternoon Swingers" and we had lots of laughs together. We took our young kids with us and they were cared for by a lovely lady named Alice, who worked in the nursery at the bowling alley. The couples often got together for parties on the weekends which were a lot of fun, as well.

After we moved to Lark Avenue, Walt worked in his three-car garage nearly every night after dinner and always had an entourage around him. He then got involved with buying wrecked Corvettes and restored and resold them, fourteen Corvettes over the years, as I recall. He and his friend, Dick Kuny, were always in competition as to which was a better car, a Ford or a Chevy. Walt favored Fords until he got involved with the Corvettes. Dick always remarked how he "knew he'd win him over to Chevys one day."

This routine got old with me over the years. For his birthday one year I bought him a membership at The Back Wall Racquetball Club. He played several times a week and he became an "A" player. Once on that roster, he played more often. I was a mediocre player, preferring tennis to racquetball, but he and I did play occasionally.

We joined Park Hills Country Club and both April and Betsy swam on the swim team in the summer. The first year Betsy was only three years old but could swim about half of the length of the pool. She'd stand on the starting block and jump in and swim halfway down the lane. When she got tired, she'd swim over to the side and say "I'm ready to get out now," and the lifeguard would lift her out with a big hook that fit under Betsy's arms.

I remember the first time Betsy participated in a relay race. She was about six years old and her first tooth had fallen out which caused a bit of a lisp. She got up on the starting block and Kathy King, one of the parents, was standing on the other side of Betsy's block. This kept the block from falling into the water when the swimmer dove in.

Betsy was new to this. She turned around with her little toothless smile and asked, "Mitheth King, are you thwimming too?" Kathy got a chuckle out of that remark.

Walt's parents always were available to stay with the girls if Walt and I went out Saturday evenings. We'd often go to dinner and then dancing at the Red Arrow or the Rustic Isle. Sometimes we'd see a movie, but for the most part, our lives weren't aligned.

For several years Walt's parents spent the weekend at our house caring for the girls when Walt and I went to Atlantic City to celebrate our anniversaries. I remember there were clubs open all night long with dance bands. One of our favorites was The Melody Lounge on St. James Place.

The Bistro was another popular dance club where we saw the famed drummer, Buddy Rich, perform one evening. Buddy knew the owner of the Bistro and just happened to be in town and the owner invited him to play the drums much to everyone's delight.

Walt and I usually stayed at the Algiers or the Holiday Inn. We went to the Atlantic City Race Track, and to the Steel Pier. One time we took a barfy boat trip out of Captain Starn's in the Atlantic City Inlet.

In 1974, the summer Betsy was born, we borrowed a two-room tent and went with two other couples to Assateague Island in the Chesapeake. A ferry took us over to the beautiful island where wild ponies run on the beach. The first few mornings, April and her friends fed apples and carrots to the ponies, and we took walks and enjoyed the sunshine and the beach.

Then the rains began. Betsy was an infant and cried a lot and the sand beneath the tent became cement. There was only so much you could do in a tent and the signature phrase for those several days was "Hey Dad, Mom's crying again." I couldn't wait to get home, but we were bound by the ferry schedule. That was one very long weekend.

When the girls were older they came to Atlantic City with us for our anniversaries, and we rented a beach house in Brigantine for a week. They loved the beach there and the penguins at the Steel Pier in Atlantic City. The Diving Horse was a major attraction and one year, it was simply closed as being inhumane. There was a haunted castle on the pier in Brigantine and all of us were scared when the characters in that place that leaped out at you!

One summer we bought a pop-up camper and a 15' runabout boat and spent weekends at Glendale Lake relaxing and fishing. Some of our friends went camping also and we had a good time for several summers. Betsy liked to fish and always wanted to have a "bobber" or two or four on her line, and I remember well her continually saying "Where's my bobber? Where's my bobber?" and Walt would help her reel in a little till she could see that the bobber was still tied to her line.

Walt and I shared many good times but we also had our difficulties. Our lives slowly drifted apart and we separated several times over the years. We'd get back together, but things were never the same. Our last vacation together as a family was in 1979 when we spent a week at Niagara Falls. I filed for divorce shortly after that vacation, and we lived apart nearly two years until the divorce was finalized.

CHAPTER THIRTY-EIGHT

I married a second time in late August 1981. We packed our belongings and moved to Ocean City, New Jersey. My husband and his sister owned a duplex there. The second floor was rented and we would be living on the first floor. We each had two daughters who had all been good friends and gotten along well from the time we started dating. The six of us spent the last two weeks together at the shore before school began.

My daughters intended to stay in New Jersey with us. His daughters were returning to Altoona to live with their mother. When it was time to register April and Betsy for school, April said she wanted to return to Altoona to start high school with her friends. Betsy wanted to stay with me in New Jersey, so I enrolled her in the Ocean City Primary School.

Several weeks later, my husband's sister arrived at the Jersey house. She said she was staying in New Jersey. She and I started doing "change-overs" on the weekends. We cleaned rental units Saturday mornings after the weekly tenants left. Check-out was 10:00 AM. The new tenants would be moving in at 2:00 PM so we had several hours to have the rentals cleaned. We each were able to clean two units within that timeframe. We were well paid through rental agencies.

It wasn't long till all the things my new husband and I thought we had in common, we didn't. The marriage became rocky. My new husband and his sister had a very close relationship and I was an "outsider." They'd stay up late and drink. There were always empty liquor bottles in the trash can outside.

I saw an ad in the Ocean City Sentinel Ledger for a part-time typist position for an insurance company. The company was Scibal Associates in Somers Point. I was hired and worked for Barbie Scibal, and she and I became good friends. The office was small and there was no desk for me. I had a typewriter on a card table in a corner and sat on an Abbott's milk carton and did my work. That suited me just fine. Everyone in the busy office was friendly and fun to be around. I thoroughly enjoyed being away from Ocean City four mornings a week. I appreciated being out of the fray.

Countless trips were made back and forth from Ocean City to Altoona. My husband's sister had left their mother in Altoona to run the family business. Their mother had hired help but really wanted her children to take over the business. Neither of them were interested. She didn't understand why.

Christmas was spent in Altoona jockeying kids around but for the most part, it was enjoyable. After the holidays I thought our lives would smooth out. Instead the marriage continued to deteriorate, and I knew I needed out of it as quickly as possible. This marriage was a major mistake. More importantly, I needed a full-time job with benefits. I called Barbie Scibal.

Barbie told me that John Realer, the Risk Manager of the Claridge Casino Hotel in Atlantic City was looking for an Executive Secretary. She gave me John's office phone number and suggested I call him and apply for the job. John and I spoke over the phone and made arrangements to meet personally the following week. My husband and his sister drove to Altoona for the weekend.

After making arrangements with Walt, I withdrew Betsy from the Primary School. I drove her back to Altoona to live with her father and April until the end of the school year. There were a lot of tears. Betsy was only seven and upset.

I returned to New Jersey and met with John the following morning about the position. I completed an employment application and after his review and our discussion about the job, he hired me. He asked how soon I could start. "Immediately," I told him. He then took me on a tour of the facility and gave me a very lengthy casino license application to take home and complete as soon as possible. He said I could start work the next day with a preliminary hotel license the Claridge could issue.

I had nowhere to live but at the duplex. Thankfully, my husband and his sister weren't there. I knew, however that it was just a matter of time till they returned to the shore.

The next morning I arrived early at the Claridge. I went through the hotel licensing process. John made introductions for me with everyone in nearly all the departments we'd be working with, as well as the on-site Casino Control Commission and the Division of Gaming Enforcement representatives. John joked around and told everyone I was a "little country girl from Altoona". John was born and raised in Yeadon, Pennsylvania outside Philadelphia. Compared to Philly, he said Altoona was "in the sticks!"

My first week at Claridge went well. Each night on my way home from Atlantic City, I'd stop at Barbie's new office in Northfield to type insurance reports and correspondence for a few hours. She had given me the office key and sometimes she'd pop in to see how I was getting on. I was so grateful for her referring me to John. I really liked my job. I made extra money from typing and opened a bank account in my own name.

The tenant upstairs in the duplex was a single man who left pie tins with grilled bluefish for me outside the foyer door several times a week. I wrote a note and taped it to his door thanking him for sharing his fish with me and for his kindness. I was very glad there was someone else in the house in case of emergency.

I got my casino/hotel credentials within a week which gave me access to every part of the casino and hotel. John even walked me across the catwalk above the stage in the theater. I was a wreck, not liking heights very much. That made John laugh because I had a death grip on his hand.

Our office was located across the hall from the Entertainment office. I became very good friends with "Charli" Charlesworth, the Executive Secretary to the Entertainment Director.

I was just getting settled in at our office, when we were advised we had to temporarily move out of the hotel. The Facilities Department was making major renovations. We were moved a block down Indiana Avenue to the "Eastbourne", a motel that was eventually to be razed. In the interim, several Claridge offices were renting space there, including Risk Management.

The "office" was dreary, very dated from the '60s, and rather ugly. It had really ugly orange shag carpet and avocado green draperies. It smelled like a combination of Lysol and bug spray. We had packed all our files in sturdy boxes and the guys in Facilities put all the boxes, our file cabinets, desks, chairs, and everything else, on dollies. What a sight that was with the Facility personnel rolling our "office" down the sidewalk on Indiana Avenue. They were wonderful and set up our "new" office for us.

"Look," I remember John pointed out to me, "we even have a kitchenette and a full bathroom – you can even cook or take a shower here if you want!"

We both laughed. Every day we had pop-in guests, employees on their way to lunch or to the "Dirty Drug Store" across from our office on Indiana Avenue. That drug store had a long way to go on cleanliness, but whatever you needed, they had it.

John's wife, Carol, was the Hostess in the Garden Room Restaurant at the Claridge. John introduced us and we became good friends. They were a delightful couple and had two beautiful young daughters close in age to my two. I was happy when all four girls finally met in the summer. They had fun together at the beach in Sea Isle where they lived. We went back to the house for a picnic and the Realer girls taught my girls to jump rope with two ropes, called "Double Dutch".

I loved my job and the people I worked with, but I still went home at night to the duplex. Most nights when I got home, the phone would ring incessantly. I wouldn't answer, fearing it was the soon-to-be-ex or his sister. It was just a matter of time till they would return and probably put me out on the street.

Celeste Yost

KINETOSCOPE

CHAPTER THIRTY-NINE

One Saturday night there was a terrible thunderstorm and the lights went out. I had no candles or even a flashlight so I went to bed. I broke down and cried that night because I realized how God had provided a job for me working for a kind respectful family man, and after ninety days I would have benefits. Typing reports for Barbie enabled me to start saving money for a place for my children and me to live. I hoped to have them both with me by summer. I thanked the Lord that Walt cared for the girls in Altoona while I regrouped.

I cried myself to sleep and remember praying and thanking the Lord for His blessings. I had made so many mistakes and dragged my children into them with me. I was so far from God and needed to get myself right with Him. I could almost feel my mother's arms around me. I promised the Lord I would go to church the next morning and be faithful to Him.

When I awoke, it was dismal and still raining and my first thought was to crawl deeper under the covers and go back to sleep, but I didn't. I got up and got dressed and drove downtown to find a church. It was just after 10:00 AM. Most of the churches started at 11:00. I drove several blocks in the downtown section of Central Avenue and noted that the service at Ocean City Baptist started at 10:30. I could go there. Conveniently, there was one parking space near the main door. I drove up the street, turned around and came back and parked in that spot. Divine Intervention.

I entered the foyer. The auditorium was completely full and an usher asked if I minded sitting up front. I didn't. I sat in the front row and Pastor Don Phillips, the Visitation Pastor, spoke from Matthew 5, the Sermon on the Mount, the Beatitudes. When I heard *"Blessed are the poor in spirit;*

for theirs is the kingdom of heaven" I started to cry. I realized I was so far from God and was in a hopeless condition.

The message was clearly meant for me. I was among the "poor in spirit". I sobbed throughout the message. At the conclusion of the service, Pastor Phillips gave an invitation to anyone wanting to speak with him afterward, to just raise their hand. Without hesitation I raised my hand. My heart was broken and I needed to talk with someone.

After the benediction, Pastor Phillips sat with me and asked if I was okay. I told him "no", and that my life was a shambles, my children were living 300 miles away, my second marriage of six months was over, I had just started a new job, and had very little money, and I needed to move into a place of my own.

He held both my hands and we prayed together. I told him I had accepted Christ when I was nine years old and was baptized when I was twelve, I but hadn't been following the Lord for years. I was so far afield from God, how could He ever forgive me? We prayed about that and for the Lord's guidance in my life.

When I left the church it was still teeming rain but I felt encouraged and my heart was a little lighter. I drove south down West Avenue toward the duplex. The rain continued in earnest. A car coming in the opposite direction passed and made a sudden U-turn, then came up behind me beeping the horn. It was a Volkswagen, and my heart was in my toes. My soon-to-be-ex had a Volkswagen. I feared it was him. The headlights behind me flickered and I pulled off to the side and stopped. There was a knock on my driver's side window. I rolled it down and there stood Melissa Logan, the mother of Betsy's best friend in second grade, Rebecca.

Standing in the rain, Melissa spoke rapidly and asked if I remembered where her mother's beach house was and I nodded yes.

"Go there and look in the mailbox – there's a letter for you that was to go out tomorrow. Get it right away and I'll call you tonight." I was befuddled when just that fast, she said good-bye. She dashed back to her car, hopped in, made another U-turn, and was gone.

The beach house was on 42d Street just off West Avenue on a small road surrounded by marshes. I had been there several times and knew it well. The quadraplex was on stilts and I pulled in under her mother's unit and went to the mailbox. Inside was a short note addressed to me at Walt's house in Altoona.

The note said that she was worried about me and that Rebecca was so upset finding out Betsy had moved back to Pennsylvania. She was hurt that Betsy never told her about moving or even said good-bye. There was only one more line, "Here's the key to my mother's beach house, stay there as long as you have need." It was like Melissa had E.S.P.

I unlocked the door and found another note on the kitchen table. The note included Melissa's phone number and asked me to call her. I was euphoric. I knew I had to work quickly. I locked up the house and drove to 52d Street.

Once inside, I grabbed large trash bags and began stuffing them with my clothes and belongings. All my paintings and my Rockwell collection were at Barbie's because my ex and his sister threatened to destroy them.

I began singing hymns and felt light enough to fly, "Thank you Jesus, thank you, Jesus!" I got on my knees and asked Him to forgive my waywardness and to guide and direct my steps. I prayed that He take care of my children and keep us all safe. I promised to follow His direction and would change my life.

I had a Volkswagen Dasher station wagon and stuffed the back seat and the whole luggage area with the trash bags containing all my worldly goods. I took one final look inside the duplex to see if I had forgotten anything. Only my piano, but I would think about that another time. If I ended up losing it, it didn't matter. What mattered was getting my heart right with God.

I had just put the duplex key back under the doormat and gotten into my car when my soon-to-be-ex and his sister pulled up behind me in his sister's car. I was a nervous wreck and drove out of the alley as fast as I could. They were right behind me. I remember going through Ocean City, across the causeway, and onto the NJ Parkway to the Atlantic City Expressway. I took the Atlantic City exit and they were right behind me. I ran through several traffic lights and drove past Harrah's onto the Brigantine Bridge. It was dark and their headlights glowed in my rearview mirror. They would disappear and then be there again.

The rain continued and I finally alluded them. Actually, I got myself lost. I was unfamiliar with most of Brigantine, but I found a spot to park. I stayed there the better part of an hour until I felt they were gone. I drove back to Melissa's mother's beach house. I reread Melissa's letter and called her. We talked the better part of an hour. She was so gracious and thoughtful. We only knew each other for a short while and she was there to help me. We hung up and I took a hot shower and hopped into bed. That night was probably the best rest I'd had in months.

I awoke early and thanked the Lord for the sunshine and the warm place I had to stay. I thanked him for caring friends I hardly knew, who had rescued me through the providence of my Savior, Jesus. I was living proof that Jesus puts people into your life for a reason, and usually when you least expect it.

I had a pending Appeal with the Pennsylvania Unemployment office concerning their denial of my benefits when I moved from Pennsylvania to New Jersey. I spoke with a gentleman a few weeks earlier. At that time I asked if we could schedule an over-the-phone conference call sometime soon to discuss the matter.

I explained to him that I had been hired by the Claridge in New Jersey and hopefully, I would be working within a few days. He gave me his private phone number and asked me to call him so we could resolve the issue. I'd totally forgotten about the whole matter until I was going through my belongings. When I was stuffing my belonging into trash bags, I found the paperwork.

I had a made a few fiends at the Claridge, one of whom was Kathy Hodson who worked in Advertising. That morning, I asked her if I might use their small conference room to make a private call during my lunch hour. It wasn't a problem and I made the call. The gentleman I spoke to earlier asked me several questions. After hearing my circumstances, he said was going to reverse the decision. The funds would be released to me. He asked where to send the check.

I never thought I would prevail on the Appeal, but again, God intervened on my behalf. I gave the gentleman Barbie's mailing address. The check arrived within a week in the amount of $541. That was more than I expected and I noted that interest was added because of the delay in arranging my hearing. I deposited the check in my new bank account.

I took the Atlantic City Press home from work every evening and found several options for rentals in Ocean City. There was a small two-bedroom apartment only two blocks from my soon-to-be-ex's house. Not where I wanted to be; however, I could afford the rent. I needed to make some calls to learn the cost of the utilities and factor those in. I also needed first and last month's rent and a security deposit.

With the unemployment reimbursement, my Scibal checks, and my paychecks, I had most of the money. I was shy a hundred dollars. I called my sister, Trudy, and asked if she could loan me the money. She sent two hundred dollars. My sister always goes the extra mile.

The utilities were reasonable and I had the money required. I signed the lease with the Finsels who owned the house, and moved in. There were already some dishes, pots and pans and linens in the apartment. The prior tenant had left a youth bed in the smaller bedroom, so I had a place to sleep until I moved my furniture from Altoona.

I'll never forget the thoughtfulness of Melissa. I kept her letter to remind me how the Lord puts people in our lives and His timing is always perfect. In one of our conversations, Melissa told me Rebecca was so upset that Betsy was gone from school, that she asked Melissa to go to the principal's office to ask if there was a forwarding address for Betsy in their records.

Melissa was given Walt's address in Altoona. She said she knew if Walt got the letter he would contact me and make sure I got the key. It didn't happen that way, but worked out God's way in His perfect timing. I've learned repeatedly to never underestimate the power of God and how He works things out for our benefit in ways we'd never imagined.

I continued typing for Barbie in the evenings and after ninety-days at the Claridge I got a raise in salary. I paid back the loan from Trudy and deposited my additional raise money and my typing money into my savings account for moving expenses. I'm grateful for my dear adopted Mother, Ruthie, who sent me checks also and refused to accept any reimbursement. I was so very blessed.

KINETOSCOPE

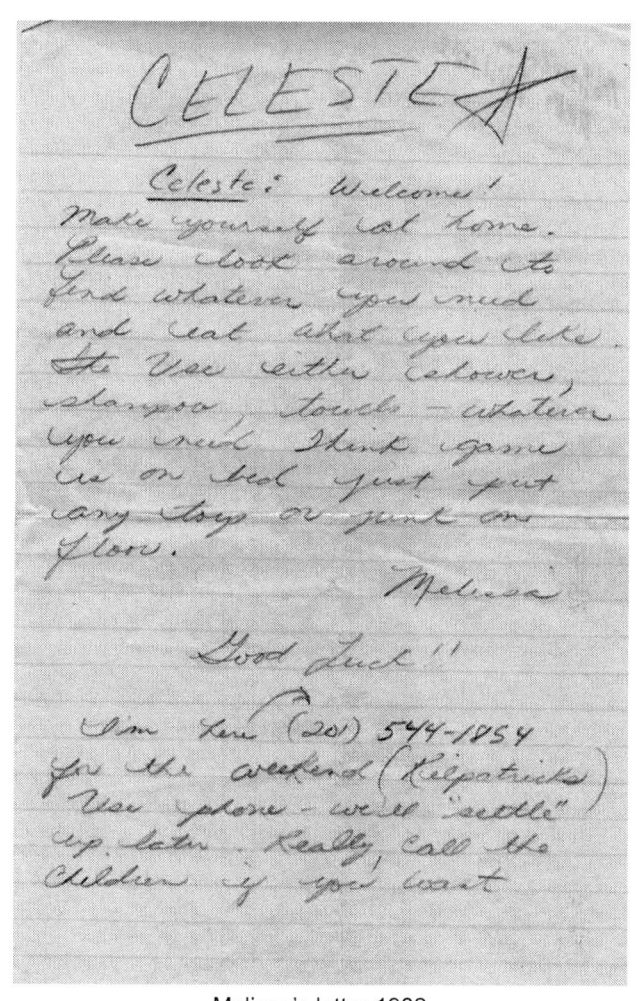

Melissa's letter 1982

Celeste Yost

CHAPTER FORTY

Ocean City, NJ 1982

I drove to Altoona several weekends the spring of 1982 to see April and Betsy and to attend April's swim meets. One of those weekends, I asked my nephew, Billy, to help me get my furniture from my soon-to-be ex's mother's apartment which he and his friend, Tyke, did for me.

The soon-to-be-ex was there and tried to stop them, but I think, one look at Billy and Tyke who both played football, he thought better of it. Billy and Tyke took the furniture to Walt's house for storage in the basement until I could come back to Altoona, rent a truck, and take all our belongings to New Jersey.

I brought my children to the shore for Easter weekend. We walked the Boardwalk and watched the Easter Parade. We swam in the ocean, and just had fun together. They both liked the little apartment and we all slept on the floor on comforters like we were camping out. I couldn't wait to have them with me when school was over. Taking them back to Altoona was difficult for all of us but they had to complete the school year. Before leaving Altoona, I met with an attorney and filed for a 90-Day No-Fault Divorce.

When school let out I drove back to Altoona for my children. I rented a U-Haul truck and we packed it with the furniture and just Betsy's belongings. There was a tow-bar on the back of the truck and Walt connected my car to it. April wanted to spend the summer in Altoona with her father, so it was just Betsy and me.

Looking back I don't know how we managed that trip. It was three hundred eight miles. We traveled the PA Turnpike, the Schuylkill Expressway, through Philadelphia, the New Jersey Turnpike, the Atlantic City Expressway, and then to the south end of Ocean City to our new home.

When we pulled up to the apartment, Betsy and I hopped out of the truck. The next-door neighbor came out and said "I don't believe my eyes!" I didn't believe it either.

My friends from the Facilities Department at Claridge helped us move in. Because I didn't have a table, they got me a large round one from the Claridge cafeteria that was going to be discarded. They even went to my soon-to-be-ex's house for my piano and hauled that up to the second floor.

The only piece of furniture that couldn't make the turn at the top of the stairs was an Early American sofa that was too large. The first floor had no tenants and I asked the Finsels if I could keep the sofa in the downstairs apartment. They offered to buy it from me in exchange for reducing my rent the next month.

I was so appreciative for the willingness of everyone who helped me. The guys from Claridge were happy with a spaghetti dinner and a couple cases of beer in payment for their hard work. I was living on a shoestring and they knew it. God bless them.

Betsy spent part of the summer in Altoona with her father. When she returned to New Jersey, I hired the daughter of one of my neighbors to take care of Betsy during the day while I was working.

When school began in the Fall I found an ad for after-school care. Mrs. Petnick was her name and she lived across the street from the Middle School. She also cared for several other children after school. The children came to her house from the school, did their homework, watched tv, or played games until the parents retrieved them.. Betsy took her own snack for after school every day. She liked chicken and stars soup, goldfish crackers, and a juice box. Always the same items.

A year later in July 1983, the Claridge held its annual company picnic at Lake Lenape Park. Betsy and I were going. The facility had playgrounds and offered swimming, a nice beach, water skiing, and paddle boats. They had music and dancing and lots of picnic food all day and all evening in an open air pavilion.

Betsy and I were just leaving the apartment when the phone rang. It was April. She was very upset and asked me to please come and get her. She said she was in Snow Hill, Maryland with a neighbor girl who lived across Lark Avenue. She said she wanted to leave Maryland and come home. She was calling to ask if I could come and get her. I had no idea where Snow Hill, Maryland was and asked her for the street address. She put someone on the phone to tell me.

That woman gave me a hard time. She said the arrangements were with April's father, not me, and she had to wait to hear from him.

I persisted and finally got the address. I asked my next-door neighbor about this trip. He gave me a map and told me to take the Cape May-Lewes Ferry to Lewes, Delaware, and go from there to Snow Hill. He said since it was the middle of July, I should call and make a reservation on the ferry. I made the reservation and off we went "on an adventure", I told Betsy. Betsy was a very amiable child and used to say she was my best date and would go anywhere, anytime, with me. This was one of those times.

I had asked some passengers on the ferry about this particular address and no one was helpful. When we got to Lewes, I followed the map to Snow Hill. I pulled into a gas station and there was a police car there. I asked the officer if he could help me find this address.

"Well," he said, "you're very close, but there are a few turns to get to this street, just follow me." He put on his flashing lights and we followed him. When we arrived in front of the house behind the cop car with lights flashing, April came running out the door with her little gym bag. The woman I had spoken with on the phone came out onto the porch. She never said a word. She thought we had a police escort and went back into the house. Now that's what I call "Divine Intervention".

"You need to get right back on that ferry as soon as possible. You'll be taking the last trip back to Jersey," the officer said. "Follow me and I'll get you on the fastest route."

I was so happy to see April and she and Betsy giggled and laughed together. I enjoyed just listening to their chatter, and having both my children with me again. I asked April if she had many clothes in that little bag and she did not. We made it onto the last ferry in Lewes. After we were again in New Jersey, we stopped at the Shore Mall. April needed clothes.

I tried calling Walt for several days, but got no answer. It was over a week later that he called to ask if I knew where April was. I was incredulous. "Of course I know where April is. She's in New Jersey with Betsy and me."

I explained that we'd tried to call him numerous times but never got an answer. He said he went to Florida with his friend, Jimmy, who took his daughter to Disney World. I asked if it occurred to him to take his daughter to Disney World. He said nothing.

Our apartment was a block from the beach and Betsy and April went there every day while I was working. We all enjoyed the beach in the evenings and on the weekends.

I purchased a typewriter from a small company in Atlantic City. They allowed me to make monthly payments on it. Having my own typewriter I could continue typing in the evenings at home for Barbie and also for Dr. George Godfrey, a trauma specialist.

Dr. Godfrey was a lifelong friend of Barbie's and she introduced us. He was scheduled to testify in court that week regarding a severe automobile accident and I typed his notes for him. From that point on, I worked for him whenever he needed me. He had an office in Atlantic City where I'd pick up the tapes, transcribe them at home, then drop the tapes and reports back off to his office.

Betsy was my proofreader and she earned a dime for every typo she found. I liked working at home so I could be with my children. My working relationship with Dr. Godfrey continued for twenty-eight years.

I registered April for Ocean City High School in late summer, she would be a junior. The girls and I attended the Ocean City Baptist Church regularly. I joined the Ocean City Masterworks Choir at the suggestion of our landlords who had been members for many years. I sang with the Masterworks for eight years and enjoyed every minute of it. We sang "The Messiah" with a full orchestra every Christmas. Each spring we had another classical concert.

One weekend we drove back to Altoona and brought Fifi home with us. The girls and I really missed having her with us. She was getting older, but quite excited to see us.

The Lord had truly watched over us and blessed my socks off, starting with the job offer at Claridge. I loved the job and after ninety days, I got a raise. Ninety days after that all employees received an across-the-board raise.

In the Fall of 1982, the Claridge opened a Legal Department and I applied for the job of Executive Secretary/ Paralegal to Charles Hanlon, Esquire.

I was hired at a higher salary than I'd been making. Again, within ninety days I got another raise, and another ninety days after that, another across-the-board raise.

Within a year I had doubled my salary from when I had first started at the Claridge.

I also had perks with that job. I had a Secretary, Natalie Jones, and we became very good friends. I had preferred parking in a nearby parking garage, a private office, and comping privileges. I was so blessed.

KINETOSCOPE

CHAPTER FORTY-ONE

When school began In the Fall of 1982, April took up company with a girl she met in one of her classes. I didn't care for this girl, she was too bold and too brash. I learned early on telling your children you don't approve of the company they were keeping was like saying "Make this girl your best friend!"

April and I got into quarrels about her. One night after a shouting match, April ran down the stairs, shouted that she hated me in the middle of West Avenue, and never came home that evening. I called the girl's mother inquiring if April was at her house and was told the girls had gone out, but they'd be home soon. Hours went by and no April. I called the girl's mother again. The girls hadn't returned and her mother suggested I relax and come over for a glass of wine. I declined her invitation.

I was awake most of the night. April never came home. Dressing for work in the morning, the more I thought about it, the more livid I became. I drove Betsy to the Middle School, then instead of going to work, I went back home. I gathered April's belongings together, stuffed them in trash bags and tossed them in the back of my car.

Then I drove to the high school. My intention was to withdraw her from school, then drive her to the 30th Street Station in Philadelphia and put her and her dolls and dishes on the train to Altoona. Her father could deal with this.

The woman in the high school office said she'd send someone to get April out of class. Within minutes I was told she wasn't in class. I was then asked to wait to speak with Detective John Taccarino. Moments later Detective Taccarino confirmed April was not in school and said he'd find out from some of his "sources" just where she was.

I called the Claridge and told my boss I had a family matter to take care of and that I'd be in late. About a half hour later, Detective Taccarino returned and told me he found April and he'd bring her in. First, though, he wanted to talk with me. I told him my plan to put April on the train in Philly and send her back to her father.

"Don't do that," he said, then told me all about a ten-week program they had at Ocean City High called "Diversion". The purpose of the program was to help kids who had a propensity to get into trouble. He explained the parameters of how it worked. Every morning the kids in this program had to check in with him face-to-face. He told me he'd make pop-in visits to the various classrooms throughout the day. This ensured the kids were in class and not at the Pickle Barrel, a popular hangout near the high school.

The Diversion kids were not permitted to go out after school unless accompanied by a parent. On Saturday mornings they were required to get to the Ocean City Police Department by 8:00 AM "under their own steam". Once there, they'd get their assignments for the morning. These kids worked until noon. They picked up trash on the beach, washed police cars, washed windows and swept and mopped the various schools, and did any other job the police had for them to do.

Detective Taccarino told me this program has been very successful and that he thought April would benefit by it. Currently there were fifteen kids in the program. Then he told me that April and her friend had spent the night on the beach. Sleeping on the beach in Ocean City was a violation of a City Ordinance. He intended to let April know about that.

I had calmed down considerably by then. I really did not want to send April back to Altoona. I agreed to allow him to put her into this program. He brought April in and I was shocked to see her. She had the most beautiful black hair, but now she had a wide blonde streak down one side. She was wearing someone else's clothes that were too small for her. She was barefoot. I was smart enough not to comment about any of it.

John explained the Diversion program to April and said that rather than going back to Altoona, he thought she'd benefit from this program. He asked if she was willing to participate. He told her that he knew she and her friend had slept on the beach which was in violation of a City Ordinance and involved a fine. If she agreed to be in the Diversion Program, the fine would be waived. April agreed and it wasn't long until she and John became good friends.

When the weather turned cold, April was assigned to work in the Police Department office. Her job was inputting information into their data base. That task was not only interesting, but enlightening to her. She told me that two kids that past summer had been sleeping in the sand dunes on the beach. In the morning when the City came with the equipment to groom the sand, they were nearly run over. She learned, too, by doing the data entry, that even in this friendly town, there was still much crime.

By the end of the ten weeks, April was so different. Her grades were improved which permitted her to be back on the high school swim team. She was looking for a part-time job after school and on weekends.

April swam for the high school swim team and she and Betsy swam for the Community Center team. I spent every Saturday timing lanes or writing the ribbons at the meets. When the season was over, April was awarded the gold medal for the best swimmer on the Girls' Ocean City High School team.

I met a friend at the Claridge who said she'd decided to join the US Army. She told me about President Reagan's affordable housing program for the military. I was very interested in that program and read more about it. I then made an appointment to speak with someone at the Naval Reserve office in Atlantic City. I wanted to learn more of the details of the program. Both my brothers had served in the Navy so I wanted to pursue that branch of the service also.

The Naval Officer gave me lots of hype about the advantages of being in the Navy. He explained all about President Reagan's program which appealed to me. I took a written test and a typing test and passed. He said, based on my legal background I was qualified to be processed into the US Navy Reserve as a Legal Yeoman.

He required copies of my Birth Certificate, the girls' Birth Certificates, my Divorce Decree, and my Will. I provided them. At that time I learned more about being in the reserves. The Recruiter said if I got called up for active duty, regardless of the stipulation in my Will that my brother, Girard, would be Guardian of my children, the girls would be placed with their father, if he was living.

There were no loopholes around that and, thus I abandoned the Navy idea. I often regretted that I didn't persevere and enter the Navy. I remember my brother, Girard, saying, "It's too bad about the custody circumstances, the Navy would really do you good – considering you were spoiled as a child and never had any discipline growing up!" Not funny!!

I started having problems with my Volkswagen Dasher station wagon shutting off when it felt like it. I had it looked at by several mechanics in Ocean City and no one could resolve the issue. I found an ad in the Sentinel Ledger that a local dealership was offering used cars for no money down.

April, Betsy and I went looking at their lot and decided upon a Chevy Chevette with affordable payments. We bought the Chevette and I sold the Dasher to the owner of a fish market in Ocean City. With that money we bought a new sofa with a pull-out bed.

In the spring of 1984 the girls and I found a larger apartment at 1045 Asbury Avenue. It was also on the second floor but with an outside entrance. There were two second floor apartments back-to-back. Ours faced the alley and underneath was a carpet warehouse. Underneath the apartment facing Asbury Avenue was a real estate office.

The rent was more money than our prior apartment but it was twice the size and April and Betsy had a huge bedroom to share. They also had their own full bathroom. We had a washer and dryer, a microwave and a dishwasher, for which we were all grateful.

I received a large tax refund that year and surprised the girls with a trip to Disney World during spring break. We spent a week in Florida and stayed in a hotel in Kissimmee and shuttled back and forth to Disney World for three days.

We spent the rest of the week lounging at the hotel pool and visiting our former next door neighbors in Juniata, Arlene and John Edmiston. They had moved to Bradenton. They lived near "the world's biggest cow" and April took a dozen pictures of that cow. We had a wonderful time. I believe it was one of our best vacations ever.

April worked all summer at Spadafora's Seafood Restaurant and the Atlantic Book Store during the week. On weekends she worked in the prepping area at Cousin's Restaurant. Betsy had a lot of friends and we lived a block and a half from the beach, so she was at the beach everyday. We bought a used longboard at the Surf Shop and both girls learned to surf. We'd go to the beach when I got home from work. I learned to surf too, not nearly as well as either of them, though.

We divided the girls' bedroom with a folding screen I had found in the alley in someone's trash. They each decorated their respective sides of screen. I had to laugh at the difference between my two daughters. On April's side were pictures of rock stars, sports figures, and cartoons. On Betsy's side there were clippings of the first heart transplant by Dr. Christiaan Barnard, and other scholarly items. How could these two be so different, yet so much alike? I love them both the same!

We all liked the spaciousness of the new apartment. We could keep the windows open at night and feel the cool breeze from the ocean. We were glad to be in the rear apartment because Asbury had a lot of traffic and was noisy. The apartment was conveniently located two blocks from the beach, in the center of town, within walking distance of our church, lots of shopping and restaurants. We had easy access off the island across the causeway to the Atlantic City Expressway. Both girls were within walking or biking distance to their respective schools and to the Community Center for swim practice.

We had adopted a cockapoo at the Ocean City Shelter when Betsy and I were living in the smaller apartment. Her name was Kimmie. When we moved downtown we took her with us and shortly after we moved in, she ran out the door and down the steps.

We called her but she didn't come back. It was dark out and I went one way and the girls went another way looking for her. We all went home and the girls went to bed. I went out again alone and found her along the side of West Avenue. She'd been hit by a car and left there. The police came and took her away.

A couple weeks later, April was home from school and the Ocean City Shelter called to ask if we could take in a rescue dog. The Ocean City Shelter never euthanized any pets, but they did not have enough room for another dog.

They knew about Kimmie being hit by a car and thought we might be interested in another dog.

The dog in question belonged to a family moving to a home where no pets were permitted. April called me at work pleading her case, "Could we adopt her, Mom? She's really cute!"

"We'll see when I get home," I replied.

"Well," April said, "she's here now. Can't she stay? She's a schnoodle, her name is 'Ralphie', she's so cute, and she and Fifi get along really well…"

And that's the rest of that story. Ralphie was ours and she and Fifi became two little friends who got along beautifully.

Ralphie and Fifi 1984

Celeste Yost

CHAPTER 42

January 1985

One of my Claridge friends, Debbie Wescoat, invited me to go to a ski club meeting one evening after work. The meeting was in Cherry Hill, New Jersey. The President of the Club was Charlie Gazarra, who worked in the Security Department at the Claridge.

Ellen, another friend of Debbie's, came also. She and Debbie sat up front in Debbie's van and I sat in the middle seat. We drove to Absecon to pick up Debbie's fiancé, Ken. He was an Atlantic City Fireman who was just coming off a three-day shift. Ken's nephew, Ralph, came out the door with him. Ken introduced Ralph to Ellen and me then he hopped into the long seat in the very back of the van. He wanted to stretch out and sleep. There was no place else for Ralph to sit but beside me. We all chatted on our way to Cherry Hill.

The meeting was interesting and we were given paperwork regarding future ski trips with the club. Ralph and I had a few drinks and got acquainted. I remember he commented on my boat shoes and asked if I liked to sail. I told him I'd never been sailing, and that I just have the shoes. He asked if I might like to go skiing with him some Saturday in the Poconos. The drive was about three hours from New Jersey.

"I have two daughters who swim on swim teams." I explained, "and they have meets early every Saturday morning. One of them swims first and the other one swims last, so I can never plan anything on a Saturday. I help time the lanes or write out the ribbons and we're there for hours."

"Well, if you ever have a free Saturday, call me," Ralph said, "and maybe we can make arrangements to go." We exchanged phone numbers.

A couple weeks later, on a Friday after swim practice, the coach informed the swimmers that the meet the next day was canceled, so they had a "Bye". That was unheard of for their teams as long as my kids had been swimming.

I called Ralph that night to ask if it could work out for us to ski the next day. He said yes and offered to take the girls, too. "We need to leave my house at 4:00 AM so we can get to Jack Frost when the snow is freshly groomed. Then we can go for dinner on the way to Big Boulder in the late afternoon, and then do some night skiing."

My skiing experience was strictly at Blue Knob Ski Resort near Altoona, Pennsylvania and I'd only skied a few times. April and Betsy both went on ski trips with school groups, so I told them Ralph had invited them to go, too.

They looked at me as though I had two heads and April said, "Are you kiddin'? We don't want to get up at the crack of dawn! We want to sleep in and stay in our pajamas all day! We've never ever had a Bye before."

Ralph gave me precise directions to his house and I arrived at 4:00 AM in the dark. He lived in Northfield, three towns away from Ocean City. We chatted the whole way to the Poconos, learning about each other. We arrived when the resort opened for the day.

The first run down Jack Frost, I skied to the bottom and got into the lift line. I felt dizzy and overheated and told Ralph that I thought I might faint. He looked at me, probably thinking "what's wrong with this girl?" then calmly said, "Well, then, give me your poles so you don't stab me on the way down." He took my poles and caught me as I fainted.

I put some snow on my cheeks and the back of my neck, and felt better. I told him I was a fainter and could tell when it was coming on, and just lower myself to the floor or the ground.

He just nodded. I had no idea what he was thinking, though.

In the late afternoon, we took our last run and enroute to Big Boulder, stopped for dinner. We had a nice meal and then continued on our way for night skiing. We were nearly to Big Boulder when I realized I had left my sunglasses at the restaurant. Ralph turned around and drove all the way back to the restaurant and found them still on the table where we had dinner.

I was impressed that he didn't say "forget about them, they're only sunglasses," or some other trite phrase. They were Ray Bans and expensive and I was glad to have them back. I was really impressed with his thoughtfulness.

We skied in the evening and when I was tired I went into the lodge at the bottom of the mogul run. I sat at a table by the window and ordered a glass of beer and a peppermint schnapps while Ralph took a few more runs. I watched as he deftly skied the moguls and went back up for a final run. He was a very good skier and I was mediocre, yet he spent the whole day skiing at my pace, certainly not his!

On the way home I asked him why he just didn't ski at his own pace all day instead of hanging out with the likes of me. He laughed and said, "I wanted you to like me." No problem there, I liked him from the night we first met.

As I drove home from his house that night, I felt a rumble in one of my tires. I pulled into the parking lot of a Seven-Eleven Store. It was late and snowing. I called Ralph and he came right away to help me. He looked at the tire and said he'd come back in the morning and take care of it. Then he drove me home to Ocean City.

The next morning he took the wheel off the car and realized I had hit the curb making a three-point turn at his house and damaged the rim. He took it to a Gulf station and a guy he knew worked there. He put the wheel on the tire rack and hit the damaged rim with a sledge hammer. The tire held air and Ralph drove my car to my apartment. I invited him to stay for dinner.. That's the least I could do for his chivalry.

After he went home, I asked the kids what their impression of him was. They both said he was nice, but April added that he was "sorta' Felixy'" like Felix Unger of the Odd Couple. Betsy shook her head solemnly in agreement. Later they told me he reminded them of Richard Dreyfus who starred in "The Good-Bye Girl".

That winter, Debbie was planning a ski trip to Mt. Snow, Vermont with some girls she worked with from the Claridge. She asked if I wanted to go, too. I could never afford a trip like that and declined. Ralph found out about the trip from Ken and offered to pay for my trip. He said he would also stay at my apartment and look after the girls and the dogs in my absence.

The weekend was a lot of fun. There were six of us and we laughed and had a great time. When I got home, Ralph told me he had replaced the exhaust system on my car, changed the oil, and filled the gas tank. I guess he wanted me to like him. His kindness made me like him more than I did already.

In the early spring we jogged on the Ocean City Boardwalk together almost every evening after work. We enjoyed each other's company. In late September Hurricane Gloria pushed its way north from the Outer Banks and hit South Jersey. Ocean City had a lot of high water damage. Before the storm arrived, Ralph invited us to come to his house on the Mainland because Ocean City always flooded.

He also invited my friends, Jimmy Pappas, "Crazy Jimmy", and his son, Jimmy Jr. to stay at his house. They lived in Strathmere, a connecting island from Ocean City to Sea Isle City. Jimmy was a commodities broker and Ralph and the two Jimmies talked stocks and commodities. Jimmy was happy to be able to connect to the markets without interruption. Ralph and the two Jimmys became good friends.

In the Spring of 1985 April graduated from Ocean City High School. Walt came from Pennsylvania and Ralph, Walt, Betsy and I attended the graduation held at the High School football field. We all then went to dinner at Pearl Garden Chinese Restaurant, the girls' favorite place for celebrations. The attraction for Betsy was the PuPu Tray and the little paper umbrellas they put in the drinks. One time when we were there, Betsy's umbrella got too close to the PuPu Tray and caught fire. That was interesting! She doused it out herself with her glass of water.

I had applied for a PELL Grant for April to start summer classes at Atlantic Community College. What a complicated process that was. Her classes were held in the mornings and began shortly after graduation. She was busy with school in the mornings and working afternoons at Atlantic Book Store on the Boardwalk. On the weekends she waitressed at The Flanders Hotel also on the Boardwalk.

Walt had given April an old Dodge Dart and with the money she saved from working, she traded it in on a Volkswagen Beetle. What a Godsend when she could drive. She took Betsy everywhere she needed to go and ran errands for me, as well.

Ralph and I were dating regularly mostly on weekends. I had a lot of transcription work and sometimes we would jog together on the Boardwalk. Afterward he'd stay for dinner then go home. I had to transcribe medical reports in the evening for Dr. Godfrey.

April took her college courses a few mornings a week and Ralph noticed she never brought a book home. He asked me about it. I hadn't really noticed at all, I was up to my neck and floating in medical transcription, and working a full time job at the Claridge every day.

At Ralph's prompting, I called April's professors to find out how she was doing. Two of them told me they didn't know, because they didn't know her! That sparked a big controversy between her and I. I told her she better get to class and complete all the assignments and take any tests she had missed. I let her know in no uncertain terms, that if she didn't pass these courses with at least a "C" I would be on the hook for her entire tuition. That would not make me happy.

God bless her, she did take care of those missed assignments and tests and passed the courses. Then she decided college was not for her. She didn't return for the Fall semester. A few years later, however, she took Criminal Justice courses at the same college and did very well. She loved the studies. She always had her homework done. She did well on the tests. She even had her required project completed several weeks ahead of its due date. "Look, Mom," she said, "it even has a cover!"

Ralph had a 27' Catalina sailboat and invited us all to go sailing with him one weekend. He kept the boat in the Frank Farley Marina in Atlantic City. None of us had ever been sailing so it was a new experience. April didn't care for it so much because she felt seasick before we even left the dock. Ralph gave her Dramamine and she fell fast asleep.

I remember when we returned to the dock and were tying up, April woke up and thanked him for taking us sailing. She told him she had a wonderful time! We always laugh about that because she slept the entire afternoon. Betsy, on the other hand, enjoyed sailing and Ralph let her handle the helm for a while. She thought that was really special.

Throughout the summer of 1985 I met most of Ralph's sailing friends, including Eddie Stanton. Eddie raced his sailboat, "Serendipity," in the annual Heart Cup Race off Atlantic City every summer. Eddie had bought the hull and the deck of a 34' Seafarer and installed the engine and completed the interior himself. He often sailed alone but needed crew and ballast for the Heart Cup races. Ralph and a couple other guys were the crew, and some other women and myself were ballast.

I knew nothing about sailboat racing, but I caught on to the ins and outs as we raced all week. Eddie registered for other races that summer including races from Atlantic City to Ocean City and Atlantic City to Cape May. We crewed with Eddie in the Heart Cup and the other races for several years after that and always had a lot of fun.

I remember one race from Atlantic City to Cape May when the weather was awful. We seemed unable to make headway beyond Wildwood, recognizable through the mist by only the giant Ferris wheel on the Wildwood Boardwalk. We were rocking and rolling and I was getting cold and feeling barfy. I went into the head and we were struck by a wave and I fell forward and hit my forehead on one of the hatches. I put on heavier clothing but was unable to walk the length of the cabin to the companionway because it was so rough. I crawled through the cabin and then up the companionway to the cockpit.

Ralph was at the helm and called down to me that it was time for lunch, and asked that I make the sandwiches. Eddie, on the other hand, saw that I had cut my forehead in two places on the hatch fixtures and said, "There's blood in her eyes! Forget about your lunch, I'm calling the Coast

Guard and having her airlifted off this boat. She needs medical attention!"

I did not need medical attention, I had two small abrasions on my forehead above my eyes, and they definitely weren't airlift worthy. Eddie came below and got me a pillow and blanket and a warm washcloth for my forehead. He proceeded to the galley to make lunch for "Captain Bly" and the rest of the crew, including me.

Ralph's parents owned "Elusive", a Catalina 30' sailboat and his Uncle Ken owned "Summer Breeze", a 34' Hunter, and they were docked on the same pier as Ralph's boat. We all used to sail on the weekends and have dock parties when we all got into the marina afterward. We shared whatever snacks we had by putting them out on our dock boxes for "grazing". Banjo Bill docked his sailboat, the "Digger Too", across the dock from us. He entertained everyone with his banjo.

By mid-August I realized I'd never gotten my Final Decree of Divorce from my second husband. I called the Court and was advised that "the other party" never signed the paperwork. I knew he worked at a Wawa in Ocean City. I went there on my way home from work one evening and told him if he didn't sign the papers, I'd refile and state the specific reasons for our divorce, thus making the 90-Day No-Fault null and void. A few weeks later I got my Decree in the mail. The matter was finally over.

KINETOSCOPE

Summer 1985 Ralph & Celeste on Evening Star II
Frank Farley Marina, Atlantic City, NJ

Betsy left end arms raised
Ocean City Middle School Cheerleaders 1985

Celeste Yost

Betsy & April Ocean City Community Pool
Swim Team 1985

Betsy left end first row Ocean City Middle School Cheerleaders 1985

Ralph and I had a Halloween party at my apartment in Ocean City following Hurricane Gloria. We invited about twenty friends and had an enjoyable evening. We dressed as Popeye and Olive Oyl.

Popeye and Olive Oyl Halloween 1985

Celeste Yost

CHAPTER FORTY-THREE

A new beginning , Ocean City, NJ 1986

On January 16, 1986 Ralph took me to The Sweetwater Casino, a quaint little restaurant established in 1928. This restaurant was located in the woods along the Mullica River in Sweetwater, New Jersey. I'd never been there before. The lights were dim with candles at each table, fine linen tablecloths, and an intimate atmosphere.

We ordered dinner and Ralph ordered a bottle of champagne. We talked and drank some champagne and then he took my hand and said he wanted to discuss something important with me. He asked me to marry him. I was shocked and my first thought was "I cannot get married three times!"

He said, "You don't have to give me an answer now. You can take as long as you like."

All the differences between us popped into my head at once. First of all, he was nine years younger than me, he had never been married before and never had children. I had two children and one of them was a teenager. He was Catholic and I was a Born Again Christian, he was a Democrat and I, a Republican.

When dinner arrived we made small talk, ignoring the obvious "elephant in the room", his proposal. After dinner I excused myself and went to the powder room. The matron was a stately older woman. As I washed my hands, she remarked that I looked pensive and asked that I please sit down on the settee with her. I sat down and she took my hand in hers and asked what was bothering me. I told her about the proposal and that this would be my third marriage.

She simply nodded. I explained all the differences between us and said, "He told me to take as much time as I needed to decide.

"Do you love him?" she asked. I said I did, but remarked about the age difference, and how he'd never had children of his own, and that I had two daughters, and so on.

"Would you like my advice, Dearie?" she asked, but before I could respond, she said, "You should marry him. You love him, he loves you, and he cares about your daughters."

I nodded and she added, ". . . and besides, you're not getting any younger!"

We both laughed and she hugged me and suggested I give him my answer as soon as possible, perhaps over dessert. "He really wants your answer now, you know!"

That comment gave me pause. I went back to the dining room. Ralph looked pensive and I was a little nervous.

I took her advice and over crème brulee', my favorite dessert, and finishing off the champagne, I told him, "Yes, I want to marry you, too."

He started to laugh and asked, "Okay, what happened in the ladies' room?" I told him about the matron and our conversation. He kissed me and said, "I'd like to meet her!"

"I thought you might," I replied.

My engagement ring belonged to "Mom Dot", his grandmother on his mother's side. The ring is beautiful and is precious to me because I just loved her. She was so witty and fun to be around. She called herself "Mother Hen" which was appropriate, she enjoyed being with her family. Soon my children and I were going to a part of her family.

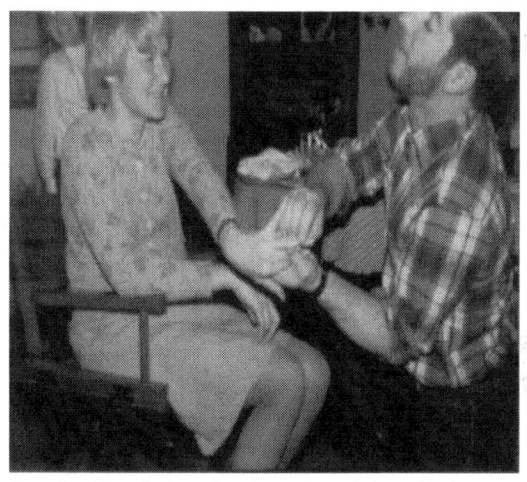

April took the photographs of our official
engagement

Ralph wanted to get married as soon as possible. He suggested Flag Day in June which gave us five months. He believed five months was sufficient time to sell his house, find a house for us, make settlement, move in, and then have a wedding.

His house in Northfield was smaller than my apartment in Ocean City. He put it on the market and the four of us started looking for larger houses while snow was still on the ground. I was bound to a Lease in Ocean City till the end of May.

I suggested a September wedding which would give us time to find a house and get settled in before school started for Betsy. Ralph wasn't thrilled, but agreed. Looking for houses in the winter is probably the worst time ever, but we looked at seventeen houses. We finally found one we all liked. The house was located in a beautiful neighborhood on Wilson Avenue in Linwood, New Jersey, on the mainland between Ocean City and Northfield.

We learned the history of the house. It had been built by a couple years earlier and they had gotten divorced. The home belonged to the wife and she rented it out for ten years. We learned it now had been vacant for seven months.

The house itself was an eighty-foot long rancher. It needed a lot of work inside and out but we were up to the task of making it our own. We signed a contract and invited Ralph's parents to come over and take a look at it. When his mother stepped inside the foyer and looked around she said, "Oh, it's awful! Don't buy it!"

It was pretty awful, but we thought it had possibilities. Outside it needed a new roof, a fresh coat of paint, and replacement of the driveway which was badly cracked. Roots from two large maple trees between the sidewalk and curb had grown under the driveway and the apron was falling apart. There was hardly any grass in the front yard and the grass in the back yard was up to my knees and full of beer bottles and cans – about a hundred of them. We learned from the next door neighbors that once a place looks abandoned, it becomes a hangout for kids.

Ralph's house sold right away and a few months later we made settlement on both houses the same day. At the settlement table the seller looked familiar to me. She thought I looked familiar to her, as well. As it turned out, she was the owner of "The Famous Shop" in Atlantic City and had sold me my wedding dress. She was a lovely lady and she wished us happiness in her former home.

Somehow the house looked bigger on the outside than on the inside. We counted all the windows and realized there were two more windows on the outside at the far end of the house. April hoisted herself up to look into one of the windows and discovered another large room that had been framed for what looked like a master suite.

The first order of business for Ralph on settlement day was to rent a machine called "The Big Rip Off". That machine was used to peel up indoor/outdoor carpeting and linoleum. He spent the afternoon and most of the evening stripping off a layer of indoor/outdoor carpeting plus two layers of linoleum from the country kitchen and adjoining laundry room.

That project revealed a wet rotted floor in the laundry room from a leaking washing machine. The pull-down stairs to the attic were in the laundry room. The attic was empty, but it also lacked flooring. Ralph took measurements in the laundry room and the attic and bought enough plywood for both projects.

April, Betsy, and I were tasked with going through the myriad packed boxes and putting everything away in closets, cupboards, and dressers. Other items were to be stored in the attic once the additional flooring was laid. We opened and labeled each box accordingly.

Our first weekend in the house, Ralph bought fencing and borrowed a fence post digger and he and a few friends put a fence around the back yard to keep the dogs in. Fifi and Ralphie were happy to be outside without their leashes.

Betsy was still in school in Ocean City and I drove her to school every morning before heading to work in Atlantic City.

April brought her home every afternoon. Betsy turned twelve in June and would be entering Belhaven Middle School in Linwood in the Fall. We hoped she'd make new friends from Linwood over the summer.

At first she wanted to take the bus back and forth to Ocean City. She stood on Shore Road at Poplar Avenue holding a sign she made that said "BUS". Depending upon the driver, the bus would stop for her or pass her by. She was tiny for twelve years old so maybe the bus drivers didn't think she was old enough to ride the bus alone.

She eventually stopped going to Ocean City and made friends with our neighbors' kids. By the time school began she was comfortable because she knew at least the kids her age in our neighborhood. One of the Genova kids who lived on our corner offered her a ride to school.

When winter turned to spring, Ralph and his friends tore off the old roof and replaced it. Ralph then spray-painted the exterior of the house and we had all the windows replaced, including the large picture window in the living room. We had the window sills and trim wrapped with vinyl and bought new front and back doors. Inside, we had the kitchen flooring installed and new appliances delivered.

Ralph's friend from work, George Hartranft, gave him a slider that he had just removed from a guest house he bought in Ocean City. Ralph was happy to have it and the two of them cut a giant opening in the addition for the slider. Having that slider provided easy access in and out when Ralph was ready to start working on the master suite. He had already removed some of the framing that was there and designed a new floor plan.

Ralph was thinking ahead about our honeymoon in the Chesapeake and made arrangements for me to go to sailing school for a week at Great Oaks in Fairlee Creek. My friend, Marlene Baichl, went with me. Her husband, Franz, had just bought a sailboat and thought she should take the class, too. We both passed the course and at least learned how to tie a bowline, a sheet bend knot, and a clove hitch, and how to raise and lower the main and jib, and steer a steady course.

In my absence, Ralph and George, built a double closet in the existing master bedroom and turned a smaller closet into a half bath. Ralph then refinished the hardwood floors in the two smaller bedrooms for April and Betsy.

The Ocean City apartment building I lived in had gone into receivership and I now had a new landlady who had just bought the place. She advised she was raising my rent. I asked to be let out of the Lease early. Ralph offered, in exchange, to give the apartment walls a fresh coat of paint, if she provided the paint, which she did. God bless him! As if he had nothing else to do.

I had been contacted several times by Jim Butler, Legal Counsel at Harrah's, who offered me a job as his Paralegal. I had been at Claridge for five years and thought that perhaps working for Harrah's which, was owned by Holiday Inn, might be a good move for me. I met with Jim and he offered me all the perks I had at Claridge as well as a raise in salary. I accepted the position and started working the middle of May.

Our wedding took place September 13, 1986 at Zion United Methodist Church, Egg Harbor Township, New Jersey in front of two hundred forty wedding guests. The reception meal was held in the church hall and the wedding cake was served at our house.

Fran Eisele from the Claridge did the catering and her husband, Ule, the Claridge Pastry Chef, made the cake and brought it to our house in the back of his VW Beetle and put it together in our kitchen. He never told us what the cake would be like and it was absolutely amazing. Every bit of the lace-work was made of sugar and put together in our kitchen, and it was delicious. He also baked a Groom's

Cake, an Italian Rum, at Ralph's request. I don't think either of us had a bite.

Our wedding was simple and lots of fun with old friends and family reminiscing and chatting with new friends and both families getting to know each other. Banjo Bill played the banjo and everyone was singing. Crazy Jimmy Pappas, one of my first friends in New Jersey, came to our wedding with an entourage of his friends dressed for a parade. Jimmy got down on one knee and serenaded my sister, Gretchen. It was a perfect day.

Girard gave me away   Rev. Peterson officiated

Jim and Lorraine Yost

KINETOSCOPE

Ule's wedding cake   Betsy's sign for the stern

Ken & Jason Wescoat, Girard, Ralph, Celeste, April, Betsy,
Murph Brangenburg and James Roscher

Crazy Jimmy and his band of merry makers serenading Gretchen

Banjo Bill played everyone's favorites

    Ralph's parents, Jimmy and Lorraine, offered us their Catalina 30' sailboat, "Elusive," to use on our honeymoon. It was larger and more comfortable than the "Evening Star II". I didn't really know the difference three feet would make in a sailboat, but after two weeks on Elusive, I understood.

    We had beautiful weather and so much fun everywhere we went. There were so many interesting places to see and things to do. We walked through quaint little towns like Oxford and Cambridge. We stayed in Annapolis a few days and toured the Naval Academy. We enjoyed breakfast at "Chick and Ruth's" where the food was great and their son came to each table doing magic tricks. Every morning everyone in the place stood and said the Pledge of Allegiance.

We enjoyed eating crabs at every port. We enjoyed a wonderful honeymoon, very relaxing and peaceful. On the way home we had a romantic dinner at Schaeffer's Canal House in Chesapeake City. The lights of the restaurant are dimmed when a large boat comes through the canal.. They announce all the details of the boats, their home port, their cargo, the ships weight, and destination. That experience was a highlight for each of us.

We were married exactly one month when Ralph had the Catalina 27 hauled out for the season. There had been a crack in the keel joint that had been repaired twice by the manufacturer that was cracked again. My husband was not happy and called me at work one day and said he was trading the boat in and buying a new Catalina 30.

I was surprised and my first question was "Can we afford this?" I was concerned about the multiple projects we had planned for the house, but he assured me we would be able to buy the boat and do all the projects.

That weekend we went to the Catalina dealership in Delaware where Ralph had bought the Catalina 27 a few years earlier. There was no question that we both loved everything about the Catalina 30, since we'd sailed Ralph's parents' boat for two weeks on our honeymoon.

We were both excited about the new boat and Ralph wanted a spinnaker package. When it came down to the actual sail-away price, the haggling with Tom Haigi began. He was the owner of the dealership and was accepting the

'27 on trade. He and Ralph went back and forth over the figures. They were at an impasse over $2,000 that Ralph wanted taken off the total. Tom wasn't budging and Ralph wasn't either.

We had driven three hours to get there and we'd been at the dealership several hours. According to my watch, it was time to head home. I was looking at the price sheet and saw that the spinnaker package cost exactly $2,000. As the new Mrs., I suggested that we just not get the spinnaker. Tom Haigi said "That's a great idea!" Boy did I get a look!

Needless to say, we ordered the boat, including the spinnaker package. On the way home, my new hubby informed me that from now on, he wouldn't need my help in negotiating anything involving money.

The boat arrived at the dealership in the winter and Ralph went to Delaware to install the electronics. In the spring, "Obsession" was launched from Delaware City. Ralph and our brother-in-law, Frank and our friend, Franz, took the boat to Cape May. They stayed overnight, then brought the new boat to Atlantic City the next day.

We kept the boat at the Farley Marina on Pier 3 a few slips away from Ralph's Uncle Ken's boat and Ralph's parents' boat. Everyone in the family had a sailboat on the same pier.

CHAPTER FORTY-FOUR

Our honeymoon in the Chesapeake
September 1986

Our honeymoon was over and it was back to the real world and back to work. Betsy was happy at her new school and made new friends. Jimmy Pappas, a commodities broker, hired April as a Wire Operator at PaineWebber. I continued working at Harrah's during the day and typing for Barbie and Dr. Godfrey at home in the evenings. Ralph began working a flex-time 10-hour day/4-day week at the Tech Center. He had every Friday off.

The days flew by, the projects were completed, and soon it was our first Christmas as a family. We all went out to the tree farm to find the perfect Christmas tree. Ralph chopped it down and we brought it home. It was the most beautiful tree ever. We decorated it with the ornaments of my childhood, the Rockwell collectibles from Grandma Ruthie, and all the ornaments and garlands the girls had made through the years.

Ralph had a few ornaments of his own, including a Santa face surrounded by flashing lights. Suffice it to say, it was gaudy. April and Betsy called it "Psycho Santa". We had a cozy fire in the fireplace and Fifi and Ralphie curled up near the hearth and slept soundly.

Our first Christmas as Mr. and Mrs. was a blur to me. I can't remember what gifts we gave the girls, but it was probably cash because they both loved to shop. I don't remember what I gave Ralph, but I think it was a ski jacket. Ralph's gift to me was my first computer, a Leading Edge that had 512 KB, a monochrome screen, and held floppy discs.

In my stocking was the best gift of all, a note from Santa that said "Quit your job!"

I could have danced in the streets. I was very happy to give my two weeks' notice to my boss at Harrah's. None of the promises he made at my interview had come to fruition and within the first month I regretted leaving Claridge.

My last day at Harrah's, Ralph took me to work and picked me up at noon. I had a half-day to use before leaving the job. Our car was packed and we were off for a weekend of skiing at Mt. Sunapee in New Hampshire.

Snow was coming down lightly in Atlantic City and the further North we traveled the snow became heavier and the scenery more beautiful. We stayed in a hotel in Boston and drove to Mt. Sunapee in the mornings. The slopes were like picture postcards and the skiing conditions were perfect. Our weekend seemed like a second honeymoon to both of us just a few months after the first one.

The Leading Edge opened a whole new world for me. I could now do my transcription work at home during the day in my pajamas. I liked this better than working in an office all day and typing all evening. I could easily edit documents and save my work on floppy discs.

We bought a printer/FAX machine and scanner/copier and I went to the Atlantic County Court House and registered my trade name, "Shore Transcription Services". I continued to type for Dr. Godfrey, and a group of doctors in Egg Harbor Township, and Scibal Associates.

Around 1989 Debbie Wescoat and I attended classes at the Academy for Culinary Arts at Cape Atlantic Community College. We planned to open a catering a business together. We "kept our day jobs" as they say, and took evening classes. The course required 300 hours in the food service industry.

I applied for work in the cafeteria in the Belhaven Middle School two hours a day, two days a week. Working in a school requires all employees to be fingerprinted. I went to the Linwood Police Station for that. The officer taking my prints had a hard time getting them. He asked what I did for a living. I told him I had a transcription business and typed legal and medical reports.

"You must have typed your fingerprints off," he said as he scrubbed a stiff little brush over my fingertips, and finally got a passable set of prints. I was good to go.

We registered our catering trade name with the county, as "Simply Special". Our first job was a spring luncheon for the honor students of Elizabeth Ann Seton Catholic Church in Absecon, New Jersey.

My mother-in-law, Lorraine, and Debbie's daughter, Jessie, helped us that day. Her son, Brian, sliced all the meat for us. Our first job was a whirlwind but we were very pleased with the outcome. The school booked us for the same luncheon the following year.

We catered all summer for fishing charters and parties on individual boats. We catered a wedding and Christmas parties in people's homes. Christmas was very busy for us with take-out orders for sandwiches, salads and pastries.

In the spring and summer we catered for Stone Harbor Country Club functions We also cooked and served a luncheon for 100 under a large tent at the Atlantic City Polo Grounds.

"Simply Special Catering"
Ralph's sister Denise's Baby Shower

In the summer of 1987 we sailed "Obsession" to Block Island, Rhode Island for two weeks. Ken and Debbie put Betsy on a train bound for Bridgeport, Connecticut where we met her. She sailed home with us through Long Island Sound, through the New York river system, and down the coast to Atlantic City. This was one of many sailing trips we took on the Catalina 30' over the next twelve years.

Bridgeport, CT   Long Island Sound, NY

In the early summer, Atlantic City sponsored an annual boat parade, "The Blessing of the Fleet". Each boat entered was decorated with a particular theme. Awards were given for the best decorated boat.

Ralph's parents and their friends won that contest every single year! They decorated their boats with themes like "The Flintstones," a "M.A.S.H." unit, "Ninja Turtles", and "Hawaiian" themes.

We entered "Obsession" in the event one year. Our theme was "S.S. Popeye". We won a bronze boat clock, and I'm sure Ralph's parents took first place."

1987 Blessing of the Fleet,
Atlantic City, NJ Boat Parade Pat Cahill, Betsy, Kathy McFadden, Celeste, Ralph , Heather Remer , Lou McFadden

Every summer for eight years Ralph and I volunteered for the "Around the Island Swim". The event is an international open-water swimming competition sponsored by the City of Atlantic City. Swimmers came from all over the world to swim in this 22.5 mile event around Absecon Island. All the surrounding towns offered their lifeboats for this event. The lifeboats had two rowers and were assigned to a specific swimmer. Their job was to keep the swimmer on course. The swimmer's coach was in the boat to encourage, and supply food and water to the swimmer. This was also a rowing competition among the lifeguards.

The start was in Gardner's Basin in Atlantic City. The swimmers lined up in the water and at the start gun, they swam out the inlet to the Atlantic Ocean, south along Atlantic City, past Ventnor, Margate and Longport, then around the jetty to the Back Bay, swimming in the calmer bay past all those towns to the starting point.

Swimmer, Angela Maurer and her coach Shila Sheth from Germany stayed at our house for several years when Angela participated in the competition. We became good friends and our home was their home during the Swim each year. Angela was an excellent swimmer and took first place in the women's division every year but one, which was nearly a tie. The swimmers won medals, money, and recognition in the open water swimming events around the world.

The "Around the Island Swim" eventually ended because of lack of funding from the City of Atlantic City and other businesses who supported it.

Back in the 1970s, there was little financial support for this international event. Atlantic City Mayor Jim Whelan swam it alone in 1978 to keep the momentum of this event alive. That action on his part brought a lot of attention back to this wonderful unique event.

SOUTH JERSEY CHAMPIONS
Andrew Funk sets a record, leads Ventnor to lifeguard title. **Page D1**

AUGUST 9, 2003

The "Funk Hunks" as we nicknamed the Funk twins, Ventnor, NJ Lifeguards
They rowed together in the Lifeguard Championships each summer and set a record in August 2009.
They also rowed in many Around the Island Swim Events

Celeste Yost

CHAPTER FORTY-FIVE

My Christmas gift to Ralph in 1988 was flying lessons with Jack Philp. They started in the spring of 1989, and Ralph made his first solo flight in August that year. He and Jack became good friends and Jack, who worked for Trane Air Conditioning, helped Ralph install central air in our house that summer. What a Godsend that air conditioning was in the sweltering heat and humidity of a New Jersey summer.

Ralph loved flying and joined the FAA Flying Club. His membership gave him access to the three club planes, the Tomahawk, the Piper Archer and the Piper Arrow that had retractable landing gear. Jack taught him to fly all three.

Ralph also took lessons for a seaplane endorsement. He went to Ken Mills' Flying School in Philadelphia every week for a month until he mastered the technique of flying and landing a seaplane. Aaron and I went along to watch. Ken took Aaron out in his little boat to help set the buoys on the Delaware River.

During the winter when Ralph couldn't fly, he started working on the addition. The master bedroom was large and we had double closets. There was a full bath and an area we hoped to make into a sauna. Ralph had cut the doorway from the addition into the rest of the house and fortunately, the floors line up perfectly.

In the spring, the carpeting was laid and the only thing left to do was to paint the louvered closet doors, which Ralph was spray-painting in our back yard. We had already been sleeping in our new bedroom and had transferred our clothes into the closets. The room would be complete when the closet doors were painted.

One afternoon I went up to the attic to look for a specific box that contained letters and photographs of my family in Germany. Several years earlier I had tried to contact my

Aunt Frieda's daughter, Annelies, but never received a response. I marked that box and set it aside in the attic. My intention was to try and connect with Annelies using the address on the most current correspondence to my Father. That date was twelve years earlier.

I eventually connected with Annelies at Christmastime 1988. Our friend, Rudy Dalinger, translated my letters into German for Annelies. When I received a response from her, Rudy translated her letters for me. Her letter said was happy to hear from us and that she still lived at the same address. She sent photos of herself and her older sister, Lotti. She enclosed also, photos of her daughter, Bettina, and Bettina's daughter, Annett. Annett drew some pictures of Donald Duck for Betsy.

In one of her letters Annelies told us that she and Lotti, were planning to come to America for a ten-day visit. There were many German government stipulations about traveling out of East Germany, especially travel to the United States.

Germans could travel only if they were going abroad to celebrate a "round numbered" birthday or anniversary. The German government required the actual invitation to the party, as well as the exact date and location of the event. They even had to provide the geographic areas in the United States they would be visiting.

I was so excited to finally meet my German family. I called all my siblings and told them we'd like to get together when Annelies and Lotti came to visit. The "round numbered" birthday worked out well, for Artie would turn 60 years old in April of 1989. All my siblings were excited and wanted to meet our cousins, too.

I sent a letter to Annelies with all the government required information, as well as invitations to Artie's 60th birthday party to be held April 19, 1989. The party would be hosted by Gretchen and Neal at their house in Altoona.

Girard and Bonnie lived across the street, Artie and Shirley would come from Georgia and Trudy and Frank would come from Louisiana. Ralph and I would pick up Annelies and Lotti in New York and after a few days, we'd all come to the party in Pennsylvania.

The communication to and from Dresden was slow and erratic. Phone calls were difficult because of the language barrier. The only information we had was from Annelies's most recent letter. It said she and Lotti were flying from Prague, Czechoslovakia. We knew no details of their travel plans, not the exact date, the airline, flight number, arrival location, or arrival time. We only knew they were flying to New York.

We had one day's notice when we received a telegram in our mailbox which gave the details. Things were totally different than we expected. Annelies was now coming alone and was flying from Warsaw, Poland. The name of the airline wasn't given, nor was the flight number. We did know she was arriving the next afternoon at Kennedy Airport in New York. Ralph verified the airline, flight number and arrival time.

I gave the guest room a once-over cleaning and put fresh linens on the bed and in the half-bath and full bathroom. We left shortly after lunch for Kennedy Airport the next day.

The flight from Prague was scheduled to arrive around 4:00 PM, but was delayed and it was nearly six o'clock in the evening until Annelies had her luggage and was through Customs. This had been a very long day for all of us.

Communication was difficult. Annelies spoke no English except for a few basic words and we spoke no German, except for what I learned in high school and from my father as a child. We did have a German/English dictionary with us which was somewhat helpful, but not so in the car at night.

Annelies was tired and hungry and we stopped to get a bite to eat and use the restroom before we continued to New Jersey. Friday evening in rush hour traffic out of New York City in a nightmare. Annelies was clearly upset with all the traffic and kept motioning for Ralph to slow down. She put her coat over her head on the way home.

When we arrived home Annelies was tired and had a cold. I fixed her something to eat, she had a hot bath, and went to bed. She slept late the next day and had a terrible cough. I went to the drugstore and bought cough syrup and cough drops for her.

She refused the cough medicine because she had her own medication with her. She was afraid to take any medicine in America, and we understood.

The weather was warm and the flowering crab in our front yard was starting to bloom so we decided to take a walk on the bike path. The three of us walked by City Hall on the way. When Annelies saw the police cars in the parking lot, she again put her coat over her head. She was insistent that we go back home, and we did. She was visibly shaken and showed us in our bi-lingual dictionary that the police were not good people.

With the dictionary we were able to communicate basics to each other. Ralph asked to see her ticket for the return flight. When he looked at it, he realized she did not have a return flight. She had a 30-day visa to be in the United States. We were surprised about that, we thought the visit was for ten days. Working for the FAA, Ralph had connections in Washington and was going to look into how to get a flight scheduled for her within the thirty day visa period.

It took many phone calls through various channels to resolve the issue but within a few days, Annelies had a reservation for her return flight to Germany in a month.

During the day when Ralph was at work I took her to the Boardwalks in both Atlantic City and Ocean City and showed her around Linwood. She loved shopping and I took her to the grocery store and to the Mall. When she was excited to buy something, we made the purchases. We introduced her to our friend Rudy, who translated for each of us, for which we were grateful. I did my transcription work at night after she was asleep.

Rudy told us the impression Annelies had of America was that all Americans were wealthy. People drove big cars everywhere and had multiple telephones and televisions in their homes. She was amazed by the abundance and variety in our grocery stores and marveled at the beautiful produce and meats.

We went to the Mall several times and she wanted to look in every shop to see everything. She put her hands to her face like she was wearing glasses and commented, "Meine Augen!" meaning "My eyes!" We found ourselves only looking up key words in our German/English dictionary. We could communicate fairly well, but a running conversation was next to impossible.

Trudy and Frank arrived at our house about a week later. They stayed a few days with us then they drove to Washington D.C. with Annelies to show her the sights at the Nation's Capitol.

Everyone arrived in Altoona for Artie's 60th birthday celebration. The party was a lot of fun and Annelies was happy to meet all the American Lipperts, and they were happy to connect with at least one of our German relatives. I'm glad Ralph took a family picture.

Girard and Bonnie took Annelies shopping and sightseeing around Altoona, and to the Horseshoe Curve and to their cottage in Raystown where they had a picnic.

Annelies spent her last few days in America with Gretchen and Neal and they drove her to the airport in New York for her return flight home.

Annelies Funke's visit to America
Artie's 60th Birthday, April 19, 1989 Rob, Trudy holding Ben, Gretchen, Artie, Annelies, Neal behind Annelies, Frank behind Shirley
: Cathy, Girard, Celeste, Eileen
Jarrett and Billy

We all had taken Annelies shopping and bought things for her to take back to Germany, but she couldn't take all of it with her. I packed and mailed several boxes to her in Dresden. She called a few weeks later to tell us her packages had arrived and thanked us again for the wonderful visit and gifts.

My sister, Trudy, and her son, Steve, had gone to Dresden in 1988 to visit Annelies when the border was once again open. Over the years Trudy had corresponded with our cousin, Karlernst Lippert, who was the son of our father's brother, Arthur. Karlernst had married and he and his wife, Gertrud, raised their family on the outskirts of Wittstock in an area named Biesen.

Karlernst had been ill and Trudy had hoped she and Steve could take the train from Dresden to Biesen to meet him and his family. She asked Annelies if they could do that. Annelies told her no because there was no train from Dresden to Biesen. Trudy was very disappointed. Karlernst died shortly thereafter and she never had the opportunity to meet him and his family personally.

In October 1989 the East German government was under increasing pressure to reform the government. There were mass demonstrations in Dresden, Leipzig and East Berlin. Erich Honecker was forced to resign his DDR party leadership position. This was the beginning of the end of a divided Germany.

President Ronald Reagan had visited Berlin for the first time on June 11, 1982. On his second visit in 1987 President Reagan made his historic speech in front of the Brandenburg Gate in which he said, "Mr. Gorbachev, tear down this Wall!"

On November 9, 1989, during a news broadcast, an East German government spokesman mistakenly announced that the citizens of DDR would now be permitted unrestricted travel between East and West, effective immediately.

Hearing that long-awaited news, swarms of East Berliners, in an attempt to get into West Berlin, overwhelmed the unsuspecting border guards at the Wall. The guards were unaware of the announcement. The citizens of both sides of Berlin were demolishing the Wall. Over the next few months the Berlin Wall would almost completely disappear.

Pieces of the Berlin Wall were for sale and my friend, Vera, whose daughter and son-in-law were stationed in the Army in Germany, bought me a package containing pieces of the Berlin Wall.

A large piece of the Berlin Wall was presented to President Reagan as a gift. It is displayed in the courtyard of the Ronald Reagan Presidential Library in Simi Valley, California.

Fragments of the Berlin Wall given to me by my friend, Vera Taggart

Commemorative piece of the Berlin Wall
Ronald Reagan Presidential Library
Simi, California

CHAPTER FORTY-SIX

During Betsy's junior year at Mainland High School in 1991, Ralph had a conference in Cocoa Beach, Florida during spring break. The three of us flew there together in the Archer. The trip wasn't exactly the "spring break" Betsy had in mind. We went to the Kennedy Space Center to watch the publicized launch. Unfortunately, the launch scheduled that day was scrubbed. We still had a good time just being at the launch site. The weather was beautiful and Betsy and I lounged around at the pool and went shopping while Ralph attended meetings.

Betsy and Ralph packing the Arrow for Cocoa Beach, FL 1991

Kennedy Space Center Spring Break 1991

Near 6:00 PM on Wednesday, July 31, 1991, Ralph, Ken Wescoat, Franz Baichl, and Gordon Nichols boarded "Obsession" with all their gear and sailed her out the Atlantic City Inlet. Their final destination was Northeast Harbor, Maine which could take several days. The weather was beautiful. They sailed all night through the shipping lanes toward Block Island.

Friday August 2, they arrived in Provincetown, Massachusetts for fuel and water. They'd had a great time surfing the waves with the spinnaker up since the first day out.

Their second day out didn't go as well. They had the boatspeed at 10 knots. The wind caught the spinnaker at a wrong angle and blew it out. Below is a photo of the spinnaker before the trip. No picture exists of the blow out.

This photo was taken off the coast of Atlantic City - circa late 1980s

The crew arrived at Northeast Harbor, Maine on Saturday evening around 9:00. Several days later Gordon and Franz flew home. Debbie arrived by car in the afternoon and I flew into Bar Harbor Airport around 6:00 PM and took a cab to Norteast Harbor.

Ken and Debbie sailed with us about a week. None of us had ever been sailing in Maine before. We were eager to explore all the areas we'd only read about. I kept a ship's log of our travels on waters with interesting names like Penobscot Bay, Eggemoggin Reach, Vinalhaven and Christmas Cove.

On August 12 Betsy and her boyfriend, Bill Leeds, drove to Camden to sail with us for a few days. They arrived just as Ken and Debbie were leaving. Ralph needed to replace a broken bracket on Obsession so we walked into town to Wayfarer Marine. The bracket was almost $100 and Ralph paid with an out-of-state check. He showed his ID and the owner said,"That's not necessary, your name is on the check. The part should be here in a couple days."

The four of us went out to dinner at the Dockside Café. Afterward we had dessert at "Cappy's", a bakery and ice cream shop. We took pictures of the beautiful tall ships and schooners in the harbor. On the way back to the boat we picked up a few groceries. Everyone was tired and we talked a while then settled in for the night..

The following morning we sailed from Camden across Penobscot Bay to Hurricane Island, home of "Outward Bound." This international program is a one-of-a-kind team-building and self-sufficiency experience, specifically for teenagers and young adults.

On our way we met a lobsterman selling lobsters off his boat. We bought four beautiful lobsters and put them in a large stock pot with ice. When we arrived at Hurricane Island, we picked up a mooring and dinghyed ashore.

We were given a map and some information at the main desk. We were told the island is granite and that Dr. Gastin, who owned the island, was building a new house on the summit and it was worth the hike to see it. As we hiked we were intrigued to see with our own eyes just what Outward Bound is all about.

In the woods we saw tall wooden structures where competing teams climbed up one side and came down the other side on ropes. We watched competing groups scaling the cliff walls. Sets of paralleled telephone poles were suspended from trees about twenty feet from the ground. Partners on poles across from each other were clipped to safety wires overhead. The held hands with their partner on the opposite pole. The task was to walk across the sixty-foot poles holding hands, replying upon each other. That was amazing to watch.

After a long day and we dinghied back to the boat. I made a salad and we steamed our lobsters for dinner. They were delicious. We sat and talked in the cockpit a while after dinner then settled in for the night.

In the morning after breakfast Betsy and Bill took the dinghy and rode around the island taking more photos. We sailed back to Camden and just relaxed. We had dinner on the boat and walked to Miss Plum's for ice cream.

We asked around and found a place where they packed lobsters for traveling. The next morning after breakfast, we said goodbye to Betsy and Bill. They picked up lobsters and headed back to New Jersey.

Ralph picked up the bracket from Wayfarer Marine and installed it. The day was cool and overcast and we sailed to Long Cove to anchor for the night. We woke up early the next morning and saw otters swimming around the boats in the anchorage. They were so comical, we had breakfast in the cockpit so we could watch their antics.

KINETOSCOPE

As we continued south, the sky became darker and by noon it was starting to rain. We talked to fellow sailors on the radio as we traveled and discussed the weather. We learned that a big storm was heading up the East coast.

I had read in one of the local newspapers that an international quilt exhibit was being held in the historic village of Wiscasset. The little village was about fifteen miles up the Sheepscott River. Ralph was totally opposed to that idea, not wanting to travel fifteen miles up a river just to look at quilts.

However, his decision changed when he again checked the forecast and saw that really bad weather was coming our way. He decided that Wiscasset might be a safe haven to ride out the storm. We motored up the Sheepscott River to the center of town where there was a small anchorage. The rain had started when we arrived. Someone told us that one of the granite moorings in the anchorage was available. Its owner was away and we could use his mooring, which we did and were grateful it was available.

The weather changed rapidly and we learned that Hurricane Bob was heading north right behind the storm. We donned our raingear and took off the sails and the boom and off-loaded our gear. Everyone in the harbor pitched in helping one another secure the boats and offload belongings.

One man helping us owned a Bed & Breakfast and said they had one room available, and that if we wanted to stay there, we could have the room. That was a Godsend.

We took our gear to the B&B and formally met Ray and Lynn Jenkins, our hosts. We walked downtown to find a place for lunch. Most of the shop owners had already secured plywood over their windows, taken down awnings, and brought in furniture. The only business open was "Red's Eats", a small silver trailer along Route 1. We ordered two burgers and sat outside in our raingear. The rain dripped off our hats and made our sandwiches soggy, but we enjoyed them nonetheless.

The electricity was out everywhere in the village and the rain continued to pelt the house. Newlyweds on their honeymoon were also staying at the B&B. Lynn made a wonderful roast beef dinner, topped off by a homemade huckleberry pie for dessert. The six of us had dinner by candlelight.

Around midnight there was only drizzle. All six of us walked down to the town dock. Practically the whole town was there already. We all were watching the boats in the harbor bobbing up and down. The eye of Hurricane Bob was passing over us.

The next morning we went to the service at the local church. We had more heavy rain and stayed another night at the B&B. By the following morning "Bob" had weakened and was downgraded to a tropical storm. We attached the boom and hoisted the sails and helped others get their boats together. We learned the quilt exhibit would be held the following weekend. We thanked our hosts and our new friends and headed south toward home.

"I think if I could tolerate the winters, I'd love to live in Wiscasset." That comment got ony an eyeroll from my husband.

We stopped at many unique small towns, one of which was Brunswick, the home of the Naval Air Station. We went to Biddeford Pool, a large tidal pool located off the south coast of Saco Bay and walked through the town of Biddeford. Kennebunkport was only a few miles away, so we stopped there and took a bus tour of the town. The tour included passing by the home of President and Mrs. George H.W. Bush. We sailed on Penobscot Bay and Casco Bay.

KINETOSCOPE

We visited the little towns of Bath, Vinylhaven which is on Fox Island, Yarmouth, Kittery and Freeport.

In Freeport when we docked, L.L. Bean had a complimentary shuttle to take everyone into town. We had a sailbag full of laundry with us and were directed to a local laundromat. Afterward we visited the L.L. Bean store and they offered to keep our laundry for us while we went out to dinner. We walked through the town and had ice cream at Ben & Jerry's. The Bean shuttle took us back to our boat. Our last stop in Maine was Kittery.

We continued making our way south and anchored in Inner Harbor in Glouster, Massachusetts. The anchorage was small and there were eddies causing the anchored boats to swing wierdly. We were awake most of the night to be sure we didn't hit another boat or that they didn't hit us. We were up early to leave the next morning. The fishing boats were coming out. One boat saw us watching and the captain headed directly for our bow. I thought he would hit us, but he veered off quickly and missed us by inches. We left immediately and had breakfast on the way. Folks in Gloucester were not friendly to strangers.

We stopped in Plymouth to see Plymouth Rock and tour a replica of the Mayflower which carried had 102 passengers and about 30 crew members from England in 1620. We left Plymouth and motored through the Cape Cod Canal and crossed Buzzards Bay to Cuttyhunk Island. We had been there before and were sad to see the stacks of empty lobster traps on the town dock. The greenery of the entire island was now badly burned from the salt water from the hurricane. There had been a large windmill at the top of the only hill on the island. It was an icon and was destroyed by Hurricane Bob.

We helped a boater entering the harbor who could not get his engine started. We towed him to his slip.

"Do you like lobster?" he asked.

"We do," we told him, "but we're sure there are no lobsters here now."

"Not so," he said and went alongside the dock and pulled up his trap and put two lobsters in a bucket for us. "Thanks for the tow!" he said. We anchored for the night and steamed those delicious lobsters for dinner.

At 5:30 AM we weighed anchor and headed to Block Island. That was a long trip. We anchored in the Great Salt Pond. The weather was hot and sunny and the pond was rough with waves. Many boats there were damaged by the storm. We had dinner at Smuggler's Cove. Through every area there were boats wrecked onto the rocks and houses and businesses damaged. The devastation was disheartening.

The final leg home was an overnight passage through the shipping lanes from Block Island, Rhode Island to Barnegat, New Jersey. We took turns at the helm and we, especially me, were very grateful for the auto pilot. We arrived in Atlantic City on August 30, greeted by our good friend, Jay Gray. Jay was out sailing and heard us on the radio. He sailed near us by the inlet and tossed flowers to me from his boat to ours.

"Welcome home!" he hollered, as Ralph sailed right past the inlet.

"What are you doing?" Jay and I asked the captain. Ralph replied,"I want to dry the sails!"

I said, "Dry the sails? After we've been awake 30 hours? You better turn this boat around and head in!" Jay laughed, and the captain headed for the inlet.

We were happy to arrive home safely. We have fond memories of that trip. It was one of the best and most exciting sailboat trips we'd ever taken, not to mention, it was the longest!

CHAPTER FORTY-SEVEN

Betsy graduated from Mainland High School in the spring of 1992. We'd been looking at colleges for her in the prio Fall. Betsy's first choice was North Carolina State. Ralph flew us to Raleigh, North Carolina to visit the campus. The tuition for out-of-state students was considerably more than for in-state students. We also visited Rutgers in New Jersey, which was her second choice.

Betsy & Roark Stahler Mainland HS Graduation 1992
Linwood, New Jersey

We suggested her first year be at Stockton State College near Atlantic City so she could live at home. She agreed and took her initial courses at Stockton. She worked part-time at Olympia Sports and Dairy Queen. Ralph's favorite job that Betsy had was Dairy Queen. That was because the workers were allowed to take home any mistakes! He loved that perk!

Betsy settled upon an in-state college and transferred her credits to Rowan University in Glassboro, New Jersey. Glassboro is about an hour's drive from Linwood. Her major was Microbiology.

She shared a quad suite on campus and joined the Delta Zeta Sorority. She and her suite-mates, all Delta-Zeta members, became lifetime friends and still get together at least once yearly.

Ralph and I continued flying and sailing for many years. We liked to fly to "The Three Little Bakers Dinner Theater" in Wilmington, Delaware with our neighbors and friends, Ted and Elaine Stashak. The cab ride from the airport to the theater cost more than our av-fuel, but flying at night was spectacular.

One of our favorite spots was Tangier Island in the Chesapeake, with a narrow landing strip next to the Bay. Landing was a little dicey if the weather wasn't perfect. We flew the scenic Hudson VFR Corridor in New York and many places locally in Atlantic County.

Aerial view of the Hudson River VFR Corridor
New York, New York

In 1993 I took the AOPA Pinch-Hitter's Course from Wayne Rumble who taught me how to fly from the passenger seat. We used the Flying Club's 2-passenger Tomahawk for my actual flying lessons. When I first met Wayne he knew Ralph and I were flying often and asked what instruments I knew about in the cockpit. I told him the gas gauge and the clock and laughed. He said "Well, we're going to do better than that."

Six lessons later I had learned to take over the controls in an emergency, how to call the tower and give my location and tail number. Most of all, I learned to land the plane in a "survivable crash". Although I never flew at night, I remember learning about the VASI lights for night landing: "Red over white, you're all right; white over red, you're dead."

I never attempted a night landing, but it was good information nonetheless.

Celeste Yost

CHAPTER FORTY-EIGHT

April married Richie Smith in May 1990 at Zion United Methodist Church in Bargaintown, New Jersey. April was now a Labor Relations Specialist at the Claridge Casino Hotel in Atlantic City. Richie was working at Johnson's Appliances in Ocean City. The newlyweds lived close by us in Somers Point.

On November 1, 1992 our first grandchild, Aaron Richard Smith, was born. When Ralph and I went to the hospital nursery to see him for the first time, we asked the nurses which baby he was. One nurse said "Oh, that's 'Surfer Boy', wait till you see him!" She brought him out and we were surprised to see a blonde baby. He was a beautiful baby and, indeed, a "Surfer Boy".

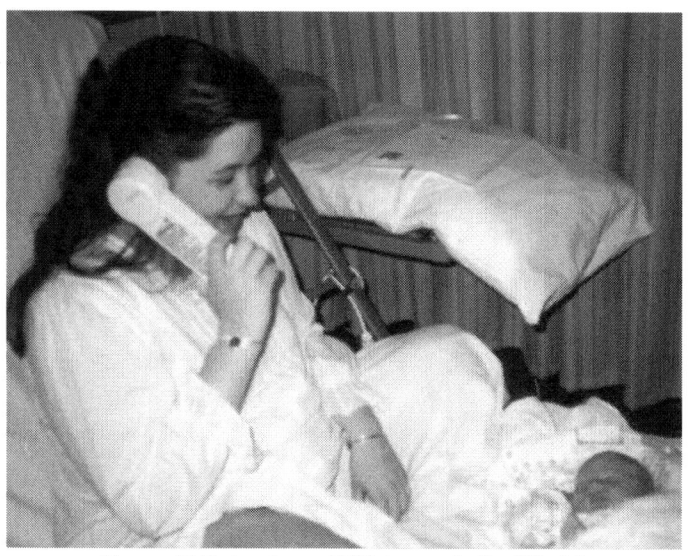

Happy Birthday Aaron!! Welcome to the World!
November 1, 1992

Aaron 3-1/2 months old and Gram

What a joy it was for me to have a baby to cuddle! While April and Richie worked I had the pleasure of caring for Aaron every day until he started pre-school. We moved a crib and playpen and tons of toys and books into my office which worked out nicely with Shore Transcription.

I had gained two more clients, another doctor's office and a local lawyer who lived nearby. He needed pleadings prepared and typed once in a while. I liked him a lot but he was unorganized. He'd often give me the files and ask me to write the pleadings and have them ready for him to take to court the next morning. He'd tell me he would stop by at 4:00 PM to drop off the materials so I could work on them and have them ready for him to pick up on his way to court.

One time he was a no-show and when Ralph was getting into his car at 6:30 AM to go to work, here comes Lou. He was riding his bicycle to drop off the file and the tape he wanted transcribed. Fortunately, I was up and working when he arrived. He said he had to be in court by 8:30.

I was able to have the pleadings ready and printed for him. I included my invoice with the documents as I normally did, only this time I added "$10 A.T." to the total.

Every time he gave me work (always at the last minute) I would add "$10 A.T." to my invoice. Finally after months of this, he asked what "A.T" meant and I said "Aggravation Tax" and he just laughed. I told him he is my worst client and that I like him a lot but he tortures me with this last minute stuff and he just said "Okay," and paid the extra $10. I operated that home-based business for twenty-three years.

Every day I delivered my work to the various offices. Of course, Aaron was with me, and everyone wanted to hold him. He was adorable and a very good baby. Sometimes I'd put Fifi in the playpen with him and the two of them would nap side-by-side in my office.

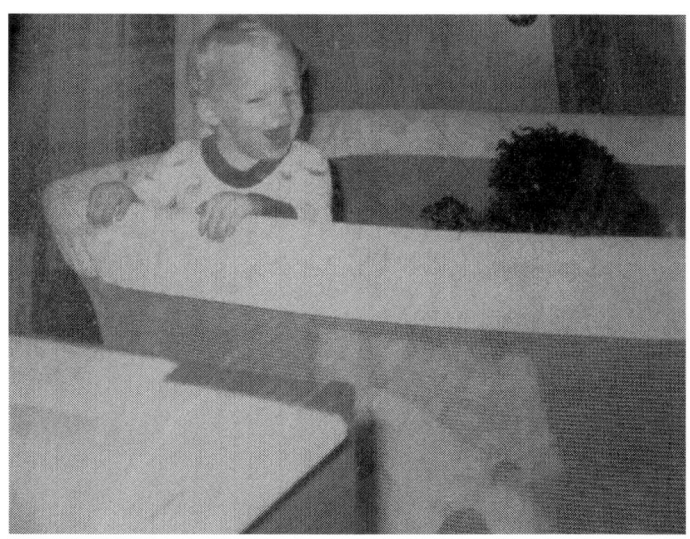

Aaron and Fifi 1994 – are they ready to escape?

In the Fall of 1994 we got a letter from my cousin, Uwe, from Germany. Uwe is the son of Karlernst and Gertrud Lippert and they live in Biesen, outside of Wittstock, Germany.

They asked if they could come and visit us in January when Uwe had a vacation from his teaching position at the Music Academy. We had never met them and were very excited. Of course they were welcome to come.

My sister, Trudy, was staying at our house while her husband, Frank, an airline pilot, was in Philadelphia for his job.

Uwe, Christine and their oldest son, Alexander, arrived in New York one very snowy January day. Ralph borrowed his parents' station wagon and he and Trudy picked them up at the airport in New York. I had work to do and was watching Aaron and stayed home. Ralph drove them through Manhattan so they could at least see a little of the "Big Apple" on their way to our house. The weather was terrible and we had an ice storm the night they arrived.

Uwe had a movie camera with him and we walked all over the neighborhoods. He took videos of everything, all the while, narrating in German. We had a wonderful time with them. We took them to visit Betsy at the Rowan campus and spent some time with her. We also went on the Atlantic City Boardwalk and into the casinos. Uwe played the "Big Bertha" slot machine that took silver dollars, and he won almost a hundred dollars. He was very happy about that.

Every casino at that time had some sort of special buffet each day. We went to the Seafood Buffet at the Taj Mahal. We had gone through the massive buffet line for our dinner, and afterward, Ralph got up and announced "Ich verden suchen Nacht."

When he returned with several desserts, everyone at the table was laughing and Ralph asked, "Was ist der Spass?"

which translated means, "What is the joke?" Christine had one hand over her mouth laughing and pointed at me to tell him and I said "You just told everyone at the table that you were going to get naked." That has been a running joke among us for many, many years.

We had a wonderful visit and our cousins invited us to come to Germany that summer. We had previously booked a trip to Israel for December and could not do both. However, we promised we would definitely come to visit. Uwe's grandfather and grandmother were my father's oldest brother, Arthur, and his wife Hedie. They had only one child, Karlernst, who was Uwe's father.

Uwe and Christine Lippert January 1994, Linwood, NJ

In December 1994 we flew to the beautiful country of Israel for a 10-day teaching tour with Marvin Rosenthal. Marv is a Messianic Jew. He was born a Jew and accepted Christ as his Savior and became a Born Again Christian. We rose early every morning for breakfast then got on the bus. We traveled and went sightseeing all day. In the evening we returned to the hotel for dinner and lectures afterward. The lectures were so interesting.

Just being in the Holy Land was the most amazing experience. Our trip was doubly special because we were there during Hanukkah and Christmas. The whole country is no larger than the State of New Jersey. It's astounding to see what the Israelis have done with the desert. The country is lush and green. We went to all the historic sites, the Via Delarosa (the way of the cross) the route Jesus walked to Golgotha bearing His cross. We had a communion service at the Garden Tomb.

We took a cable car to the top of Megiddo. Megiddo is a "Tel" which means an archeological mound of many civilizations over hundreds of years. There are twenty-six levels of civilizations comprising the Megiddo Tel. Many battles and wars were fought there. In one battle the Israelites took their own lives rather than surrender or allow their enemies to kill them.

Megiddo is translated Armageddon. Christians believe, according to the Bible, it will be the site of the final battle between Jesus Christ and the Kings of the world who are against Israel. Megiddo is a World Heritage Site. Some of our group walked down about 3,000 steps to the bottom.

Less than a mile away from Megiddo was the Megiddo Kibbutz where we all spent the night. The accommodations were Spartan but very clean and the gardens were beautiful.

The following day we went to the Hotel Nirvana located next to the Dead Sea. The hotel had an indoor salt water pool. The salt content was so high we floated on top of the water. We rode a camel in Jerusalem and enjoyed grilled St. Peter's fish on a cruise across the Sea of Galilee. This was the most memorable tour we've ever taken.

We walked the strand in the evenings after Marv's lectures along with just about everyone else in our group. Israel is a beautiful country and I'd love to go back sometime again.

KINETOSCOPE

Floating in the Dead Sea salt water pool at the Nirvana Hotel
Jerusalem, Israel 1994

Jerusalem 1994

St. Peter's Fish grilled on a boat crossing the Sea of Galilee

Celeste Yost

CHAPTER FORTY-NINE

In the summer of 1995 Betsy was working for the law firm of Michael Weiss in Northfield, New Jersey. She loved her job and all the people she worked with. Betsy had turned twenty-one that summer and she and three other friends were going to Somers Point for "wings" at Charlie's, a popular neighborhood eatery.

We were unaware that afterward, the son of the owner of Charlie's, C.J., invited everyone out for a boat ride. He suggested they go to the Deauville Inn in Strathmere, a summer tourist town between Ocean City and Sea Isle City.

Around 11:00 PM that evening our phone rang and I answered it to hear "This is the Sea Isle City Rescue Squad, is this the home of Elizabeth Zapo…please hold…"

"What?" I ran to the bedroom to wake Ralph and we waited till the caller came back on the line.

"Is this the home of Elizabeth Zapo.."

"Yes! Elizabeth Zapotoczny!" we both said. The caller proceeded to tell us there had been an accident and Elizabeth was on her way to Shore Memorial Hospital with the Sea Isle City Rescue Squad.

We asked what happened and were told there was no additional information, except she was to notify the family.

We got dressed and went to the ER of Shore Memorial We waited nearly a half hour until Betsy's friends, Jon and Amy, arrived just ahead of the ambulance. They were both upset and Amy was crying.

Betsy was brought in strapped to a body board with her head, arms and legs immobilized. We were very upset but didn't want to alarm Betsy. I asked her if she could wiggle her fingers and toes, fearing a spinal injury. She could move both fingers and toes, and told us she was in a lot of pain.

The resident ER physician took x-rays which showed a spinal issue, but Betsy needed a MRI. "We can't do an MRI this evening, there's no staff available to do it." the attending physician told us. Betsy was put back into the ambulance and transported to the Atlantic City Medical Trauma Center where she was admitted. Their MRI machine was broken, they told us. They said they would make arrangements to transport her to a MRI facility in Absecon the next day. We were not happy that she had to, once again, be put into the ambulance and driven to another facility the next day.

In talking to Jon and Amy we learned what happened. They were leaving the Deauville Inn at flood tide with a full moon, and the Ocean was higher than usual for those conditions. C.J., driving boat, headed toward Ocean City, but he didn't realize he was out of the channel. His boat struck the south end of the Ocean City beach. Betsy was seated on the center console. Amy was on a side seat, C.J. was running the boat, and Jon was standing beside him.

On impact with the beach, Jon was thrown forward and fell on top of Betsy, injuring her back. Early the next morning Betsy had the MRI at the facility in Absecon. When they returned with the films, the surgeons at the Trauma Center reviewed them. Her thoracic spine was fractured in three places at the T-11 and T-12 vertebrae.

The surgeons at Atlantic City Medical Trauma Center had mixed thoughts on how to treat these injuries. One surgeon wanted to operate immediately and had the paperwork ready for us to sign. Another suggested putting her in a Jewett brace and getting her up and walking immediately. We thought that would be the lesser of the evils until we could get better educated on what to do. So she was put into a Jewett brace and helped out of bed and started walking with the nurses.

We spoke to Dr. Cristini who had treated Betsy ten years earlier for a buckle fracture of her upper arm. We asked what he would do if Betsy were his child.

"I'd take her to see Jerry Cotler at Jefferson University Sports Hospital in Philadelphia. He's the best," he said and he offered to make the appointment with Dr. Cotler for us. We agreed completely. We were able to obtain all the studies for our appointment with Dr. Cotler two days later. We went home and researched Dr. Cotler's credentials which were glowing. He had the reputation of being "the spine guru of the Northeast". He specialized in treating sports injuries. He was highly respected and at the top of his field.

"Don't say anything until I've reviewed the studies," Dr. Cotler said, holding the various x-rays up to the light.

"Two vertebrae are injured, the T-11 and T-12, the T-12 in two places." He pointed out the injuries.

"How would you treat her?" we asked.

"When and how did this occur?"

"Three days ago in a boating accident," and we told him how it happened.

"She should have been brought here right away, she needs to be put in traction. Had we gotten her right after the accident it would have been better."

"What's involved with traction?" we asked.

"It's barbaric. We drill holes through her bones above both knees and insert screws which will be part of a pulley system. Sand bags will hang off each leg to stretch the spine. Her head will have a halo apparatus with a weight hanging off it to keep her stable. We'll put her in a special rotating bed. The next step will be to start with a bubble under her spine to arch it. We'll continue adding bubbles as we see the progress of moving the vertebrae back into place.

"What is being done right now?" Dr. Cotler asked.

"She is in a Jewett brace and they have her up and walking."

"That's how we treat injuries in third world countries. I suggest she be transferred here as soon as possible so we can get this traction started. The longer we wait, the more the bones can crumble like crackers breaking upon each other."

Betsy was transferred to Jefferson Hospital late that evening. She was put into traction within hours of her arrival. We went to the hospital in the morning and she was in a rotating bed with the sandbags just as Dr. Cotler had described.

She was on pain medication and in and out of sleep so we just stayed with her in her room. She hadn't eaten anything and said she was hungry for cinnamon discs and peanut butter cups. We went out to get them for her. Betsy slept most of that day.

We went back and forth to the hospital every day. I called my fellow transcriptionists and asked if they could take my clients. We often helped each other. Dr. Godfrey hired a transcriptionist to come to his office. He had used her several years earlier and I was happy that his work was getting done. I needed the freedom to care for Betsy.

We arrived at the hospital early that morning and were told Betsy was being put into a body cast, and that we could be with her. They had to remove the screws in her thigh bones and we weren't there for that, but we saw the bandages on her legs.

We watched as the team of doctors put her into a soft jersey knit tube. Then they laid her on a framework. Four of them worked together making the cast around her. They cut the cast to fit her. It covered her upper chest to her hips and it had a swayback tilt to the spine to keep her spine straight.

She looked almost like she was pregnant. A circle about the size of a dinner plate was cut into the cast at the belly.

Betsy was miserable and could barely stand because of the holes drilled into both legs where the sand bags were hung. We stayed with her all day and Ralph went home and I stayed with her all night. She couldn't sleep and we talked and we sang and we prayed. I turned her onto one side and propped her up. Shortly thereafter, I turned her onto her other side and propped her up. This went on all night long. Neither of us got any sleep.

At 4:00 AM Dr. Cotler and his entourage of interns entered Betsy's room. Dr. Cotler was not pleased.

"What are you doing here, Mama?" he asked me. I told him that Betsy asked me to stay and that the nurses provided a roll-away bed so I could be with her. He told me, in no uncertain terms, that Betsy was going to "live" in this cast for several months and she will have to get used to it. He clearly did not appreciate that I was there. I never stayed overnight again. We came in the mornings and went home after dinner.

Betsy was released from the hospital a few weeks later. She received home therapy. In the fall, she returned to college in her body cast. The Delta Zeta sorority mascot was a turtle. Betsy's cast was a perfect "costume" for the DZ float in the annual parade. She was on the Dean's List that semester, as I recall.

In early December she was out of the body cast and into a corset brace. By New Year's Eve she was out of the brace and going to parties with her friends. She had recovered from a serious injury without having surgery, truly a blessing from the Lord.

In the spring of 1996 Betsy and nine other Rowan students were chosen to work at the Coriell Institute Cell

Repository in Camden, New Jersey. She was excited to be chosen and enjoyed the work they did there.

Betsy graduated from Rowan College in the spring of 1996 with a degree in Microbiology.

Betsy's graduation from Rowan University 1996
Glassboro, New Jersey

When Aaron started pre-school at Education Station in Somers Point I went back to work. April dropped Aaron off in the mornings and I picked him up in the afternoons. He was smart and loved pre-school. He learned so much there, including sign language and Spanish.

I applied for a job as a paralegal working for the law firm of Schreiber & Friedman. The office was conveniently located in Egg Harbor Township. It was only about five minutes from my home and another five minutes in the other direction from the pre-school.

I worked for Marc Friedman, who was the Solicitor for Egg Harbor Township. My job was interesting and I enjoyed working with Marc and the Township personnel, as well. I was still typing Dr. Godfrey's medical reports at home in the evenings.

I worked for Marc for several years and enjoyed every minute of it. After my 50th birthday, however, I just wanted to work at home in my pajamas. I was available to help Marc if he needed me, but for the most part, I worked at home.

CHAPTER FIFTY

Following college graduation Betsy moved to a brownstone in Philadelphia. She got a job working for Yoh Pharmaceuticals. After nearly a year, she was disheartened by the tedium of the job. She had heard about Laura Jacobs, a job recruiter in downtown Philly. She made an appointment to seek other options in the pharmaceutical industry. Laura had other ideas and hired Betsy as a recruiter in her office, salary "on commission."

After several months of not receiving her full pay on time, as promised, Betsy interviewed with a different recruiting company, T. Williams Consulting. The partners took her to dinner and offered her a very good salary with many benefits. She accepted the job which entailed working on-site at various companies and either promoting from within or recruiting from the outside. Her job was interesting and diversified and she enjoyed it and worked there for several years.

Also graduating in 1996 Aaron, our grandson graduated from Education Station Pre-School.

Aaron and Miss Michelle
Education Station Graduation 1996

My surprise 50th Birthday Party July 1997

Ralph and the girls threw a surprise party for me for my fiftieth birthday. He and I had gone flying that day and when we got home, the living room was full of many of my friends I had not seen in ages. How very thoughtful of them to come, and how sneaky of the girls and my husband to plan it. I was totally surprised.

Uwe and Christine Lippert were celebrating their twenty-fifth wedding anniversary in September and we were invited to the party. We were very excited about the trip to Germany and, especially, about meeting all our aunts, uncles and cousins on my Father's side of the family.

We landed in Munich and took a commuter plane to Berlin where we were met by Uwe and Christine. There's a six hour time difference "across the pond". For us it was the middle of the night but it was morning in Berlin.

We waited at the bagging area and our luggage wasn't there. We were told it wasn't on the plane from Munich, but they would bring it to us in Wittstock that evening.

We had reserved a rental car at the airport which turned out to be a red "Twingo" economy car.

When Ralph saw the car with its little tiny wheels and its little tiny steering wheel and the name "Twingo", he was not happy. He said he was not driving a car all over the country that sounds like a dessert. We exchanged it for the only car they had left, which was a bright green Opal that made Uwe burst out laughing. He immediately named that car the "green bean" or, as they say in the Fatherland, "groen Bohne". We never saw another vehicle like it anywhere in our travels.

Uwe drove us to center-city Berlin and down the world famous street "Unter den Linden" lined with the beautiful linden trees. We saw the Brandenburg Gate and markings of where Checkpoint Charlie at the Berlin Wall were located. We had an early lunch at an outdoor eatery and then went shopping in downtown Berlin. Christine was looking for another dress at the newly opened Lafayette Department Store. There would be a second party to celebrate their anniversary the following week.

Uwe & Christine Lippert's 25th Anniversary
Celeste, Ralph, Sven, Christine, Uwe,
Kenny, Alexander & Gertrud
Wittstock, Germany 1997

The basement of the Lafayette had a huge restaurant and market. We had dinner there and ice cream from a street vendor when we came out of the Lafayette. Ralph and I were stuffed with food and sleep-deprived. Uwe took us back to the airport to pick up our Opal. I rode home with Uwe, requesting the back seat so I could lie down, and Christine rode with Ralph who was following Uwe on the autobahn.

Uwe took off in his BMW and Ralph took off behind him in the "green bean" which was left in the dust with the power of Uwe's "Beemer". When we arrived in Biesen, a village outside of Wittstock, Uwe's mother, Gertrud, had dinner ready! Ralph and I were so full and so tired, but the table was set and the meal was prepared and we all sat down for another meal. Shortly afterward our luggage was delivered by the airport as promised.

The following morning family members and friends began to arrive. Ralph had been downstairs having coffee and came up to wake me. "Everyone is arriving for the party, and no one is having breakfast until you come down."

I quickly got dressed and went down to meet the family, which was a delightful experience. We met Uwe's sister, Rosita, and her husband, Paul, and their children, Astrid, Jens and Ryck who came from Rostock. Our cousin Karsten and his girlfriend Erica came from Koblenz. They both spoke English fluently, as did most of the younger cousins. They learned English in school. Uwe and Christine's three sons, Alexander, Sven, and Kenny, were fluent in English. We relied on them for translating which they did and had fun doing it. Ralph and I each carried our own Langenscheidt (dictionaries) everywhere we went.

The party started around 4:00 PM with hors d'oeuvres, followed by a late full course dinner and dessert. The music, dancing and fun continued into the wee hours. There were

KINETOSCOPE

lots of jokes made about the anniversary couple and everyone had a wonderful time. Ralph, Gertrud and I walked home two blocks around 1:00 AM. We were all very tired and glad to go to bed. The party stragglers came home at daybreak. Those Germans love to party!

The next day Uwe and Christine showed us all around Wittstock, a seven hundred year-old village with a wall around it. Wittstock is one of the few villages where the wall is still intact The streets were cobblestone and the architecture just beautiful.

The following day we said our goodbyes and traveled to Potsdam where the WWII Armistice was signed by Harry S. Truman, Josef Stalin and Clement Attlee, representing Winston Churchill. We learned that most of the historic attractions in Germany are closed on Mondays.

The next day we drove to the Sans Souci Palace in Pottsdam. The grounds and the palace are breathtaking. What I remember most was a huge sleigh in one of the rooms that was totally covered with seashells. Photographs were not permitted inside, however, with or without a flash.

The following day we headed south to Dresden to meet my cousin Annelies, her friend, Gerhard, and her daughter and granddaughter Bettina and Annett Funke. We were invited for Kaffe and Kuchen (coffee and cake) which was always at 4:00 PM when you were entertaining guests. We later went out to dinner and met Annelies' sister, Lotti, her son Wolfram, and my cousin Kurt.

The following day Annelies took us to her brother, Willy's, house. Willy was named after my father. He was born the year my father left Germany to emigrate to America. Willy and his wife, Annelies (another Annelies Funke) showed us pictures of my father as a child and pictures of their family.

Willy and Annelies invited us to dinner that evening at a beautiful restaurant in a park. There we met their family. Korin and her husband, Gerd have two daughters named Michaela and Sylvia. Christina is divorced and has a son named Robin and a daughter named Isabel.

Dresden is one of the most beautiful cities in Europe. On that visit, the Frauenkirche which had been nearly totally destroyed by firebombing in WWII, was in the process of being restored. Piles of numbered stones lay about in the zentrum and it was hoped that within five years, the church would be completely rebuilt. We stayed in Dresden a few days and saw all the tourist sites. Zwinger Palace is an art gallery, the Green Vault is where the crown jewels are on display, and the Semper Oper, is a beautiful opera house.

We visited with our cousins at their various homes and, of course, saw my father's home when he was a child, 30 Langenstrasse in the Dresden Alt Stadt.

We next drove south to Nuremburg where the WW II War Trials were conducted. The following day we drove on the Romantic Road to Rothenberg, which is a very scenic highway. We continued south to Munich.

We were traveling in September, and that's when the Germans celebrate Oktoberfest. The Hotel Atlanta, where we stayed, was within walking distance of the world famous glockenspiel in the town center. At noon and at 6:00 PM the clock plays music while life-size carved figures come out to dance and have jousting matches. We went to see and hear it at noon the next day. It's very old and very beautiful.

We went to the Hofbrauhaus (Hitler's hang-out) and saw the Clydesdales out front, and we could pet them. Inside was an om-pah band. Some of the songs I knew from my childhood were being sung, and I could sing along with the rest of the revelers.

We went to the dinner variety show upstairs which featured singers and dancers dressed in native costumes, and whip crackers, and Alpenhorns. We so enjoyed everything about Oktoberfest. However, it was there we learned that the big celebration of Oktoberfest is really outside the City of Munich in an area called Thereisienwiese – a short ride on the metro – the metro station is in the center of town.

The next day we took the metro to Thereisienwiese and when we arrived we were right in the middle of about thirty-five huge tents. Each tent is sponsored by a particular beer company. They come from all over the world. What a party! Music, dancing, live entertainment, great food – like those long white radishes that are cut in curls and served with lots of salt on big plates. There's lots of beer from different breweries from all over the world, and pretzels as big as your head. The waitresses carry three giant full liter mugs of beer in each hand, it's something to see! They have grills going with all sorts of food and whole fish roasted over charcoal on stakes in the ground.

We went to Neuschwanstein Castle, which is the castle Walt Disney recreated as Cinderella's Castle in Disney World. It's located in Hohenschwangau in Bavaria. We also went to Oberammergau, a lovely little town in the Bavarian Alps which puts on the "Passion Play" every ten years. Almost all the homes and businesses in this town are painted with fairytale characters or religious depictions.

We took a cruise on the Rhine River and saw the Lorelei Rock and the Riesling grape vineyards growing almost perpendicular on the mountainsides.

We knew we would return to Germany some day, and we've made a total of seven trips to "the Fatherland". Each time we visit our family and then take in other cities we'd not visited before. We took Ralph's mother with us one year and

Aaron, after taking three years of German in high school, came to Germany with us over Christmas vacation his senior year. Another year after visiting our family, we took the train from Dresden to Prague, Czech Republic, the oldest city in Europe. We stayed a few days sightseeing. What a gorgeous city it is. The Vltava River runs through the center of the town.

    Germany is especially beautiful to me. I never imagined I'd meet anyone from my father's side of my family. I'm so blessed to have met so many precious cousins from four generations. Anyone younger than thirty speaks English and they love to come visit us here in America. My siblings and I live in different locations so it is fun for our relatives to experience different parts of our beautiful country.

CHAPTER 51

On July 4, 1999 we held our first sibling reunion at our house in Linwood, New Jersey. We had not all been together since our father's funeral in 1970. We had such a wonderful time, we decided to continue taking turns at each other's homes as long as we could travel.

The ten of us enjoyed a total of eight reunions at our house in Linwood, NJ, Artie and Shirley's home in Lilburn, GA, Trudy and Frank's home in Lafayette, LA and in our hometown, Altoona, PA at both Bonnie and Girard's and Gretchen and Neal's homes. We were so very blessed to get to know one another and reminisce about our childhoods.

Our first Lippert sibling reunion, Ocean City, NJ 1999
Artie, Gretchen, Trudy, Girard, Celeste

Lippert sibling reunion 2003
Horseshoe Curve, Altoona, PA 2003
Frank, Trudy, Artie, Shirley, Bonnie, Girard,
Celeste, Ralph, Neal, Gretchen

Our eight reunions were wonderful and I'm so thankful for them. The weekend of August 4, 2001 Bonnie and Girard hosted our third sibling reunion which coincided with the Bathurst Family Reunion, my mother's family. That gathering was held at DelGrosso's Park in Tipton, PA.

We had a wonderful time at both reunions that same weekend. We'd not been together with our cousins in many years. The only living sibling of my mother's was my Aunt Junette Burchner, and she was the Queen of the Reunion.

Our cousins came from all over the United States, as far away as California and some living in Altoona. We laughed and talked about childhood memories and Grandma's house in Penns Creek. What a wonderful time we all had.

Many thanks to our cousin, Imogene Henck, for putting together a beautiful keepsake reunion booklet.

KINETOSCOPE

Artie Lippert and Leonard Bathurst
Bathurst Reunion
DelGrosso Park, Tipton, PA
August 4, 2001

Lippert "hooligans" August 4, 2001
DelGrosso Park, Tipton, PA

Over the years, we've lost three nieces, Lynne Renee Hollabaugh-Sparkman, daughter of Girard and Bonnie, Pamela Ann Lippert, daughter of Artie and Shirley, and Wendy Wendel Todd, daughter of Trudy and Frank. We've lost both our brothers, Artie and Girard, Gretchen's husband Neal, and Artie's wife, Shirley.

As for the German side of the Lippert family, we have only one living first cousin, Annelies Funke, Willy's widow. My cousin Willy was born the same year my father emigrated to America. He was my father's namesake. We were so privileged to have met him on our first trip to Dresden in 1997. We have numerous second, third, and even some fourth generation cousins in various locations in Germany.

As for the Bathurst side of the family, my grandparents and my mother and her siblings have all died, but we have numerous cousins to the fourth generation living in all parts of the United States. The last family gathering was our final Bathurst Family Reunion in 2001.

In the summer of 1999 the FAA Technical Center in Pomona, New Jersey and the EAA, Experimental Aviation Association located in Oshkosh, Wisconsin, were working together on a research project that utilized an experimental aircraft.

The Young Eagles Youth Program of the EAA in Oshkosh, guided by their mentors had built a single engine GlasAir GlaStar aircraft from an FAA approved kit. The electronic avionics package contained some new concept systems that were to be evaluated by the Research and Development group of the FAA at the FAA Technical Center in Atlantic City, New Jersey.

Ralph was the project manager from the FAA Technical Center. He and several others from the FAA headquarters were manning the exhibit at the Oshkosh Air Show that year to explain to others about the project. The static display utilized a special portable generator and power converter (built by the FAA Technical Center) required to operate the avionics while the aircraft was not flying. Ralph brought it with us when we flew to Wisconsin.

Ralph was looking forward to flying into Oshkosh where the airplanes look like they're strung on a kite tail stretched to Chicago. They land on different colored spots painted on the runways and taxiways and he wanted to try that. It was not to be. There were no car rentals available in Oshkosh so we flew into Milwaukee instead. There, we rented a car and drove to Oshkosh.

We watched from a window in a tall building near the tower as all makes and models of airplanes landed four-abreast using the runways and the taxiways. Each pilot carefully listened to the air traffic controller in the tower directing the pilot onto which colored spot to land in which particular lane.

None of the pilots spoke at all, and when they understood their indicated landing position, they were to "waggle their wings" and then land. It was something we'll never forget. We were mesmerized watching them.

Privately owned airplanes in line to land
at the Oshkosh Airport Airshow 1999

Celeste Yost

FAA & EAA Joint Research Project Crew
Oshkosh, Wisconsin July 1999
Ralph left end of the group

Research Glasair Glastar airplane kit built by the
Young Eagles Youth Program of the EAA
The FAA Technical Center in NJ provided the avionics

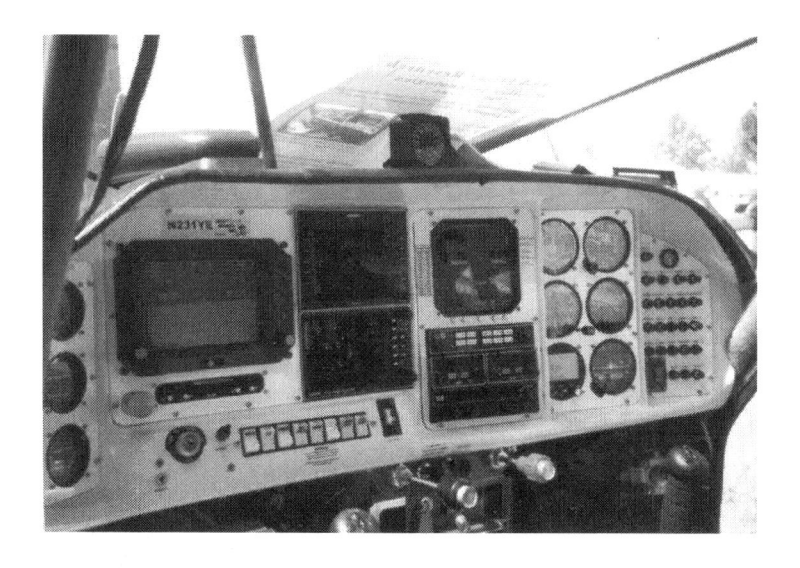

My birthday was that week and Ralph surprised me with a helicopter ride over Oshkosh which was awesome. Neither of us had ever been in a helicopter and it was very exciting. It was amazing to see the thousands of tied-down airplanes nose to nose. There were more than 10,000 planes and 500,000 Air Show attendees in Oshkosh that week.

Exhibition Day at Oshkosh Air Show 1999
One day prior to opening

Celeste Yost

Opening day Oshkosh Air Show 1999

Happy Birthday to me!

Seaplane mooring at Fond Du Lac

Later that evening we took a shuttle to Fond Du Lac where the seaplanes were moored. We met people from all over the country at a big barbecue. Ralph was talking to a couple guys who owned seaplanes and said to me "That guy over there says he'll take you up for a ride in his seaplane for your birthday."

"Which seaplane is his?" I asked, and we walked around till we found it. To me, it looked neither flightworthy nor seaworthy. There was a hose in the back leading to the gas tank, and the plane wasn't kept in very good condition.

"Are you crazy?" I asked, "Look at this! I'm not getting into this plane, and besides the condition of the plane, your new best friend is a tad inebriated from drinking all afternoon."

"Well, I just thought since I couldn't take you up in Philly, this would be a good opportunity."

"Well, I'll take a pass on this thoughtful gift, thank you anyway."

My bestie from Roosevelt, Jr. High, Ruthie Davis, lived in Stevens Point north of Oshkosh. When I told her we were coming to the Air Show for a week she said she'd come and pick me up and take me to her house for a couple days.

She drove 85 miles to pick me up, then back again! What a friend!! We had the most wonderful time. We'd not seen each other except at high school reunions over the years. It was so great to just be with her. Ruthie got out her class yearbook and we went through it page-by-page. Many of our classmates were no longer living, I'm sad to say. We discussed our memories from our Jr. High years also. What fun we had together.

When the Air Show closed Ralph drove to Stevens Point to get me and the four of us went out to dinner. We had a great time laughing and talking with the Davis's.

Who could possibly leave Oshkosh without a Wisconsin "Cheesehead"? Not me!! Ruthie was the perfect model!

Ruthie Davis wearing an official
Wisconsin Cheesehead!

CHAPTER FIFTY-TWO

We sold our sailboat, "Obsession," in the Fall of 1999 after sailing her for twelve years. We were boatless until spring when Ralph bought a new Parker fishing boat which we named "Say Good-Bye". We kept her in Snug Harbor, Atlantic City. Ralph loved to fish for striped bass in the Delaware Bay and we enjoyed every delicious bite of those wonderful fish.

Striped Bass from the Delaware Bay
caught on the Parker

Betsy married Michael Barron in November 2001 and their son, John Robert Barron, nicknamed "Jack", was born December 30, 2002. Their daughter, Reese Elizabeth Barron was born April 13, 2005. They lived in the Philadelphia area and I drove back and forth from New Jersey quite often to visit, or to bring the grandkids down to our house for a few days.

When the children were a little older Betsy and I would meet at the Babies "R" Us store at the Deptford Mall, Deptford, NJ, which was halfway between us. I'd bring Jack and Reese down to our house on Tuesdays for a few days.

They came for "Adventure Wednesday" when Aaron joined us, too. We always went out to lunch and then to Stockton College for the Children's Summer Theatre. We always went to the beach, too, if the weather was nice.

Aaron holding his new baby cousin, Jack
January 30, 2002

Jack and Reese summer 2005

Ralph's birthday present (to us) was "Striper the Wonder Dog", a Portuguese Water Dog born September 13, 2002 on our anniversary. Ralph named her Striper, the nickname for striped bass. He and I flew to Traverse City, Michigan to bring her home in late October. She was the cutest little dog out of a litter of seven puppies. We flew her home in a little

KINETOSCOPE

traveling case that fit under the airplane seat. We introduced Striper to our little poodle, "Holly", and they were so funny together. They were both the same size for about two weeks. Striper followed Holly all around and laid down on her little bed, so Holly laid down on Striper's big bed.

Striper was a lively little dog and when she was nine months old we took her to Carol Kyle's Dog Training School. We diligently worked with her and she was easy to train. She was very smart and caught on quickly. She was a well behaved dog and a joy to be part of our family. We once made a list of how many words she understood. She knew a lot of words!

This photo of Striper was featured
on a Portuguese Water Dog Calendar

Holly with her carrot and Striper with her bone

One of my favorite pictures of the grandkids
L-R Reese, Jack and Aaron

In 2008 we sold the Parker and bought "Rosetta" a 41' Defever trawler from John and Kathy Jeidy. We picked her up in North Carolina. We renamed her "Say Good-Bye" and docked her at Great Oak Marina in Fairlee Creek, Maryland. We stayed there for a year and then relocated to North Point Marina in Rock Hall, Maryland.

We joined MTOA, Marine Trawler Owners Association and the Chesapeake Bay Cruisers groups. We had great fun over the years traveling with these special boaters every weekend and every vacation.

Say Good-Bye on the Chesapeake

We'd been in contact with a realtor from Southwest, Florida for over a year. Her name was also Celeste. Each week she'd send us new listings. In late summer of 2011 we flew to Cape Coral, Florida and Celeste showed us potential houses for three days. We settled in October on the home we now live in.

Ralph retired from the FAA December 7, 2011, Pearl Harbor Day. We had been packing boxes for months and had a tractor trailer from ABS U-Pack brought to our house.

With the help of family and friends in New Jersey we were packed and ready to head for Florida in two cars the next day. We traveled two long days until we reached our new home.

Ken and Debbie brought us chairs,
a table & meals and Jay took us to buy a tv
and twin beds for the guest room

Two days later, our furniture arrived. Friends came over to help us unpack the boxes in the truck and help set up the furniture.

Our furniture arrived two days later

KINETOSCOPE

Unpacked and waiting for the trash truck

Grateful for dear friends, Jay and Charlotte and Ken and Debbie for helping us

Home Sweet Home

In May 2012 we drove to New Jersey and launched Say Good-Bye from Hancock Harbor Marina in Greenwich, NJ and headed to our former home port, Snug Harbor in Atlantic City. We spent two weeks there getting the boat ready to embark on a 6,000 mile boat trip known as The Great Loop.

We kept "Two Loopers and a Portie", a daily blog of our adventures on Say Good-Bye, and had about 35 followers.

The following is a summary of our Great Loop Trip:

OUR GREAT LOOP STATISTICS

We began The Great Loop in Snug Harbor, Atlantic City, NJ on May 23, 2012 and we arrived at our home in Cape Coral, FL on November 11, 2012 where we spent the winter.

On April 15, 2013 we left Cape Coral to complete the Florida to New Jersey final leg of The Great Loop. We arrived back at Snug Harbor, Atlantic City, NJ on May 21, 2013.

We traveled 5,868 statute miles for a total of 900 engine hours. We used 1,771 gallons of diesel fuel at an average cost of $3.89 per gallon and a total fuel cost of $6,842. We made 13 fuel stops in the United States and 1 fuel stop in Canada.

Our average daily water consumption was 45 gallons. Our trip was 209 days long. Of those days, we traveled 149 days. We locked through 157 locks. We stayed at free docks or on free moorings 51 nights. We stayed at paid docks or moorings 93 nights. We anchored out 65 nights. We visited 2 countries, 18 states, and 159 cities.

What we've learned:

We can live well with a whole lot less than we ever thought.

Most people we've met on and off the water have been very friendly and hospitable.

We've learned that a 41' boat can be quite a cozy little home for Two Loopers and a Portie.

WE ALWAYS WANT OUR PETS TO LIVE FOREVER, SADLY THEY DO NOT...

Blog Entry May 28, 2013: We took Striper to the University of Pennsylvania Hospital this morning. They performed an ultrasound which confirmed she was bleeding internally from tumors surrounding her liver and spleen. They gave her two months to live. We opted for euthanasia and said our farewell to her this afternoon. We are heartbroken.

Striper the Wonder Dog
September 13, 2002 – May 28, 2013

Celeste Yost

CHAPTER FIFTY-THREE

A view through my kinetoscope . . .

My parents were kind to everyone and my mother, especially, welcomed all our friends to our home. When I was a kid, we played restaurant on our front porch using my mother's china dessert molds to serve "dishes" involving sand, leaves, berries and flowers. Afterward we'd drag out the garden hose and spray the whole porch off as we slid around in the puddles of water.

My father built a big sandbox out back under one of the apple trees and we made buildings and roads with the sand and used twigs for trees. We always had a bucket of water handy to mix into the sand to make houses formed in small plastic containers. Sometimes we dribbled the wet sand through our fists to make tent-like structures.

My mother let us have circuses in the backyard and we did tricks on the "jungle gym" and flips on the swings. We hung upside down by our legs and then did "skin the cat" on an adjustable bar at the side of our house. Mother even let us jump around pretending we were trampoline artists. We had nothing to jump on but an old mattress on top of old bed springs in the back yard. When the junk man came to take it away, my friends and I were heartbroken; my parents, on the other hand, were not.

Of course, my mother was our best customer, always willing to sit in the "audience" as we performed. She never failed to bring out snacks like popcorn and Kool-Aid. Her specialty was little popsicles in ice cube trays. They were made with orange juice and each had a maraschino cherry frozen inside. We held them by a toothpick frozen in the center, and ate them quickly before they melted.

We rode bikes and had bike parades and played Robin Hood in the little woods across the street. The older kids used real arrows in their bows. The folks weren't too keen on that but I don't remember anyone ever getting hurt.

My parents probably doted on me, the surprise baby, and Girard often reminded me that I was a spoiled brat. His bedroom had a closet near the entrance door to his room. When both the closet door and the bedroom door were open, the glass doorknobs could link together and were difficult to separate.

When I was little, he used that closet as a torture device. He took great pleasure in putting me inside and rigging those two doorknobs together so I couldn't get out. My claustrophobia, as I grew older was probably his fault from the trauma of being trapped in that closet. I can barely put a sweater on over my head without small signs of panic. I totally blame that on my brother.

One afternoon, Daddy, Girard and I went to Musser's Bicycle Shop and I selected my very first bike. It was a blue twenty-six incher. It was a used bike for $15. I was short and it was too big for me. Even adjusting the seat as low as it could go, my feet were barely able to reach the pedals.

Consequently, I learned to ride standing up. Daddy and Girard spent lots of time holding onto the back of the seat running along with me down Southey Avenue. I stood up pedaling until I was tired and my father would grab the handlebars and stop me. Eventually I learned how to keep my balance standing up, but it was a while until I could ride while seated. My mother was a big believer in buying everything a little bigger than you really needed, because eventually, "you'd grow into it."

My parents were avid readers and passed on their love of reading to each of us kids. They each always had a book going. My mother became an avid Bible reader once she was saved and she even took a Bible course several evenings a week for about a year. She graduated from Altoona Bible Institute.

We all had our own Bibles and memorized verses in the original King James Version. To quote Pastor David Jeremiah, "our family had a "drug" problem." Every time you turned around, we were being "drug" to church. That's how it was at the Lippert household as I was growing up.

We attended Altoona Bible Church which originally started out in the National Guard Armory over town somewhere. When I was in third grade, I joined Pioneer Girls as a Pilgrim. As I got older I became a Colonist, and finally an Explorer. I liked the Christian group of girls. Memorizing scripture was a major part of the program. We earned badges for various crafts and community projects.

I played the piano for our youth group. Girard was one of the leaders for Boys Brigade and worked in the sound room for the Sunday morning radio broadcasts. My father built wooden speakers for the church and my mother started a new Sunday School class for ladies her age which they called the "Deborah Class". It was named for Deborah who was the only female Judge mentioned in the Bible.

Mother loved to study God's word and enjoyed working on her Sunday School lesson plans at the dining room table which always had to be cleared to set the table for dinner.

Mother also loved all the classics and we memorized poems like "The Walrus and the Carpenter" and "The Owl and the Pussycat", and "Listen to the Story of the Burglar Bold."

After dinner each evening when I was little, we stayed at the table and my mother read to us. It was just a chapter each evening, but I loved listening to her voice inflections for different characters in the books.

My sisters were older and dating and it was their job to wash and dry the dishes before they were allowed to go out on dates. Sometimes I got in trouble with them for being too pokey about finishing dinner. That delayed their departure with their boyfriends who came to the house for them. Later I'd hear them complaining about it, but they never complained to my mother.

At Christmastime every year, mother read "This Way To Christmas" to us. I liked that story, particularly the part about the locked-out fairy. I have the original book that was given to my mother by her friend, Alice Fair, in 1925, the year my mother graduated high school.

My father was an avid reader also. He had two favorite books that I particularly remember that he reread from time to time, "David Harum" and "Heart of Gold". I have his copy of "David Harum" published in 1899, the year he was born. He also loved Ellery Queen and Agatha Christie mysteries.

Daddy taught us all how to count to a hundred in German. We learned German prayers, poems, and songs. I remember "Hoppe Hoppe Reiter", as he bounced me on his knee. I was much older when I learned it was a morbid poem about a "Bumpity Bumpity Rider", which did not end well for the rider.

Years later when Ralph and I were at the Old Europe Restaurant in Georgetown, Washington DC, a petite blind woman was entertaining the patrons during the dinner hour. She sang a plethora of German songs, accompanying herself on the piano. I found myself singing along. How do I know these songs? I thought to myself, but I knew the words auf Deutsch.

When we'd finished dinner, we stopped to tip the songstress and we chatted a bit. I told her I was singing along but couldn't figure out how I knew the words. She laughed and took my hand in hers and told me "From your childhood, of course!" I'm sure she was right.

When my friends and I were learning to read at Baker School, Mrs. Bushnell took her twins, Molly and Becky, and me to the library. In the summer the library had a special program where the goal was to read your height in books. The librarian would measure us when the program began. She wrote our names and our height on an index card that she kept in a special box. Each time we borrowed a book she'd measure the thickness of the book, then write the number of inches on our card. When the summer ended, If you read your height in books, you earned a special ribbon.

Everyone walked to Baker School together when I was growing up, older and younger kids alike. Coleridge Avenue was the main street to our school. We were so lucky to have two little stores on our route. Zimmie's was on one side of the street and Schmiittle's was on the other side. The two were within a few blocks of each other.

Zimmie's had a huge glass candy case which dazzled your eyes with every kind of penny candy you could think of. Zimmie was patient with each little customer and put our purchases in small brown paper bags.

The Schmittles were a very nice couple and I remember Mrs. Schmittle answering the phone "Clover Farm" in a sweet cheery voice. They also sold penny candy and put our selections in little paper bags, but Zimmie's had more candy selections.

When we arrived at Ward Avenue, the patrol boys walked out in the street with their flags to stop the traffic so we could cross safely. After crossing, we lined up on the sidewalks in front of the school waiting for Mr. Kern to ring the school bell.

A terrible accident happened when I was in third grade, I believe. We had lined up to wait for the bell to ring. Jeff

Spence climbed a horse chestnut tree in the grassy area between the sidewalk and the curb in front of our friend's house. The sidewalk was lifted up from the tree roots. Jeff fell out of the tree onto the sidewalk and died. It was a sorrowful time for his family and all of us who saw it happen and also those who didn't.

The Sachs family who owned the tree cut it down immediately. I remember that incident as if it were yesterday and just how broken-hearted everyone felt for the Spence family. Jeff was a nice boy.

Every spring, the Jaffa Shrine Circus came to town. Our next-door neighbor, Floyd Evans, was a Shriner and gave us tickets to the show. My father took me one year when my mother was ill. We ate hotdogs and cotton candy and peanuts. I remember he bought me a live chameleon to pin on my shirt. I was so intrigued by this interesting little creature that turned colors to match your clothing. There was a little ribbon around the belly of the chameleon that had a small safety pin attached so you could pin the ribbon onto your shirt. I remember my shirt was pink and my chameleon turned pink to match.

When we got home, I put him in a little bowl and the next day he was gone. What a search that was! We did finally find him in the house. My mother then suggested he might be much happier living outside. I thought he'd like living in my mother's herb garden, but after a day or two he was gone. He must have found a new home.

Miss Moore's First Grade Class
Baker School 1953
Top: Miss Moore, Paula Fried, Allison Mayberry,
Terry Kelly, Gloria Hite, Joan Beerman,
Regina Fitzgerald, Karen Ford, Mr. Keirn
Middle: John Prosperi, Molly Bushnell
, Milanie Unger, Becky Bushnell,
Celeste Lippert, Terri Bastian,
Gene Madden, Sam Magee
Bottom: Steve Eiche, Lee Petsonk,
Chuck Myers, Jack Titleman, Kip Keirn,
Andy Ellis, Johnny Hicks and Kenny Ferguson

One year stands out in my memory. I was in third grade and the Shriners gave out free circus tickets to various schools, including Baker. The tickets were for a performance the next afternoon instead of attending school. My fellow classmates and I were all excited about that. Going to the circus was a whole lot better than doing arithmetic at school!

I was given a ticket with the rest of my classmates. When I showed my mother the ticket, she told me she couldn't take me the next day. She had a doctor appointment and since our grade didn't have school after lunch, I went with her to her appointment.

The following day when I came home for lunch, my mother suggested we have lunch at the circus. What a surprise! We had hot dogs and popcorn and a fun afternoon together. I got to ride the elephant outside the Mosque. Riding on its back on a sort of platform with other kids was lumpy and bumpy. So bumpy, in fact I told my mother it seemed like the elephant's bones were coming apart. She laughed and told me when we got home she'd show me some pictures of elephants and their bone structure.

When I went to school the following morning, my mother gave me a note for Miss Clapper. The note said, "Please excuse Celeste from school, yesterday afternoon. We went to the circus. Thank you, Pauline Lippert."

Miss Clapper read the note, and wrote one back for me to take home at lunchtime. My mother was wrapping fresh meat when I came in and I gave her the note. The note said my absence yesterday was unexcused because Circus Day was the day before.

My mother tore off a small piece of the meat paper and quickly wrote another note to the effect that we were unable to go on circus day because she had a doctor appointment, and that she took me the next day instead. She asked Miss Clapper to kindly excuse the absence.

I thought I'd probably get in trouble with Miss Clapper, but when she read my mother's note, she put it in her desk drawer. She smiled at me and said "Please tell your mother thank you."

In the summer when school let out, Baker and Whittier Elementary Schools had a Carnival together. I remember there were games and refreshments. Most of all I remember losing $5 worth of tickets – ten strips – somewhere in the six blocks between the school and home. My parents were not happy. My father and I walked up and down Coleridge Avenue but the tickets were gone. My parents had to pay for them. I didn't go to the carnival that year. My father told me this is "a learning in appreciation" for me. I wasn't sure what that meant and didn't ask.

That summer I learned to swim at Mountain Lake. Girard and some of his friends were taking their younger siblings there, too, so I was allowed to go with him. Mountain Lake had a nice beach and the swimming area was large. In the middle of the lake was a big stationary wooden raft with ladders on each side. In the middle of the raft was a very high sliding board that you could climb and slide down and land in the water. The slide was gigantic to my friends and me.

The water was freezing. After all, it was Mountain Lake, and it was slow going with my brother teaching me to swim. I was both cold and scared to be where my feet wouldn't touch the sandy bottom.

After a while when I saw the other kids had conquered their fear, another kid and I swam from the sandy beach to the big raft. I was proud of myself because I was able to climb up by myself to catch my breath. I waved to my brother from the raft and I don't think he could believe his eyes. He swam out to meet me and after a few trips down the big slide, we swam back to shore together. I was so excited! I could swim!

From that summer on, if I got good grades on my report card, my parents bought me a summer pass for the Lakemont Park Blue Island Pool. My friends from Garden Heights and I used to walk from the neighborhood down through the woods on a path that led to the back entrance to the park. The pool was close to the pathway. We went nearly every day.

Celeste Yost

CHAPTER FIFTY-FOUR

When you're little, the summers seem so long. I remember our whole bunch of kids riding our bikes behind the mosquito sprayer on hot summer nights. We played kick the can and badminton and croquet in our side yard. We played four-square and a game called 7-Up. We had hula hoops, pogo sticks, scooters and stilts. We made character notebooks and listened to records by Elvis Presley, the heart throb of every ten-year-old girl. We had diaries where we wrote our secrets and locked them up with tiny keys that we hid in our sock drawers. We danced the jitterbug, and listened to the Top Ten Songs on the radio every day.

In the Fall of the year the school kids collected different kinds of leaves. Our mothers ironed them between two pieces of waxed paper to preserve them for our leaf books. The best place ever for collecting leaves was Lakemont Park. The varieties were unusual and there were signs identifying the types of trees, including their scientific names. You got extra credit if you added the scientific name to your leaf book.

The Fall meant the apples, pears, cherries, and grapes would be ripe in our yard. I was little when I would pick up the fruit from the ground. My job was to sort out what was perfect and what was bruised and put only the good fruit in bushel baskets. Any bruised fruit went on my father's compost pile. As I got older, I was climbing the trees and picking the fruit. I remember one particular golden pear on a branch about as thick as my mother's little finger. "Crawl out there, Lestie, you're little, and you can climb out and reach that beautiful pear!" I did pick that pear and got off that branch quickly before it broke, which was a minor miracle.

We took many bushels of our apples to Mattern's Orchards near Newry to have them pressed into cider. We had a big wooden crib for apples, carrots and potatoes in our cold cellar in the basement which was covered with straw. When you wanted a crisp apple they were readily available, and the potatoes and carrots from the garden were fresh all winter long.

My mother canned spiced apples and applesauce, cherries, peaches, and pears. She also made grape juice. The grapes stained everything purple, including the pots. Often the grape juice would turn to wine and the ceramic corks on the tops of the bottles would pop and grape juice and, sometimes, glass, would be on the basement floor. We could hear those loud cannon-like pops from our living room.

I helped my father in his vegetable garden and my mother canned tomatoes, green beans, peas, and beets, and we made pickles from the cucumbers. Broccoli and cabbage grew nearly all winter in his garden.

Girard, Neal, and my father often went hunting and came home with deer and sometimes rabbits. My father enjoyed rabbit pie that my mother made for him from Grandma Lippert's German recipe. I couldn't even think of eating rabbit pie. Venison was another matter. My mother soaked it in a vinegar mixture to tenderize it and she made the best roasts ever.

One winter when I might have been five years old and Girard was twelve, he took me sled-riding with him up to Halleck Place where all the kids were. All day we'd get a good start in the woods, then cross Ruskin Drive, and head down Halleck Place. We wanted to take one last run from up in the woods beside Tommy Stephenson's house.

It was dusk outside and the lights were on in the houses. We could see Mrs. Stephenson setting her dining room table for dinner as we pulled the sled a little beyond their house. I lay down on the sled and Girard was on top of me guiding the sled and we flew down that worn icy trail out of the woods.

It was too late to do anything when we heard chains clanking and Girard saw the mail truck coming our way on Ruskin Drive. He pushed my head down and laid his head on mine sideways, and we went right underneath that mail truck! Back in those days the mail trucks were high off the ground, but I can't imagine how two of us zipped underneath without being killed. That evening, Girard wanted to take the longer "sidewinder road" which turned onto Browning Avenue. That would save us from walking an extra block home. By the time we got to the end of Browning Avenue, my brother was cajoling me to keep this event to myself. He said "We could be in a lot of trouble if Mom and Dad find out."

We started walking over the little bridge on Coleridge Avenue, pulling the sled. Lo and behold, here came our parents, hugging each other slogging along in the deep snow. My mother was crying by the time we met them.

Mrs. Stephenson had seen us go under the mail truck, but didn't know what happened to us after that. She called my parents right away and told them the mail truck never stopped and just kept on going. Our parents left our house immediately to find their two decapitated children somewhere along the sledding route.

They both hugged us and my father picked me up and carried me home. My mother had her arm around Girard as he dragged our little sled. They didn't say very much, but when we got inside, they said plenty, especially to my brother.

"What were you thinking, Tyke? Your careless actions could have killed both of you," said my mother and began crying all over again. My father took Girard upstairs to his room and they had a little talk which I am sure was effective because Girard refused to take me sledding ever again. I was sad about that.

Looking back, we were so blessed to have Mrs. Stephenson alert our parents. After our friends' parents found out about that mail truck incident, nobody was allowed to sled ride down that little trail next to Stephenson's house anymore. Every kid I knew had to be home long before dusk, too.

I still have that Lightning Guider split runner sled. My brother gave it to me years ago as a remembrance of one exciting day! I love him for giving me that sled. You never see a split runner anymore and it's a keepsake with a history.

My parents were big on education and learning about music, dancing, art, and reading. At some point in my grammar school years, I took elocution from Mrs. Savage. It was Mr. Savage, her husband, who sold my parents the side lot next to our house on Southey Avenue.

The Savages were very gracious people who never had children of their own. I remember learning tongue twisters and "Little Orphan Annie came to our house to stay, she washed up all the plates and cups and brushed the crumbs away."

My father made a big wooden clock that he used to teach all of us how to tell time. When I was old enough to learn, he replaced the hands so they would move easier. Telling time was a difficult concept for me. How can it be one thirty when the big hand is on the six, and there was no "thirty" on the clock? And the three was "fifteen"? My father would just shake his head.

My mother's timely (no pun intended) purchase of a Cinderella watch for me, hastened my learning process and I finally "got the drift" as they say. That was much to everyone's relief, especially my father's. My mother told me it was because I exasperated him to no end.

I remember "Aunt Dot", not really my aunt, but one of mother's close friends. She had all sorts of pets, one big outside dog named "Stuffy", lots of cats, birds of all sorts, and tropical fish. Aunt Dot gave us some of her tropical fish, black mollies, and angel fish and a little bowl of guppies.

My mother was intrigued with the fish and so was I. I liked to feed them and help to clean the bowl – we got some snails for that -- and a loach. I remember when one of the black mollies was going to have babies and my mother was keeping a watchful eye on her. When she started to deliver the babies, they dropped from her body one at a time in a long stream. Lo and behold, an angel fish gobbled them up as each of them floated out of their mother.

My mother was appalled and reached into the bowl and grabbed that angel fish between her thumb and fingers and shook it and said "Stop it!" Then she marched upstairs with the poor thing and flushed it down the commode. Don't mess with my mother, especially if you're a predator fish.

I came across my old "Ponytail" autograph book in a box in the attic one day some years ago. I sat down to read all the entries from my friends and teachers from Jr. High and I found my mother's message to me written in 1960. This was two years prior to her death. There's not a day that goes by that I don't think of her and my father. I hope I have lived up to their expectations.

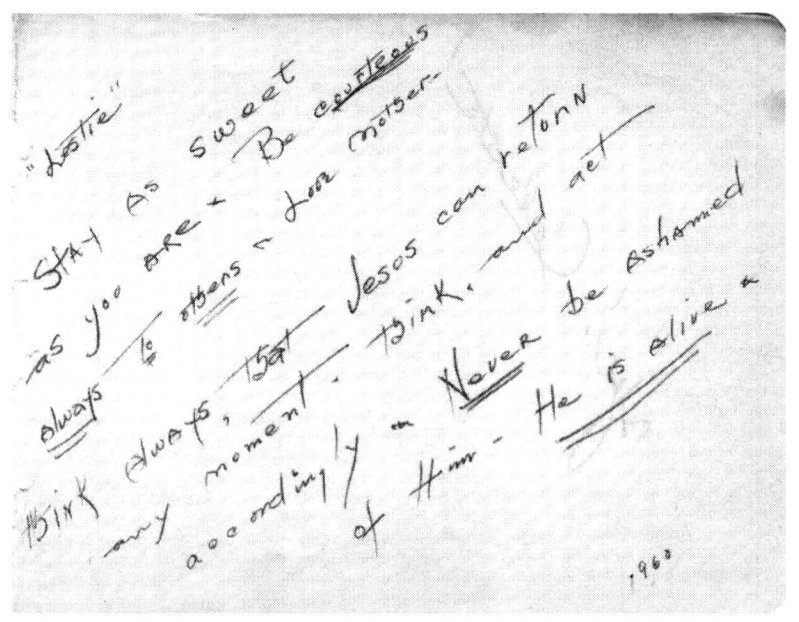

My mother's entry in my autograph book 1960

CHAPTER FIFTY-FIVE

Over the years I've had a number of very interesting jobs. I worked for Joule' Temporary Services at various positions in a variety of situations. I worked for many lawyers, a builder, a company that sold heavy equipment, and a detective agency. Each offered me full-time employment, but I declined.

I took an "English as a Second Language" course from Literacy Volunteers. My first student was an Egyptian lawyer named Artif. He and his family had recently relocated to the United States. Artif was working as a cook at one of the casinos in Atlantic City. His goal was to practice law in the United States.

We met for class twice a week at the Linwood Library. I gave him a workbook with assignments to do at home. His homework was always done, and always correct. Within six months, Artif had learned to read and write English. He sometimes showed me his written language -- loops and dots that baffled me. I told him he was a much better student at my language than I was at his, and he laughed.

Artif and I ran into each other at Dr. Godfrey's office a few years later when I stopped in with my transcription. We were both surprised to see each other. He was a big man and picked me up and swung me around! The office staff laughed about that and so did we. He told me he had been working for a law firm in Atlantic City and thanked me again for being his teacher. I thanked him for being my first student.

Shortly after teaching Artif I was assigned another student whom I met with once a week at the Pleasantville Post Office. He wanted to learn how to read. We started with Basic Reading and I assigned homework. His interest lasted only three sessions. I was disheartened. He was never on time, did not have his homework done, and wasn't focused on learning to read.

At our third and final session I gave him the phone number for Literacy Volunteers. I suggested that when he got serious about learning to read, he should contact their office and ask to be placed with another volunteer.

I then applied to teach Basic Reading and ESL (English as a Second Language) at the Atlantic County Justice Facility. I was specifically interested in working in the Boot Camp section of the jail in Mays Landing. I took a required course on how to deal with inmates. I and my fellow volunteers were tested on specific situations we might encounter and how we would handle them.

I was assigned to the Boot Camp and reported to a wonderful caring man, George Onufer. I taught classes twice a week. I had one class of men on Tuesday evenings and a co-ed class with men and women on Thursdays. These particular groups of inmates had completed most of the time they had to serve. They were to be released within several months. So to speak, they were the crème de la crème of the inmates.

Our friend, John Henry, said he had a case of twenty-four basic reading books that had only 840 different words. He asked if I could use them for my class. I told him indeed I could use them. When I opened the box I found children's Bibles. Perfect!

Many of my students were from the islands, mainly Haiti, Honduras, Puerto Rico, and Jamaica. They were all very interested in learning to read. They especially loved going to the chalkboard to write. All the students were very good at figures and money values, but the reading went slower.

From my very first class, I noticed what I had learned in a Sociology class I had taken at Penn State. That is that a prison has a definite status structure insofar as inmates and prison guards were concerned. There is a hierarchy. The guards, of course, are in charge. Conversely, the inmates are at their mercy.

One evening I watched as a guard escorted my class down the hall to my classroom. He intentionally stepped on the backs of an inmate's shoes to pull them off, like a prankster might do to cause someone to fall. What a twisted mindset, I thought. It clearly shows the inmates just who has the upper hand, but it also teaches distrust and antagonism.

I experienced a similar situation. Upon arrival twice a week for two-and-a-half years I had to sign in with the guard at the front desk. Most of the time, as I walked in the door he would swivel his chair, thus, turning his back to me. I had to rap on the glass to get his attention. I'd give him my driver's license and wait until he looked it over and finally handed it back. Then I'd go to the first of three doors and wait until he decided to buzz me through. Sometimes it took me fifteen minutes to just get past him and the first of three doors, which took away from my allotted class time with the students.

The next door was simpler and when I knocked, someone was there to open the door for me. They knew I was coming. The third door led into the jail area where I taught in a large classroom with twenty students. An older guard was the last doorkeeper and he brought me a present one evening. He gave me a small can of mace to put on my keychain and a whistle.

He smiled and said, "You keep these with you while you're in that room, and if you have any trouble, you just blow that whistle and I'll be right there!" And I knew he would be.

I only used the whistle one time. I was writing on the chalkboard with my back turned and I heard a loud slap. When I turned around, one of smallest men in the class had struck the tallest man in the class across the face. I blew my whistle and three guards appeared.

Alex was the inmate who was struck by the smallest inmate in the class, Miguel. Alex wasn't hurt and just sat there dumbfounded as did the rest of the class. I learned later that this was Miguel's M.O. when he was about to be released. Breaking rules was his means of remaining locked up where he felt safe.

One of my students, John Farmer, was a big black man in his twenties. He had graduated from Atlantic City High School, but he could only read and write his own name. When the other students were doing their worksheets, John and I worked on learning the alphabet with the children's ABC song. He told me he was pushed through Atlantic City High and graduated because he was big and he was a very good football player.

We were reading together young children's Sunday School pamphlets. This one was about Peter walking on the water to meet Jesus. John read the entire pamphlet himself. I was smiling and John started to laugh, "Miss Celeste, I CAN READ!" he said it so loud that everyone in the room heard him and applauded. I gave him his own Bible and told him he had graduated into the next level. He was so pleased.

I found that when the women were released, they often returned because they got into trouble again and were sent back. Some of them told me they weren't accepted by their family members and had nowhere to go so they'd shoplift and get sent back where they at least had a roof over their heads and food. It was a revolving door for many of them and it was heartbreaking to me.

I was active with the Linwood Library and they gave me workbooks for my classes. Life Skills was added to my curriculum. That now included how to read a bus schedule, how to make change, how to prepare a budget, and write a check and make deposits.

The bank gave me a supply of check books without real checks, so I drew oversized checks so my students could practice. They learned how to keep their own records and make deposits. Most of them were very good with figures.

They learned how to compile a shopping list and read recipes and instructions on cans and boxes of food. We talked about the importance of reading laundry tags and detergent and bleach bottles before washing their clothes.

I then got the idea to start a library for the inmates, run by the inmates, right there in the classroom. It took me several months to finally get approval from Frank Mazzone, the Warden. The books came from various libraries in Atlantic County that had been "withdrawn" from circulation.

They were delivered and stacked in the hallway that led to the classroom. Those books were in the hallway for months. I spoke to Warden Mazzone again and asked if we couldn't get shelves for the books so we could get this program going.

With supervision from the prison staff (some of them not so happy about it), the inmates put together the shelving in one section of the classroom. Together, we devised a system using index cards to keep track of the books and who had borrowed them. They all worked together cataloging the books and taking turns at certain hours, checking out or checking in books. When inmates were released from Boot Camp, those who remained taught the new inmates the lending library procedure. I hope I made a difference in the lives of those I was fortunate to teach. They each made a difference in my life.

Celeste Yost

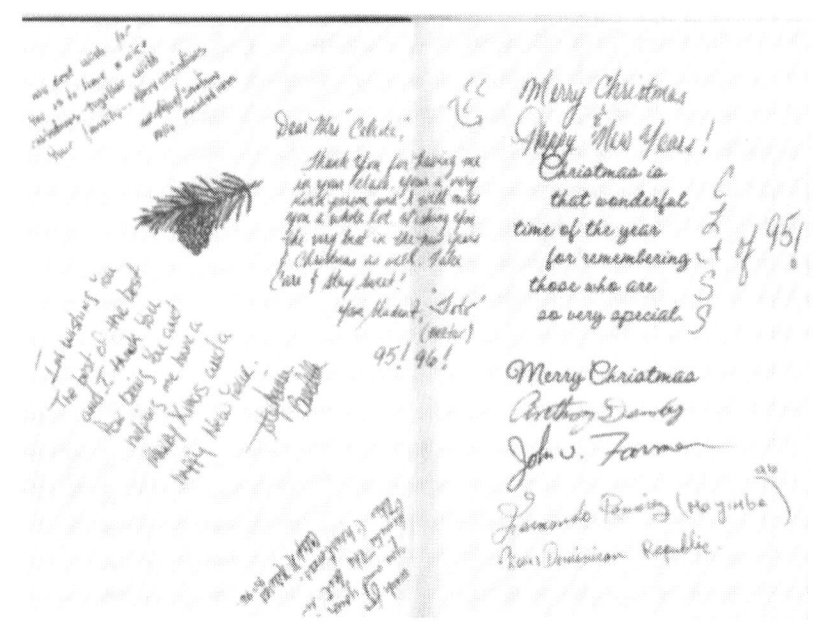

Christmas Card from the Boot Camp
Class of '95

Atlantic County Justice Facility
Volunteer Certificate of Recognition 1998

Inmate lauds boot-camp program

I'm an inmate at the Atlantic County Justice Facility. I didn't agree with the recent letter headlined, "Inmates get pampered."

I'm currently in the facility's boot-camp program. I have been a member since Feb. 15. I'm currently in the honor dorm, which is comprised of the elite inmates who want to change their lives totally around and be in the ambience of positive people who want to see you succeed, and in a program that offers true connections.

The work distribution may range from doing laundry, serving food or cleaning the local parks. All of the workers come from the boot camp's honor dorm. I'm currently the boot camp's librarian.

As per what the warden said in a July 28 letter, it's all true. We work for 16 hours every day. Part of those 16 hours may include drug/alcohol classes, educational classes, decision-making classes, and also courses through Atlantic Community College.

I have just finished taking an English course through ACC in which we were given assignments through our professor. We also had the use of an online E-mail system to communicate to our mentors. These mentors have given us some invaluable information as far as our current situation and have encouraged us to further our education. Before I was incarcerated, I was attending college in the District of Columbia majoring in computer science.

For those who are incarcerated, it's a plus to be part of the boot-camp program. This place will leave an indelible and positive effect on the majority of our lives, once released.

ANTHONY NEAL
Mays Landing

Letter to the Editor Atlantic City Press

Our children are grown now with children of their own. We now have five grandchildren. We're so proud of each and every one of them.

Wanna-be Chef Aaron, age 4   Chef Aaron age 25

Jack Barron, Jack Costello, Riley Costello,
Reese Barron and "Shady McCoy"

EPILOGUE

Writing this book has been quite an adventure for me. I'm grateful that my parents saved old letters and photographs from both sides of our family. They also saved books from our early childhoods and I am happy to own some of them. Those memories helped tremendously in putting together the timeline.

I've learned a lot of history of World War I and World War II, the Holocaust, the Roaring Twenties, the Great Depression, and how both America and Germany fared through those times.

My siblings shared a treasure trove of their memories growing up as a Lippert long before I came along. We all shared so much when we were together at eight sibling reunions traveling to different parts of the country. There was never a dull moment when we got together. We shared funny stories and some sad ones, too. What we all loved more than the stories, was that we were together. We were all very blessed and we each knew it.

Robert Frost is one of my favorite poets. This particular excerpt from Frost's "The Road Less Traveled" has a special meaning to me.

"Two roads diverged in a wood, and I . . .
I took the one less travelled by,
and that has made all the difference."
~ Robert Frost

Celeste Yost

ALSO BY THE AUTHOR

"Tried Three Times – the karmendi story"

"Confessions of a Deaf Psychiatrist"

"Elephloops and Wizzaroos"

ABOUT THE AUTHOR

Celeste Yost is a retired paralegal and freelance writer. Author of two true crime novels, "Tried Three Times" and "Confessions of Deaf Psychiatrist", she has also collaborated with her granddaughter, Reese Barron, on a children's book, "Elephloops and Wizzaroos". She and her husband, Ralph, reside in SW Florida.

Celeste Yost

KINETOSCOPE

Made in the USA
San Bernardino, CA
01 March 2019